Sustainability Standards and Global Governance

Archna Negi · Jorge Antonio Pérez-Pineda ·
Johannes Blankenbach
Editors

Sustainability Standards and Global Governance

Experiences of Emerging Economies

Deutsches Institut für
Entwicklungspolitik

German Development
Institute

Managing Global Governance

Editors
Archna Negi
Centre for International Politics,
Organization and Disarmament (CIPOD)
School of International Studies
Jawaharlal Nehru University
New Delhi, India

Johannes Blankenbach
Business & Human Rights Resource Centre
Berlin, Germany

Formerly with the German Development
Institute/Deutsches Institut für
Entwicklungspolitik (DIE)
Bonn, Germany

Jorge Antonio Pérez-Pineda
Faculty of Economics and Business
Universidad Anáhuac México
Estado de México, Mexico

Formerly with the Mora Institute/Instituto de
Investigaciones Dr. José María Luis Mora
Mexico City, Mexico

ISBN 978-981-15-3472-0   ISBN 978-981-15-3473-7   (eBook)
https://doi.org/10.1007/978-981-15-3473-7

Foreword

Sustainability standards are an important element of any strategy that aims at accelerating action towards implementing the Sustainable Development Goals and the Paris Climate Agreement. These agendas were both adopted in 2015, the year in which the collaborative work on this book commenced. Spirits were high then, and confidence in the ability of multilateralism to tackle global challenges grew again. In the end of 2019, it is a source of deep joy to see the final product and to know that it will soon be shared across the network of authors, their institutions and the communities of research and practice that they belong to.

The intellectual adventure that lured the editors and authors into writing was based on the hypothesis underlying any international cooperation initiative: putting resources together beyond national borders increases our understanding of global problems and our possibilities of implementing solutions to them. In fact, the interest in learning from others across the world in order to increase the shared body of knowledge has always been an important motive of scientific activity. And a success factor, too, as intellectual curiosity and cooperation helped to push the geographical and epistemological boundaries of the known world ever further.

Five years after the adoption of the 2030 Agenda and the Paris Climate Agreement, we know that "we are not on track" as the UN Secretary General, António Guterres, put it in September 2019 when speaking at the SDG and climate action summits. More ambition and more action are needed, domestically and globally, as well as renewed investment in international cooperation. Global greenhouse gas emissions are growing instead of falling, and global trade is stalled by tensions between what used to be strong trading partners. At the same time, companies and investors are increasingly realising that the sustainable development goals and the climate agreement actually speak the language of reason in a world threatened by unmitigated climate change, social polarization and unrest. In this situation, it is most useful to be presented an analysis of what sustainability standards are, their strengths and weaknesses, and under which conditions their potential can best be realised, particularly in emerging economies.

The questions agreed by editors and authors in 2015 which this book seeks to answer remain most pertinent: How can public mandatory regulation for sustainability and voluntary standards for the same purpose be designed to promote complementarity between public and private collective action and thus accelerate change? What is the role of global norm-setting institutions, such as the WTO, to ensure that the growing number of voluntary private standards that in fact regulate access to global trade and value chains does not create new barriers? How to ensure that sustainability standards and regulations of dominating markets support innovation in exporting firms in the South and at the same time do not hinder the creation of locally adapted rules and standards for sustainability? How to better understand the needs of smallholders in agriculture and SMEs and enable them to participate in growing sustainability markets? Do corporate social responsibility commitments and sustainability reporting help to align companies' core objectives and performance indicators with the SDGs?

The book provides some answers to these questions, which hopefully will be picked up by its readers, in academia, in public policy and companies' strategies, and in everyone's practice, to achieve the accelerated action we need. The book's insights also inevitably lead to new research questions that can contribute to new and enhanced learning processes.

I thank the editors of this book, Archna Negi, Jorge Antonio Pérez-Pineda and Johannes Blankenbach, for their dedication and perseverance, as well as all contributors, for their interest in understanding the potential and the problems of sustainability standards in making global trade more compatible with social inclusion, the reduction of inequalities, sharing benefits and significantly reducing the environmental burden of production, consumption and trade of goods and services. May this book find avid readers and practitioners ready to invest in change!

December 2019

Imme Scholz
Acting Director
German Development Institute/
Deutsches Institut für
Entwicklungspolitik (DIE)
Bonn, Germany

Preface

Complex interfaces and dynamics of a global nature mark not only the subject matter of this book but also the process through which it was produced. The unique nature of this book necessitates a brief introduction to the project from which it resulted. We believe that it represents an innovative experiment in 'knowledge cooperation' that involved a coming together of scholars and practitioners from the global South and North to jointly ponder upon the conceptual aspects of a chosen theme, enriched by empirical insights from the 'emerging economies'.

This project has taken shape under the knowledge cooperation component of the Managing Global Governance (MGG) programme run by the Bonn-based German Development Institute/*Deutsches Institut für Entwicklungspolitik* (DIE) with the financial support of the German Federal Ministry for Economic Cooperation and Development (BMZ). The MGG programme, initiated in 2007, is a training and dialogue programme designed for young professionals from the 'emerging powers' and Germany to converge under the broad theme of 'global governance' (*See* https://www.die-gdi.de/en/managing-global-governance/). The 'MGG Academy' has run for about 13 years now (until 2020), having completed 17 MGG courses so far—located mainly in Bonn. The MGG programme has created a rich alumni and partner network amongst a group of countries—Brazil, China, India, Indonesia, Mexico, South Africa and Germany/Europe—which are a part of the programme (as were Egypt and Pakistan for some years). MGG works with young professionals as well as senior experts located in government bodies, research institutions, academia, think tanks, civil society organizations, private sector organizations, etc. to jointly discuss and contribute to knowledge cooperation on issues of global governance. This book project was one such activity that emerged from 'knowledge cooperation' within the MGG alumni network, led and supported by the DIE.

The project was initiated in January 2015, when the theme for the project was finalized and a Call for Papers was conceptualized under the guidance of the three co-directors, located across three continents—in India, Mexico and Germany. The first project workshop, which took place in Bonn in May 2015, brought together all the alumni from previous MGG programmes who had sent in paper proposals. The research proposals were thoroughly assessed and the possible shape that could be given to the project discussed in detail. This initial meeting was followed by several others, such as an authors' workshop in New Delhi in April 2016, where paper contributors were invited for further discussion.

The co-directors also met on the sidelines of several other international events to which the project got closely linked as it took shape. For instance, the thematic content of the project was found to be relevant to the THINK 20 (T20) process —'the research and policy advice network for the G20'—and thus fed into the T20 Conference in Berlin in May 2016, followed by the T20 Germany Kick-Off Conference in December 2016 in Berlin.

The MGG Knowledge Cooperation project also linked up with the activities of the United Nations Forum on Sustainability Standards (UNFSS), a UN hub for informed policy dialogue and independent research on the potential as well as challenges of sustainability standards, and co-hosted the high-level launch event of the 2nd Flagship UNFSS Report in Berlin in October 2016. At this event, much discussion was held on the then recently launched (on 18 March 2016) and UNFSS-supported Indian Platform on Private Sustainability Standards. Subsequently, the Brazilian Voluntary Standards Platform was launched in May/June 2017 in Brasilia and Sao Paulo and the Chinese National Platform on VSS was launched soon thereafter in Qingdao, in June 2017. The MGG programme was represented and participated actively in both events. In September 2017, the UNFSS held various conferences on sustainability standards in collaboration with the International Trade Centre (ITC), the United Nations Conference on Trade and Development (UNCTAD) and MGG. A subsequent MGG workshop on sustainability standards took place in Mexico City in December 2017, hosted by the Mexican Ministry of the Economy, and in April 2018, the Mexican Platform for Voluntary Sustainability Standards was launched. Another MGG Conference on sustainability standards was organized in Jakarta, Indonesia, in November 2018 to explore the possibility of setting up a National Platform on VSS in Indonesia. Earlier the same year, in September 2018, the 3rd Flagship Report of the UNFSS— titled *Voluntary Sustainability Standards, Trade and Development*—was launched at the first International Convention on Sustainable Trade and Standards (ICSTS) held in New Delhi, India and contained a chapter contributed by the DIE MGG network. MGG participation in several international conferences on sustainability standards continued through 2019, including the second ICSTS that was held in Rio de Janeiro in September 2019, and an international conference on stakeholders' perspectives on sustainability standards, organized by DIE, UNFSS and the South African Bureau of Standards (SABS) in Pretoria, South Africa in November 2019.

It has indeed been timely and fortuitous that significant developments have taken place at the international as well as domestic levels—in the emerging economies— in the context of sustainability standards, including a focus on the challenges and pitfalls pertaining to them. The project has been able to create direct links with many of these new processes, thereby gaining from—and, it is hoped, also contributing to and enriching—this dialogue amongst researchers and practitioners from across the world.

Sadly, future planned activities were interrupted (temporarily, it is hoped) in 2020 by the unanticipated outbreak of the COVID-19 pandemic. It should be pointed out here that developments relating to the COVID-19 situation are not reflected in the content of this book as the project predated the outbreak and the manuscript was finalized in 2019. However, the global nature of the threat to public health, and the consequent economic and social disruptions across the world, will undoubtedly reinforce the debates relating to sustainability concerns and the role of global governance in addressing them. More specifically, incidences of workers at the bottom of global supply chains being abandoned by big brands or having to work without proper health and safety measures during the current crisis are likely to refocus the debates around sustainability standards and underscore the urgency to resolve many of the questions raised in this book—so that the world can "build back better" after this crisis.

New Delhi, India   Archna Negi
Estado de México, Mexico   Jorge Antonio Pérez-Pineda
Berlin, Germany   Johannes Blankenbach
2020

Managing Global Governance (MGG) is implemented by the German Development Institute/*Deutsches Institut für Entwicklungspolitik* (DIE) with financial support from the German Federal Ministry for Economic Cooperation and Development (BMZ). https://www.die-gdi.de/en/managing-global-governance/

Acknowledgements

This publication is a product of cooperation amongst project partners, participants and peers located across several continents and time zones, and traversing varied national, disciplinary and professional locations. It has taken large doses of patience and perseverance to reach its present form. We would like to thank everyone who participated in this endeavour of 'knowledge cooperation' on the seminal and topical theme of sustainability standards. In this 'wheel' (of knowledge cooperation), the Managing Global Governance (MGG) programme has constituted the 'hub' that connected the 'spokes' (the project participants). The German Development Institute/*Deutsches Institut für Entwicklungspolitik* (DIE), which implements the MGG programme, was the connector that brought together MGG alumni as well as researchers located at DIE to write on an identified theme of common interest.

Our foremost and sincere thanks go out to all MGG alumni and DIE researchers who have contributed as authors to this publication. Discussions that took place in Berlin, Bonn, Brasilia, New Delhi, Qingdao, São Paulo, Geneva, Mexico City, Jakarta, Rio de Janeiro and Pretoria have contributed immensely to the richness of this publication. We also acknowledge the additional lustre this project acquired from its intersection with researchers and personnel of several institutions working on the theme of sustainability standards such as the *United Nations Forum on Sustainability Standards* (UNFSS), the *United Nations Conference on Trade and Development* (UNCTAD), the *United Nations Environment* (UNE), the *International Trade Centre* (ITC), the *World Trade Organization* (WTO), the *THINK 20* (T20) process, the *International Organization for Standardization* (ISO), the *International Social and Environmental Accreditation and Labelling Alliance* (ISEAL Alliance) and the National Platforms on Sustainability/Private Standards located in India, Brazil, China and Mexico.

We acknowledge with gratitude the financial support provided to the MGG programme by the German Federal Ministry for Economic Cooperation and Development (BMZ), which made the project possible. At DIE, we thank Prof. Dr. Imme Scholz (Deputy Director), Dr. Sven Grimm (Head of Programme, Inter- and

Transnational Cooperation), Dr. Wulf Reiners (Head of Managing Global Governance), Dr. Tatjana Reiber (Head of the MGG Academy) and Dr. Ariel Hernandez (Researcher), for providing unwavering support to this project. Prof. Dr. Dirk Messner (former Director, DIE), who oversaw the initiation of this project is also gratefully acknowledged. We further thank Cornelia Hornschild, Bettina Beer, Rita Klüwer and Sabine Middecke at DIE for so efficiently handling and coordinating the publication, technical, and logistics-related aspects of the project, and the entire MGG team at DIE for providing contant motivation. Thanks to Sayan Samanta for providing helpful conceptual inputs. Finally, but most importantly, we would like to express our sincere gratitude to Dr. Thomas Fues (former Head of the Training Department at DIE) not only for his vision, patience, contribution and care towards nurturing this publication but also for having played a seminal role in holding the vast MGG alumni network worldwide together.

June 2020   Dr. Archna Negi
                                                 archnanegisingh@gmail.com
                                          Dr. Jorge Antonio Pérez-Pineda
                                                      japerpe@yahoo.com
                                                  Johannes Blankenbach
                                              johannes@blankenbach.eu

Contents

About the Editors

Archna Negi is Associate Professor at the Centre for International Politics, Organization and Disarmament (CIPOD) at the School of International Studies, Jawaharlal Nehru University (JNU), New Delhi, India. She has over 15 years of teaching experience at JNU, in which she has taught courses on international organization, law and diplomacy. She has supervised research both at Ph.D and M.Phil. levels. Her research expertise is in the issue areas of trade and environment. She was at the Trade and Environment Division of the World Trade Organization in Geneva as a Visiting Scholar for a brief period of two months in 2007. She has also participated in the six-month 'Managing Global Governance' programme at the German Development Institute, Bonn, Germany in the year 2007. She has a Master's Degree in Political Science (from Delhi University, Delhi, India) and a Doctorate in International Law (from Jawaharlal Nehru University, New Delhi, India). She is currently serving as a member of the Voluntary Sustainability Standards (VSS) Academic Advisory Council that has been set up jointly by the United Nations Forum on Sustainability Standards (UNFSS) and the Leuven Centre for Global Governance Studies (GGS) of the University of Leuven.

Jorge Antonio Pérez-Pineda is a research professor in the Faculty of Economics and Business at the Anáhuac University Mexico and belongs to the National Research System (SNI) in Mexico. He has been a consultant for Mexican and international institutions such as AMEXCID, OXFAM, Endeva, UNDP, AECID, GIZ, IICA, and a professor in other institutions such as UNAM, Mora Institute and Complutense University. He holds a B.A. in Economics from the National University Autonomous of Mexico and a Master's degree and Ph.D from the Complutense University of Madrid, Spain. He has also completed postgraduate studies at the University of Essex and a specialization on 'Managing Global Governance' at the German Development Institute (DIE), Bonn, Germany. His research interests are on the topics of private sector in international cooperation, CSR, VSS, institutionalization of International, South-South and Triangular cooperation, and financing development. He is a member of different networks and research groups such as REMECID, REEDES, GRIDESA2030 and NEST (coordinating the Mexican chapter for the last). During the time of execution of this project, he was also affiliated with the Mexican think tank, *Instituto de Investigaciones Dr. José María Luis Mora* (Mora Institute) in Mexico City, Mexico. He is currently serving as a member of the Voluntary Sustainability Standards (VSS) Academic Advisory Council that has been set up jointly by the United Nations Forum on Sustainability Standards (UNFSS) and the Leuven Centre for Global Governance Studies (GGS) of the University of Leuven.

Johannes Blankenbach works at the Business & Human Rights Resource Centre as its Berlin-based EU/Western Europe Researcher & Representative, having joined the organisation in May 2018. Prior to this, he was a researcher at the German Development Institute/*Deutsches Institut für Entwicklungspolitik* (DIE) in Bonn for more than five years, contributing to knowledge cooperation across the institute's Managing Global Governance (MGG) network with partner institutions from emerging economies. He co-chaired a research project on sustainability standards and also helped to set up the German chapter of the Sustainable Development Solutions Network (SDSN), which focuses on the national implementation of the 2030 Agenda for Sustainable Development. Johannes holds a B.A. in International Relations from Dresden University, Germany, and an M.Sc. in Human Rights from the London School of Economics and Political Science (LSE). His current research interests lie in the field of business and human rights.

Acronyms

AB	Appellate Body
ACFS	National Bureau of Agricultural Commodity and Food Standards (Thailand)
AIDCP	Agreement on the International Dolphin Conservation Programme
AMDAL	Environmental Management and Monitoring Plans/*Analisis Dampak Lingkungan* (Indonesia)
ANCE	Association of Standardization and Certification A.C./*Asociación de Normalización y Certificación A.C.* (Mexico)
AoA	Agreement on Agriculture (WTO)
APEDA	Agricultural and Processed Food Products Export Development Authority (India)
APP	Asia Pulp and Paper
APRIL Group	Asia Pacific Resources International Limited
ASEAN	Association of Southeast Asian Nations
BCI	Better Cotton Initiative
BIS	Bureau of Indian Standards (India)
BMZ	German Federal Ministry for Economic Cooperation and Development
BRI	Belt and Road Initiative
BRICS	Brazil, Russia, India, China, South Africa
CAUX	Caux Round Table Mexican Chapter
CEMEFI	The Mexican Center for Philanthropy
CERES	Coalition for Environmentally Responsible Economies
CEval	Center for Evaluation/*Centrum für Evaluation*
CITES	Convention on International Trade in Endangered Species of Wild Fauna and Flora
CIVETS	Colombia, Indonesia, Vietnam, Egypt, Turkey, South Africa
CmiA	Cotton Made in Africa
CNPC	China National Petroleum Corporation

CONAPRED	National Council to Prevent Discrimination
CONCAMIN	Confederation of Industrial Chambers of Mexico
CORE	Corporate Responsibility Coalition
COSA	Committee on Sustainability Assessment
CPTPP	Comprehensive and Progressive Agreement for Trans-Pacific Partnership
CSR	Corporate Social Responsibility
CTE	Committee on Trade and Environment
DEALTI	Farms Free of Child Labour/*Distintivo Empresa Agrícola Libre de Trabajo Infantil* (Mexico)
DEFR	Family Friendly Enterprises/*Distintivo Empresa Familiarmente Responsible* (Mexico)
DIE	German Development Institute/*Deutsches Institut für Entwicklungspolitik*
DIHR	Danish Institute for Human Rights
DOA	Department of Agriculture (Thailand)
DPCIA	Dolphin Protection Consumer Information Act
DSS	Dispute Settlement System
ECCHR	European Centre for Constitutional and Human Rights
EFTA	European Free Trade Association
EIA	Environmental Impact Assessment
EITI	Extractive Industries Transparency Initiative
EPI	Environmental Performance Index
ETP (countries)	Eastern Tropical Pacific (countries)
ETP	Ethical Tea Partnership
EU	European Union
E-WG	Electronic Working Group
F&V	Fruit and Vegetable
FAO	Food and Agriculture Organization
FDI	Foreign Direct Investment
FPIC	Free Prior Informed Consent
FSC	Forest Stewardship Council
FTAs	Free Trade Agreements
G20	Group of 20
GAP	Good Agricultural Practices
GATT	General Agreement on Tariffs and Trade
GC	Global Compact
GCMC	Global Compact Mexican Chapter
GDP	Gross Domestic Product
GFEI	Global Fuel Economy Initiative
GHG	Green House Gas
GIZ	German Corporation for International Cooperation/*Deutsche Gesellschaft für Internationale Zusammenarbeit*
GlobalGAP	Global Good Agricultural Practices
GoF47	Group of Friends of Paragraph 47

GRI	Global Reporting Initiative
GSTC	Global Sustainable Tourism Criteria
GVCs	Global Value Chains
HCV	High Conservation Value
HRDD	Human Rights Due Diligence
HTI	Industrial Forest Plantation/*Hutan Tanaman Industri* (Indonesia)
IBAMA	Brazilian Institute of the Environment and Renewable Natural Resources/*Instituto Brasileiro do Meio Ambiente e dos Recursos Naturais Renováveis*
ICCT	International Council of Clean Transportation
ICFTU	International Confederation of Free Trade Unions
ICSTS	International Convention on Sustainable Trade and Standards
IEA	International Energy Agency
IFCC	Indonesian Forestry Certification Cooperation
IFOAM	International Foundation for Organic Agriculture
IISD	International Institute for Sustainable Development
ILO	International Labour Organization
ILOLEX	ILO International Labour Standards Database
IMECA	Metropolitan Index of Air Quality (Mexico)
IMNC	Mexican Institute for Standardization and Certification, A.C./*Instituto Mexicano de Normalización y Certificación A.C*
INMUJERES	National Institute for Women
IPCC	Intergovernmental Panel on Climate Change
IPM	Integrated Pest Management
IPOC	Indonesian Palm Oil Committee
IPPC	International Plant Protection Convention
IQNet	The International Certification Network
ISEAL	International Social and Environmental Accreditation and Labelling Alliance
ISO	International Organization for Standardization
ISPO	Indonesian Sustainable Palm Oil
ITC	International Trade Centre
ITU	International Telecommunication Union
JCP	Joint Certification Programme
KAN	National Accreditation Committee/*Komite Akreditasi Nasional* (Indonesia)
LABORSTA	Labour Statistics Database operated by ILO Department of Statistics
LEI	Indonesian Ecolabelling Institute/*Lembaga Ekolabel Indonesia*
LV-LK	Timber Legality Verification Body (Indonesia)
MDGs	Millennium Development Goals
MEA	Multilateral Environmental Agreement
MEE	Ministry of Ecology and Environment (China)

Mercosur	Southern Common Market
MGG	Managing Global Governance
MIIT	Ministry of Industry and Information Technology (China)
MINTS	Mexico, Indonesia, Nigeria, Turkey, South Africa
MNEs	Multi-National Enterprises
MOAC	Ministry of Agriculture and Cooperatives (Thailand)
MOEF	Ministry of Environment and Forestry (Indonesia)
MRL	Maximum Residue Limits
MSC	Marine Stewardship Council
MSPO	Malaysian Sustainable Palm Oil
MST	Ministry of Science and Technology (China)
MTS	Multilateral Trading System
NAFTA	North American Free Trade Agreement
NDCs	Nationally Determined Contributions
NDRC	National Development and Reform Commission (China)
NEDC	New European Driving Circle
NES	Nucleus Estate Smallholder
NGOs	Non-Governmental Organizations
NIEs	Newly Industrializing Economies
NTBs	Non-Tariff Barriers
NTMs	Non-Tariff Measures
ODA	Official Development Assistance
OECD	Organization for Economic Cooperation and Development
OEIWG	(UN Human Rights Council) Open-ended Intergovernmental Working Group on Transnational Corporations and Other Business Enterprises with Respect to Human Rights
OHCHR	Office of the United Nations High Commissioner for Human Rights
OICA	International Organization of Motor Vehicle Manufacturers
OIE	World Organisation for Animal Health
OIE	World Organisation for Animal Health
P&C	Principles and Criteria
PEFC	Programme for the Endorsement of Forest Certification
PHPL	Sustainable Forest Production Management/*Pengelolaan Hutan Produksi. Lestari* (Indonesia)
PPMs	Process and Production Methods
PPP	Private Public Partnership
PTAs	Preferential Trade Agreements
PVS	Private Voluntary Standard
QCI	Quality Council of India
RASFF	Rapid Alert System for Food and Feed (Thailand)
RIL	Reduced Impact Logging
Rio+20	United Nations Conference on Sustainable Development
RSB	Roundtable on Sustainable Biomaterials
RSPO	Roundtable on Sustainable Palm Oil

RTRS	Round Table on Responsible Soya
SABS	South African Bureau of Standards
SAC	Standardization Administration of China
SAFE	Safer Affordable Fuel-Efficient
SAMR	State Administration for Market Regulation (China)
SAN	Sustainable Agriculture Network
SDGs	Sustainable Development Goals
SE4ALL	Sustainable Energy for All Initiative (UN)
SEMARNAT	Mexican Ministry of Environment and Natural Resources
SFM	Sustainable Forest Management
SINOPEC	China Petroleum and Chemical Corporation
SMEs	Small and Medium-sized Enterprises
SOAS	School of Oriental and African Studies (University of London)
SPMs	Sanitary and Phytosanitary Measures
SPS Agreement	Agreement on the Application of Sanitary and Phytosanitary Measures (WTO)
SR	Sustainability Reporting
STC	Specific Trade Concerns
STDF	Standards and Trade Development Facility
STPS	Mexican Ministry of Labour/*Secretaría del Trabajo y Prevision Social*
SVLK	Timber Legality Assurance System (Indonesia)
T20	THINK 20
TAS	Thai Agricultural Standard
TBT Agreement	Agreement on Technical Barriers to Trade (WTO)
TBTs	Technical Barriers to Trade
Thai PAN	Thai Pesticide Alert Network
TNCs	Trans National Corporations
TRIPS Agreement	Agreement on Trade-Related Aspects of Intellectual Property Rights (WTO)
UN	United Nations
UNCTAD	United Nations Conference on Trade and Development
UNEP	United Nations Environment Programme/UN Environment
UNFCCC	United Nations Framework Convention on Climate Change
UNFSS	United Nations Forum on Sustainability Standards
UNGPs	United Nations Guiding Principles on Business and Human Rights
UNWTO	United Nations World Tourism Organization
US EPA	United States Environmental Protection Agency
VSS	Voluntary Sustainability Standards
WALHI	Indonesian Forum for the Environment/*Wahana Lingkungan Hidup Indonesia*

WBCSD	World Business Council for Social Development
WHO	World Health Organization
WTO	World Trade Organization
WWF	World Wide Fund for Nature

List of Figures

6 Advances in Sustainability Reporting: What Is Missing?

List of Tables

**12 Standard-Setting in Water Use and Sustainable Development:
A Comparative Critical Analysis of Grey Water Recycling
in the Tourism Sector**

Chapter 1
Introduction

Johannes Blankenbach, Archna Negi, and Jorge Antonio Pérez-Pineda

1 Thematic Context

While accelerated economic globalization may have generated additional employment and income worldwide, it has also been one of the drivers of unsustainable production and consumption patterns across the globe. Every day, conditions of production somewhere in the world infringe on human health and wellbeing, often far away from the place where the goods and services are eventually purchased by the end consumer. Likewise, current production and consumption models exceed planetary limitations to human activity in many ways, causing irreversible damage to the environment and earth system. These impacts of economic activity are, in principle, recognized today and manifest as key sustainability concerns.

The objective of sustainability is being pursued through multiple routes at many different levels by a variety of actors. The focus of this edited volume is on sustainability standards (and sustainability regulations) as an important vehicle to make global consumption and production more sustainable. The different contributions also shed light on the link between sustainability standards and global governance. The scope of global governance has been thus described by the Commission on Global Governance:

> Governance is the sum of the many ways individuals and institutions, public and private, manage their common affairs. It is a continuing process through which conflicting or diverse interests may be accommodated and co-operative action may be taken. It includes formal

J. Blankenbach
Business & Human Rights Resource Centre, Berlin, Germany

A. Negi (✉)
Centre for International Politics, Organization and Disarmament (CIPOD), School of International Studies, Jawaharlal Nehru University, New Delhi, India
e-mail: archnanegisingh@gmail.com

J. A. Pérez-Pineda
Faculty of Economics and Business, Universidad Anáhuac México, Estado de México, Mexico

1

institutions and regimes empowered to enforce compliance, as well as informal arrangements that people and institutions either have agreed to or perceive to be in their interest. [...] At the global level, governance has been viewed primarily as intergovernmental relationships, but it must now be understood as also involving non-governmental organizations (NGOs), citizens' movements, multinational corporations, and the global capital market. (Commission on Global Governance, 1995, p. 2)

Sustainability standards and regulations, in general, are meant to achieve a spectrum of societal objectives by attaching certain criteria to commodities and their production. In theory, they aspire to achieve the social, cultural and environmental values that consumers wish to see promoted in society. Given the growing quantum of commodities crossing international borders, standards, when attached to international trade, can be an extremely effective means of promoting a certain set of values. Estimates from the UN Conference on Trade and Development (UNCTAD) show that standards and regulations have an impact on approximately 80 percent of the world's trade in commodities.

The increasing use of sustainability standards in production and trade, and across global value chains, has opened up several lines of questioning and contestation—How are standards to be defined? Who defines standards (or whose interests are reflected in standards)? How are standards to be differentiated from regulations? What could be the advantages and limitations of purely voluntary approaches? How do standards deal with the problem of competition, given the multiplicity of standards that apply simultaneously to products? How do private and public standards co-exist (collaboration or competition?) with each other in the same space? What are the differential implications of standards—(1) for the developing countries with less wherewithal to meet the financial implications flowing from the use of standards vis-a-vis the industrialized countries, who are often the sources of these standards; and (2) for big firms with absorptive capacity for additional costs and small and medium-sized enterprises (SMEs), especially in developing countries and emerging economies, who suffer from both capacity and information asymmetries? Thus, both the setting and the implementation of standards are fraught with inherent complexities.

Standards are met with a level of acceptability when they are set and implemented in a domestic setting but tend to become problematic when they operate in a cross-border context. Further, standards may be intentionally designed for protectionist purposes—in order to provide domestic producers with an advantage vis-a-vis foreign ones—thereby impeding international trade. Alternatively, they may act as de facto barriers to trade, even if they are not designed with that intention, when producers are differentially equipped to meet standards. The challenge, then, in using standards in international trade lies in achieving a balance that allows for their use for genuine sustainability reasons—environmental protection or prevention of unethical business practices across global value chains—while not allowing them to turn into instruments of protectionism.

The starting point of any enquiry is definitional; it is therefore pertinent to ask: what are "sustainability standards" and "sustainability regulations"? Given the plethora of sometimes contradicting definitions and categorisations of standards, it is not an easy task to harmonize them to a common understanding but an interlinking is possible in order to provide a common reference point. At a general level, sustainability standards have been defined as "set[s] of criteria defining good social and environmental practices in an industry of product" (ISEAL, 2015). By extension, this definition can also be applied to sustainability regulations, as the legal nature of the criteria is not specified. While it is narrow enough to distinguish sustainability standards and regulations from other types of standards and regulation, it is broad enough to cover different categories within the field of sustainability standards and regulations.[1]

The term "international standard" is also commonly referred to in research and policy. Swann makes a distinction between the "purist" understanding of the word "international" and its more limited application. In the former, a standard is considered "international" only if it conforms to a standard published by an international organization such as the International Organization for Standardization (ISO) or the International Telecommunication Union (ITU), whereas in the more limited understanding, a standard will qualify as being "international" if it is commonly used by a group of countries or within a region (Swann, 2010, p. 6). As far as defining "standards" is concerned, the main distinction that is usually stressed upon is that "standards" entail voluntary compliance, whereas "regulations" impose mandatory compliance. However, it is an established fact that it is not always easy to distinguish between the actual economic effects of both (Swann, 2010, p. 6).

Sustainability standards and regulations can be distinguished from other standards and regulations on the basis of their content, i.e. their focus on social, environmental and other sustainability challenges emanating from business activity. The 17 Sustainable Development Goals (SDGs) make clear that "sustainability" or "sustainable development" is an extremely broad concept interacting with almost all aspects of life in all countries in the world. This does not mean, however, that every example of regulation or standard setting in the world economy qualifies as sustainability related. A performance standard, for instance, may only qualify as a sustainability standard if it aims at reducing environmentally and socially harmful impacts of technical products once they are in use, e.g. energy consumption of cars and electric devices. A quality standard simply defining the size of a screw is clearly *not* a sustainability standard. However, other *quality* (and as a sub-category: *safety*) standards considerably overlap with sustainability standards if, for instance, they set limits to pesticide and other chemical residues in (food) products, thereby protecting human and environmental health both at the consumption and at the production stage. In fact, sustainability standards and regulations typically address wider environmental, social and other sustainability issues at the production stage that may or may not affect the nature of a final product: local pollution, CO_2 emissions in production, harvesting practices, social rights of workers, wages, community rights, and even financial transparency and good corporate governance.

---

[1] Some of the conceptual parts of this chapter are taken from an earlier, internal concept note for the project.

In trying to identify different categories within the field of sustainability standards and regulations, four generic forms of sustainability standards are recognizable on the basis of their *institutional origin* and *legal nature*, following Henson and Humphrey (2009, p. 5). They differentiate between (1) *public, mandatory* sustainability standards (= regulations) set by national governments or government agencies that impose legally binding requirements for general market access and (2) *private, voluntary* sustainability standards (VSS) set up by private multi-stakeholder initiatives with often global memberships to open up high-value market segments and respond to sustainability concerns. Some private voluntary sustainability standards are also set up by large individual companies, e.g. TESCO Nurture (Henson & Humphrey, 2009, p. 6). These standards may be treated as a distinct sub-category, termed company-specific voluntary sustainability standards. About two-thirds of private standards use a logo, whereas one-third rely on business-to-business implementation without a consumer-facing label (Potts et al., 2014, p. 37).

Two more categories need to be added: governments may also promulgate public voluntary sustainability standards, and private voluntary standards can become legally mandated if referred to in binding regulations (Henson & Humphrey, 2009, p. 5). This blurs the line between *public* and *private*; all the more so as some public sustainability regulations have their origins in private standards (Smith, 2009, p. 13). For instance, the Forest Stewardship Council's (FSC) instruments for zoning high conservation values areas have been fully incorporated into public regulation by China, Bolivia and others (Djama, 2011, p. 4). Similarly, the distinction between *voluntary* and *mandatory* is not always as clear as it seems, considering that voluntary sustainability standards can become "de facto mandatory in a commercial sense" if dominant companies require their suppliers to comply with them (Henson & Humphrey, 2009, p. 5; Smith, 2009, p. 17) and/or because of consumers' preferences. The effectiveness of a standard that is not legally mandatory, but de facto mandatory due to market dynamics, is certainly limited in a number of ways, for instance when it comes to legal enforceability, remediation and compensation for harm caused by non-compliance. The toughest sanction that voluntary schemes can take against an individual member is usually just exclusion from the scheme, which does not entail any immediate remediation for victims of a company's non-compliant behaviour, nor is there a possibility without appropriate legislation to hold lead firms or the scheme itself accountable for a lack of due diligence or audit failure.

The examples of the EU Timber Regulation and EU Organic Farming in Table 1 illustrate the conceptual difference between mandatory public/governmental regulations (EU in this case may be considered a supranational government) and voluntary sustainability standards, be they private or public. The Timber Regulation prescribes that all timber entering the EU market must comply with certain criteria, e.g. it must not have been illegally logged. Non-compliance may be sanctioned by EU criminal or administrative courts. EU Organic Farming, in contrast, is a public voluntary sustainability standard; any domestic or imported product that carries the description "organic" and/or the official EU organic logo is required to comply with it. However, compliance is not mandatory for all products on the market as products below this

Table 1 Different forms of sustainability standards and regulations

	Public	Private
Mandatory	Sustainability regulations *Example: EU Timber Regulation (EU 995/2010)*	Legally mandated private sustainability standards *Example: Reference to ISO 9000 in EU Directives on CE marking*
Voluntary	Public voluntary sustainability standards *Example: EU Organic Farming (EC 834/2007 and 889/2008)*	Private voluntary sustainability standards *Examples: Fairtrade, FSC, UTZ, GlobalGAP*

Source Henson and Humphrey (2009, p. 5), complemented by Blankenbach

standard may still be sold as regular non-organic products as long as they comply with basic EU food quality and safety regulations.

Apart from variations in their *institutional origin* and *legal nature*, standards and regulations as presented in Table 1 may also differ in terms of their *geographic reach* as well as in the *ambition of their formal criteria*. Thus, the distinctions to be noted are apparently not limited to those *between* the different categories of standards and regulations, but also occur *within* these categories.

From the perspective of *geographic reach*, some advanced sustainability regulations (e.g. by the EU on timber or biofuels, 2009/28/EC) take into account production and harvesting practices abroad, while others tend to focus on domestic protections. For instance, many richer industrialized and emerging economies may have adopted strict environmental and labour regulations for domestic production. These provisions, however, do not directly apply to production abroad, e.g. in poor countries where weaker sustainability regulations might be in place. Similarly, some public regulations may focus on protecting the "domestic environment and public health in the importing country against the harmful effects of consumption or disposal of [...] imported products" (Khatun, 2009, p. 8). A growing number of regulatory innovations extend this scope; for instance those striving to legally mandate corporate human rights due diligence across global value chains, which is the key operational principle of the UN Guiding Principles on Business and Human Rights (OHCHR, 2011).[2] The French Duty of Vigilance Law is a pioneering example where respect for human rights and the environment is legally mandated into transnational corporate activities (ECCJ, 2017, p. 1), in this case those of large French companies. Debates and initiatives on mandatory due diligence are currently underway in several other countries, mostly European, as well as at the regional (EU) and global (UN) levels. Voluntary sustainability standards schemes, in theory, also strive to generate sustainability benefits transnationally, especially in the global south, but their voluntary nature means that none of this is legally enforceable.

Apart from geographic reach, standards and regulations vary on the basis of *ambition*. First of all, it is notable that from a governance perspective, it is per se much

---

[2] See the Business and Human Rights Resource Centre's web portal and blog series on "Mandatory Due Diligence" at https://www.business-humanrights.org/en/mandatory-due-diligence.

more ambitious to introduce binding public regulation than to rely on corporate self-regulation through voluntary standards. In terms of the formal content of standards and regulations, the criteria that voluntary standards set may in some contexts be stricter than those of local regulations. In this volume, for instance, Brandi contends that the requirements of the Indonesia Sustainable Palm Oil (ISPO) regulation (a public mandatory certification scheme) are less demanding and comprehensive than those of the voluntary Roundtable for Sustainable Palm Oil (RSPO) standard, especially when it comes to environmental criteria. There are other contexts and sustainability dimensions, however, where "broad [voluntary] standards [...] rarely go further than local labour law" (Åhlberg, 2019), e.g. when they refer to (often very low) local minimum wages rather than requiring living wages. The question then is whether such voluntary initiatives at least provide for stronger internal assurance and implementation mechanisms, especially when compared to poorly enforced public regulations in countries with weak governance.

Having discussed definitions and classifications of standards and regulations, a preliminary look at institutional and normative frameworks for sustainability standards and regulations is in order for identifying their global governance linkages. Sustainability standards, even if many of them are private, do not emerge and operate in isolation from broader institutional and normative frameworks of global governance. In fact, there is ample evidence of interactions and overlaps. International treaties such as International Labour Organization (ILO) labour conventions and technical codes developed by international organizations such as the World Health Organization (WHO) Codex Alimentarius for food safety provide an important reference frame for sustainability standards and regulations. Sustainability regulations in general implement national sustainability laws, which may in turn result from the ratification of an international treaty (Altmann, 1994, p. 176). Similarly, private sustainability standards often refer to international norms. The formal standards of the Marine Stewardship Council (MSC), for instance, mainly build on those of the Food and Agriculture Organization (FAO) Code of Conduct for Responsible Fisheries (Santacoloma, 2014, p. 20).

The World Trade Organization (WTO) provides an additional institutional and legal framework to regulate the use and content of sustainability standards. Under WTO rules, member states "can adopt trade-related measures aimed at protecting the environment" (WTO, 2015) if these laws and regulations are "not applied arbitrarily and are not used as disguised protectionism" (ibid.). The WTO sets out a number of legitimate reasons for the use of sustainability-related trade barriers. It recommends that member states adopt internationally agreed sustainability standards—such as those originating from the Codex Alimentarius, the World Organization for Animal Health (OIE) and the International Plant Protection Convention (IPPC). If standards more stringent than the internationally laid-down ones are to be adopted, those are permitted as well, provided a scientific justification can be established for their use. These provisions, however, only apply to standards established or endorsed by public institutions, i.e. to public regulations and private standards legally mandated by public regulation. Purely private sustainability standards, in contrast, may "fall outside of this regime" (Henson 2008, p.76) as only states are subject to the WTO regime.

Therefore, the problem of the additional burden that private sustainability standards that are passed down supply chains "impose on small and medium producers and exporters in developing countries [...] have not yet been satisfactorily solved" (Santacoloma, 2014, p. 19). While the need for the WTO to address private standards has been highlighted, both inside and outside the WTO, they currently remain excluded from the regime.

It is important to note that general public and corporate policies do not fall into the definition of sustainability standards and regulations as established at the beginning but still interact with this field. For instance, Corporate Social Responsibility (CSR) strategies and reports of private companies will in most cases include a commitment to obey mandatory laws and regulations and refer to the type of voluntary sustainability standards the company uses.

Any study of sustainability standards therefore entails an engagement with the complex interface between the voluntary and the mandatory, the local and the global levels, the private and the public domains, the industrialized and the developing countries, states, intergovernmental and non-governmental processes, large and small enterprises, and producers and consumers—and the dynamic processes created by their interaction and overlap. Recent studies point to "...a policy ecosystem dominated by a proliferation of standards that complement, substitute, or compete against each other, with coordination mechanisms beginning to arise" (Lambin & Thorlakson, 2018, p. 369). The complex nature of the interactions between the multiple and varied actors need not always be antagonistic and can sometimes be complementary.

2 About the Book

The discussion above has made clear the significance of identifying "sustainability standards" as a theme of research. Further, "emerging economies" were chosen as the focus of the study as they represent countries that are increasingly engaged in international trade, yet continue to face challenges in implementing standards. This becomes a hindrance in their efforts to compete internationally at the level of industrialized countries as also in the attempt to provide effective protection to people and the environment through the use of standards. It was expected, therefore, that empirical inputs from this set of countries would yield rich learnings. The book is simply structured, with discussion divided into two main parts. It starts by broadly looking at global governance frameworks for sustainability standards and then moves to empirical studies of sustainability standards at work in specific sectoral and country contexts.

Part I, which focuses on global governance frameworks, begins with a discussion of sustainability standards in the context of the 2030 Agenda for Sustainable Development and the Sustainable Development Goals (SDGs), which were adopted by the United Nations (UN) at the summit meeting of 2015. **Blankenbach** examines the supposed interlinkages and interfaces between voluntary sustainability standards

(VSS) and the SDGs. He points out that while it is not for the first time that VSS have been a part of sustainable development agendas, it is the SDG framework that, in the most prominent way, helps shine a light on the said instrumental value of VSS in meeting sustainability objectives. This chapter explores to what extent VSS can or cannot play a role in taking forward the agenda of the SDGs. Using the International Trade Centre's (ITC) Standards Map, the chapter assesses whether specific formal VSS requirements align with one or more SDGs. **Blankenbach** finds that, in theory, a considerable number of VSS criteria correspond with the 17 SDGs but he also cautions that most assessments of the on-the-ground sustainable development impacts of such schemes have so far come to tentative or inconclusive results. He notes with concern the growing evidence of the failure of social auditing—a procedure also used to certify and verify standards compliance—in uncovering or mitigating human and labour rights abuses in companies' global value chains. Given the mutually reinforcing relationship between the SDGs and human rights, the pitfalls of certification and verification audits and lack of accountability may compromise any transformative potential of VSS, the author contends. This paper is thus a call for fundamental reform of VSS schemes, especially of their assurance and worker engagement arrangements and culture, as well as for more sustainability regulation— including mandatory human rights and environmental due diligence—for companies across their operations and global value chains.

Another significant locus of global governance where sustainability standards play out is the World Trade Organization (WTO). **Negi** provides an overview assessment of sustainability standards within the framework of the WTO. Her paper is methodologically a legal study that focuses on the rules and judicial interpretations that have emanated from the WTO in relation to standards and regulations. WTO rules have long recognized the conditional need for the use of standards and regulations by member states. Two WTO agreements—the *Agreement on Technical Barriers to Trade* and the *Agreement on the Application of Sanitary and Phytosanitary Measures*—recognize the right of member states to use standards and regulations to meet their legitimate objectives, provided trade is not restricted in a disguised fashion. The interpretations that have emerged in relation to standards and regulations from the WTO dispute settlement system have sometimes helped clarify the legal positions while at other times, have led to further confusion. Some select disputes relating to the use of standards are discussed in this chapter. Private sustainability standards are not currently dealt with at the WTO, and despite the argument having been made in favour of the WTO taking up private standards within its purview, the organization is reluctant to do so in the face of divergences between its industrialized and developing member states on this issue. The chapter also discusses the special concerns of the developing countries in relation to standards. **Negi** points to the fact that the WTO has grown organically since its inception to include newer issue areas; given the proliferation of private standards (many of which actually play out as mandatory requirements in a commercial sense), it remains to be seen whether the WTO will take on the additional responsibility of regulating private standards as well.

In the context of trade, given the sclerosis of the WTO's Doha Round and the troubles of the organization itself, there has been an increasing resort to preferential trade agreements (PTAs) to negotiate trade rules. Taking forward the trade-related focus initiated in the previous chapter, the chapter by **Berger, Blümer, Brandi** and **Chi** provides a detailed survey of environmental provisions in preferential trade agreements (PTAs) in emerging markets. In pursuing the SDGs, the authors point out, economic activity needs to be transformed to make it "consistent with environmental sustainability" and for this, an appropriate regulatory framework is required for the global economy. Because of the "proliferation" and "deepening" of PTAs, they are identified as potential loci for promoting sustainability goals through the global economy by integrating the use of both regulations and voluntary standards through PTAs. The authors point out that "...strong environmental provisions in PTAs may provide a context that is conducive to the effective implementation and use of standards and regulation that seek to address sustainability challenges" **(p. 61)**. In this chapter, the authors assess environmental provisions in emerging market PTAs to test the assumption that emerging markets (as compared to the industrialized world) are less interested in linking environmental and labour standards to trade policies. The analysis conducted in this chapter is based on an original dataset that maps environmental provisions in emerging market PTAs. The authors focus attention on five specific case studies—China, India, Indonesia, Brazil and Mexico—and develop a dataset mapping environmental provisions in PTAs, comprising nine dimensions. All full free trade agreements (FTAs) and customs unions established by emerging markets are discussed. The central finding of this chapter is that "...the PTAs of emerging markets incorporate more and more environmental provisions over time and that they tend to include more environmental content when they have negotiated and signed with OECD countries, which in turn suggests that OECD countries can still be considered as rule-makers and emerging markets still largely as rule-takers in the context under consideration" **(p. 62)**. This chapter, by focusing on PTAs, showcases the interesting regional variations that exist in the context of their sustainability ambitions.

Moving from the intergovernmental spaces, the chapter by **Pérez-Pineda** focuses on the private sector and its engagement with sustainability standards and regulations, using Corporate Social Responsibility (CSR) a link. **Pérez-Pineda** begins by revisiting the historical context of the 1980s and 1990s, capturing the changing landscape of globalization, liberalization, free trade, etc., leading eventually to the launch of the "Global Compact" by the United Nations (UN) in 2000. The chapter reviews the role of the private sector in the realm of sustainability standards, looking at context, conceptual approaches and implications. Private firms and transnational corporations (TNCs) are understood as potentially having a positive as well as negative impact on society and there has consistently been an effort—"through guides, codes of conduct and multilateral agreements" **(p. 85)**—to try and regulate their activities in order to minimize adverse impact. The UN's Global Compact represents one of the most relevant initiatives in aligning the activities of the private sector with sustainability objectives. With the growing power and reach of the private sector (which is demonstrated by the author), the demand for accountability of their activities has also grown. CSR has developed as a concept bridging this growing power with the increasing awareness of the effects of the private sector. **Pérez-Pineda** looks at a range of different forms in which standards—public and private, global and local, market-based and non-market-based—can manifest. He uses the example of Mexico, identifying three key institutions that are relevant to standards, to show how a convergence can be brought about to contribute to the 2030 goals. He concludes that given the significance of the private sector in the current times, there is a need to ensure that its activities are aligned with sustainability goals, and he argues that CSR could provide the framework for such an alignment.

A related theme is taken up by **Santos, Sena** and **Freitas** in their paper on "sustainability reporting" (SR), which argues that companies are increasingly under pressure to be more socially and environmentally responsible. CSR has emerged as a new business paradigm and "sustainability reporting" has become an important instrument of transparency and accountability. The question being asked in this chapter is whether the tool is being used to full potential? SR is a voluntary process but there is a growing tendency to make it mandatory. The authors focus on the Group of Friends of Paragraph 47 (GoF47)—a voluntary group of national governments supported by the United Nations Environment Programme/UN Environment (UNEP) and the Global Reporting Initiative (GRI) that subscribe to the idea of SR. The chapter points to the link of GoF47 with Goal 12.6 of the SDGs (*"Encourage companies, especially large and transnational companies, to adopt sustainable practices and to integrate sustainability information into their reporting cycle"*). The authors argue that SR "…has a high potential to promote good governance schemes as well as social and environmental standards…" **(p. 104)** and make suggestions on how to improve it. A major shortcoming identified in the SR process is that there is little evidence of stakeholders—governments and civil society—using SR to its full potential. Weak stakeholder participation is thus identified as the missing link between SR practices and social and environmental improvements and the chapter recommends "stakeholder involvement" in order to make SR a strong instrument of good governance.

In the last chapter of this section, **Bandyopadhyay** discusses the impact of global labour standards on export performance. Contextualizing her study in the debates around "comparative advantage", "race to the bottom" and "disguised protectionism", the author empirically investigates the effects of labour standards on the export performance of a country. The chapter tests the popular view that low-standards countries enjoy a better export performance, using a robust empirical analysis of World Bank datasets. For labour standards, the author looks at whether countries have ratified the core ILO conventions, collecting data from the ILOLEX dataset. The chapter finds, contrary to traditional wisdom, that no definite relationship can be discerned between labour rights and export performance. However, "if a richer country ratifies more labour conventions its effects on exports will be less positive than what will occur if a comparatively poorer country ratifies the conventions" **(p. 124)**. Further, the author argues that in some cases, some proxies of labour standards have a positive impact on export performance, signifying that "…countries do have an incentive to strengthen their labour conditions to improve export performance, especially if it is a poorer country" **(p. 127)**. Undoubtedly, the presence of emerging economies in the global value chains is rising, both via the supply side and the demand side participation as well as via the participation of civil society; thus their participation in global standard setting needs to be studied carefully.

A wide canvas is thus covered in the first section relating to governance frameworks, touching upon important players such as the UN, the WTO, regional trade frameworks, the private sector, GoF47 and the ILO. These studies collectively provide the backdrop for the case study based research focusing on "emerging economies" that is contained in the subsequent section. The country context includes experiences ranging from Indonesia, Thailand, India, China, Mexico and Brazil while the sectoral context spans the palm oil sector, forestry, farming, vehicular emissions, tourism, and fruit and vegetables.

Part II opens with two chapters focused on Indonesia. Interestingly, both chapters delve into the theme of the interactive dynamics between private and public standards. The first chapter, by **Brandi**, describes the "…changing landscape of voluntary sustainability standards in Indonesia…" **(p. 133)** and discusses the challenges of making global value chains more sustainable. The chapter focuses on standards in the palm oil sector, including the Roundtable on Sustainable Palm Oil (RSPO), which is a private standards scheme, and the recently introduced Indonesian Sustainable Palm Oil (ISPO) initiative, which is a mandatory government-led certification scheme. The author points out that "[t]he interaction between private and public authorities in the governance of environmental and social challenges is still an understudied field of global governance" **(p. 134)**. The chapter highlights the importance of including smallholders into certification schemes, while recognizing that this is challenging. Field research for this chapter included interviews with smallholder certification projects in Indonesia. An interesting point that this chapter raises is the potential trade-offs between the environmental and social dimensions of sustainable (inclusive) development. The chapter also suggests some ways in which such trade-offs can be managed. The findings of this study can easily relate to other sectoral examples as well.

The second case study from Indonesia is by **Kartika**, **Hariyadi** and **Cerdikwan**. This chapter focuses on the forestry sector and the practice of sustainable forest management (SFM) in the country. Two internationally recognized certifications that are available to a forest concession holder in Indonesia—the Forest Stewardship Council (FSC) and the Programme for the Endorsement of Forest Certification (PEFC)—are studied. The chapter points out that generally, these VSS complement public standards and regulation, but it also notes that multiple standards are challenging for producers due to increased compliance costs. The research is based on interviews conducted with forestry research and certification institutions in Indonesia. A variety of government regulations are assessed in order to determine whether PEFC fills the gap in what was lacking. The findings of the chapter are that PEFC seems to substitute and is preferred to FSC; they both complement government regulations, while requiring higher standards. The PEFC standard will potentially enjoy higher acceptability because its requirements are not as stringent as the FSC. The twin challenges faced by PEFC, however, are that it does not enjoy high domestic stakeholder support and it has low legitimacy as a non-state scheme.

The chapter by **Holzapfel** and **Hampel-Milagrosa** traces a "transformation of the agricultural sector in the developing countries" **(p. 163)** and points out how meeting the market requirements in high-value supply chains, has become more challenging for the developing countries. They pick as a case study a well-known private standard for good agricultural practices—GlobalGAP—that focuses on food safety but also covers aspects of environmental protection. The authors make a point similar to the one made by **Brandi**—that smallholders are particularly disadvantaged in meeting the requirements of standards. The chapter takes the example of smallholders in the fruit and vegetable value chain in Thailand and India and bases its findings on both secondary data and field work. The authors conclude from their study that mostly smallholders do not have to face GlobalGAP requirements as they serve domestic or lower value export markets and even when they do, "…it is the wealthier and more educated small-scale farmers who adopt and benefit from the GlobalGAP standard…" **(p. 180)**. During the course of their research, the authors found co-existing public and private GAP standards in both countries (APEDA's IndiaGAP and QCI's IndGAP in case of India); since the governments enjoy low credibility as a monitor of compliance, the private entities tend to introduce their own standards. The chapter points out that "[p]arallel standards, as found both in Thailand and India, lead to high transaction costs and confusion among producers, exporters and consumers" **(p. 181)** and underscores the need for harmonization. The authors also suggest institutional arrangements allowing for more smallholders to adopt local GAP standards.

Another comparative study that is carried out by **Mendoza** and **Jiahan** is between China and Mexico in the context of vehicular emissions. The comparison flows from three justifications. The transport sectors of both countries are significant contributors to overall greenhouse gas (GHG) emissions in their respective countries. Both countries rank among the ten largest automobile producers and are thus leading automobile exporters. They have to fulfil their individual commitments in combating climate change as they have committed to climate mitigation and adaptation targets under the United Nations Framework Convention on Climate Change (UNFCCC) mandate. Aside from these similarities, the standard setting and implementation process in China and Mexico has been quite different. The main dissimilarity is the adoption of different reference standards: while China has been working under the EU's regulatory framework, Mexico has set a partial homologation with the US EPA regulation. Vehicular emissions efficiency standards, the authors claim, are targeted at reaping not merely local advantages but also global advantages in the form of GHG emissions reduction. The authors show—through their case studies of China and Mexico—that "global" (EURO VI/US EPA 2010) standards cannot automatically be transposed to the emerging economies as they do not always fit the national contexts and the sectoral specificities. Rather than being treated as "one-size-fits-all" solutions, the "global" standards should serve as a reference point on which national agendas can be superimposed. **Mendoza** and **Jiahan** make the argument that vehicle efficiency standards in emerging economies should be aligned with national sustainability goals.

Moving to Brazil, the focus of study shifts to the tourism sector, in particular the use of "grey water" in this sector. The chapter by **Coelho**, **Domingues**, **Mousinho** and **Saretta** highlights the special role that tourism plays in impacting natural resource use, "responsible for a great amount of aggressive use of resources such as water…" **(p. 201)**. This chapter seeks to assess to what extent standards and regulations apply to the use of water in the hotel industry, comparing the tourist areas in two major cities—Rio de Janeiro and Berlin. The study reveals that the actions undertaken by the hotels analyzed were more to do with self-compliance rather than external pressure. Also, in most cases, they were not based on the demands of particular standards but related to the image-building of the hotel vis-à-vis its clients. The quantitative results from the study show that recycling systems are relevant for volume savings; however, most of the analyzed standards are not oriented properly to sustainability. This is a gap that could be turned into an opportunity by the different stakeholders involved (public and private). The authors propose the creation of a common regulatory framework with public and private intervention that can create benefits for both. The chapter makes a case for a strong focus on the impact of tourism on the use of water and possible standards to be developed in this area. The UN World Tourism Organization (UNWTO), it is suggested, could play a more proactive role in this. Linking with the SDGs could have a positive benefit in addressing specific issues areas like the one focused upon in this chapter.

As the summaries of the chapters above reveal, the issue of "sustainability standards" has been accorded a wide interpretation. Taking advantage of the confusion in discourse over the definitional limits, no strict definitional scope was retained for the contributions in this book. Depending on a more intuitive understanding of "sustainability standards" was a deliberate decision taken in order to gain from an expanded canvas of discussion. Thus, many of the chapters included move freely between "standards" and "regulations" and typologies of "sustainability standards" are not strictly uniform.

What is noteworthy is how studies located in different parts of the world have come up with common concerns and questions in relation to sustainability standards. A key finding that repeatedly finds mention, for instance, is that voluntary standards are clearly not sufficient to meet sustainability concerns and need to be complemented with enforceable, mandatory regulations. The fact that the dynamic interface between public and private standards, and the role of lead firms, need to be better understood in order to minimize the burden on less powerful producers emerges more than once. The special focus on smallholders is of utmost importance as there are differential impacts of standards implementation on different sizes of enterprise. Capacity limitations—in setting as well as meeting international standards—in emerging economies (let alone in other developing countries), emerges as a central theme in most chapters. Thus, many common findings have emerged during the writing and collation of this book, written from a cross-country, trans-disciplinary perspective. Multiple pathways of enquiry remain that need to be pursued in order to achieve the twin goals of attaining the sustainability objectives embodied in the SDGs through the optimal use of sustainability standards while, at the same time, watching out for the pitfalls and taking cognizance of the particular concerns of the "emerging economies".

References

Åhlberg, M. (2019). *Putting the power in workers' hands: FLEX scopes a new approach to tackling labour abuse and exploitation.* London: Focus on Labour Exploitation (FLEX). Retrieved from https://labourexploitation.org/news/putting-power-workers%E2%80%99-hands-flex-scopes-new-approach-tackling-labour-abuse-and-exploitation.

Altmann, J. (1994). International environmental standards: Considerations on principles and procedures. *Intereconomics, 29*(4), 176–183. Retrieved from http://link.springer.com/article/10.1007%2FBF02926436.

Commission on Global Governance. (1995). *Our global neighbourhood: report of the commission on global governance.* Oxford: Oxford University Press.

Djama, M. (2011). *Articulating private voluntary standards and public regulations.* CIRAD Perspective No. 11. Retrieved from http://www.cirad.fr/en/news/all-news-items/articles/2011/ca-vient-de-sortir/regulating-the-globalised-economy.

ECCJ (European Coalition for Corporate Justice). (2017). *French corporate duty of vigilance law: Frequently asked questions.* Brussels: Author. Retrieved from http://corporatejustice.org/documents/publications/french-corporate-duty-of-vigilance-law-faq.pdf.

Henson, S. (2008). The role of public and private standards in regulating international food markets. *Journal of International Agricultural Trade and Development, 4*(1), 63–81.

Henson, S., & Humphrey, J. (2009). *The impacts of private food safety standards on the food chain and on public standard-setting processes.* Paper prepared for FAO/WHO. Retrieved from ftp://193.43.36.92/codex/Meetings/CAC/CAC32/al329Dbe.pdf

ISEAL (International Social and Environmental Accreditation and Labelling Alliance). (2015). *What is a sustainability standard?* Retrieved from http://www.isealalliance.org/waypoint/what-is-a-sustainability-standard.

Khatun, F. (2009). *Environment related trade barriers and the WTO.* CPD Occasional Paper Series No. 77. Retrieved from http://www.eaber.org/node/22292.

Lambin, Eric F., & Thorlakson, Tannis. (2018). Sustainability standards: Interactions between private actors, civil society, and governments. *Annual Review of Environment and Resources, 43,* 369–393.

OHCHR (Office of the United Nations High Commissioner for Human Rights). (2011): *Guiding principles on business and human rights.* Geneva: Author. Retrieved from https://www.ohchr.org/documents/publications/GuidingprinciplesBusinesshr_eN.pdf.

Potts, J., Lynch, M., Wilkings, A., Huppé, G., Cunningham, M., & Voora, V. (2014). *The state of sustainability initiatives review 2014: standards and the green economy: State of sustainability initiatives.* Winnipeg/London: International Institute for Sustainable Development (iisd)/ International Institute for Environment and Development (iied). Retrieved from https://www.iisd.org/pdf/2014/ssi_2014.pdf.

Santacoloma, P. (2014). Nexus between public and private food standards: main issues and perspectives. In A. Meybeck & S. Redfern (Eds.), *Voluntary standards for sustainable food systems: Challenges and opportunities* (pp. 11–23). Rome: FAO/UNEP Programme on Sustainable Food Systems. Retrieved from http://www.fao.org/3/a-i3421e.pdf.

Smith, G. (2009). *Interaction of public and private standards in the food chain.* OECD Food, Agriculture and Fisheries Working Papers No. 15. Paris: OECD Publishing. Retrieved from http://www.oecd.org/tad/agricultural-trade/45013504.pdf.

Swann, G. M. P. (2010). *International standards and trade: A review of the empirical literature.* OECD Trade Policy Working Papers No. 97. Paris: OECD Publishing. Retrieved from https://www.oecd.org/tad/45500791.pdf.

WTO (World Trade Organization). (2015). *An introduction to trade and environment in the WTO.* Retrieved from https://www.wto.org/english/tratop_e/envir_e/envt_intro_e.htm.

Part I
Global Governance Frameworks
for Sustainability Standards

Chapter 2
Voluntary Sustainability Standards and the Sustainable Development Goals

Johannes Blankenbach

1 Introduction

Voluntary Sustainability Standards (VSS) have since long been used and referred to in the context of the evolving global sustainability and development agenda(s), such as the 1992 Rio Earth Summit's Agenda 21 or the United Nations Millennium Development Goals (MDGs) introduced in 2000. Discussions on the instrumental value of VSS in contributing to global development, however, have gained new ground since the adoption of the Sustainable Development Goals (SDGs) and 2030 Agenda for Sustainable Development in 2015 (UN GA, 2015). More and more VSS schemes and organisations refer to the SDGs in their official communications,[1] UN reports point to potential linkages,[2] and while VSS are not explicitly mentioned in the 17 SDGs, 169 targets and 244 indicators, they have made their way into (sub)national SDG implementation strategies. The 2016 Sustainability Strategy of the German State of North Rhine-Westphalia, for instance, includes a target to increase the market share of products labelled as organic (MKULNV, 2016, p. 37).[3]

Can VSS, or in other words, voluntary sets of "criteria defining good social and environmental practices in an industry or product" (ISEAL, 2015), contribute to the implementation of a framework as universal and ambitious as the SDGs? The 2030

---

[1]See, for example, ISEAL and WWF (2017), "How Credible Standards Can Help Companies Deliver the 2030 Agenda"; ISEAL is a VSS umbrella organisation. One of the earliest of such publications came from Fairtrade International (2015)—"Sustainable Development Goals and Fairtrade: The Case for Partnership".

[2]See, for instance, UNFSS (2016), "Meeting Sustainability Goals: Voluntary Sustainability Standards and the Role of the Government".

[3]In an earlier draft of the strategy, the target was to increase the market share of Fairtrade and similarly labelled products; the final version only refers to EU Organic Certification (a public VSS).

J. Blankenbach (✉)
Business & Human Rights Resource Centre, Berlin, Germany
e-mail: johannes@blankenbach.eu

© The Editor(s) (if applicable) and The Author(s) 2020
A. Negi et al. (eds.), *Sustainability Standards and Global Governance*,
https://doi.org/10.1007/978-981-15-3473-7_2

Agenda for Sustainable Development is nothing less than an action plan for profound transformation across the globe to improve the lives of all people while keeping the planet healthy (Scholz, 2015, p. 1).

This chapter starts off with a content analysis of VSS, based on data from the International Trade Centre's (ITC) Standards Map, to assess to what extent formal VSS requirements and processes align with the SDGs. Considering that this approach mainly captures what VSS-SDG linkages exist on paper, a subsequent section looks at what kind of real-life contributions VSS may—or may not—make to SDG implementation. This later section also links to the discussion on business and human rights, considering its intersections with the SDGs and VSS debates, respectively. The chapter ends with conclusions from the two substantive sections, including recommendations on the way forward.

2 Alignment of VSS with the SDGs: Content Analysis

It is fairly obvious why there has been increasing reference to the link between VSS and SDGs: The conditions that VSS initiatives claim to improve, sometimes even by their very name, all broadly relate to the different dimensions of sustainability. Tying them more systematically to the SDGs, which have gained traction in politics, business, civil society and the broader public in recent years, provides for a compelling narrative and, ideally, greater synergies. The 2030 Agenda also puts much emphasis on the crucial role of business and civil society in promoting sustainable development—two groups of actors that are at least formally represented in many multi-stakeholder VSS initiatives, sometimes along with local producers and public sector actors. The real influence of these different groups within a scheme, of course, varies, depending on how serious it is about multi-stakeholder—and ideally worker-driven—standards design and implementation.VSS also claim to empower consumers to take responsible buying decisions; indeed, two-thirds of VSS use a consumer-facing label, whereas one-third rely on business-to-business implementation (Potts et al., 2014, p. 37). The SDGs are very much in line with a mechanism where, in theory, consumers and end-user companies opt for sustainably produced goods to contribute towards sustainable development in their own countries as well as in other countries along global value chains. This may reflect the paradigm shift from an "aid"-centred development model for the global south (as epitomised by the previous MDGs) towards a more holistic, SDG-based approach, acknowledging global interdependencies and a need for change, especially in richer economies and societies. Whether sustainability in consumption and production as such should just be a voluntary option is of course questionable, all the more so if this option is partly based on a "jungle of certification schemes" (Verzijden, 2017) that, with their multitude, overlaps and gaps, confuse both consumers and companies. In turn, assessments of on-the-ground impacts have, to some extent, remained inconclusive, and certification and verification audits have reportedly failed human and workers' rights (see Sect. 3).

In a narrow sense, a VSS is a document that lists detailed *requirements* for good social and environmental practice in business operations. Producers, manufacturers or—depending on the scope of the standard—traders and retailers who wish to become (and stay) certified under a given VSS need to prove that they fulfil these requirements in (usually third-party) certification/verification audits, which in itself is a highly problematic practice (see Sect. 3). However, the assumption is that if VSS are to contribute to SDG implementation, their formal requirements need to correspond to at least some of the SDGs and related targets by addressing similar issues. The ITC Standards Map at www.standardsmap.org (ITC, 2017) provides a viable source for testing this as it details the requirements pertaining to over 210 VSS. From all of these VSS, 16 were included in the formal content analysis in this section, representing the "most important standards initiatives currently active in agriculture, forestry and biofuels sectors with a global reach" according to a landmark review by Potts et al. (2014, p. 3):[4]

- 4C/Global Coffee Platform
- Better Cotton Initiative (BCI)
- Bonsucro
- Cotton made in Africa (CmiA)
- Ethical Tea Partnership (ETP)
- Fairtrade[5]
- Forest Stewardship Council (FSC)[6]
- International Foundation for Organic Agriculture (IFOAM)
- Programme for the Endorsement of Forest Certification Schemes (PEFC)
- Roundtable on Sustainable Palm Oil (RSPO)[7]
- Sustainable Agriculture Network (SAN)/Rainforest Alliance
- UTZ Certified
- Global Partnership for Good Agricultural Practice (GlobalGAP)[8]
- ProTerra Foundation
- Round Table on Responsible Soy (RTRS)
- Roundtable on Sustainable Biomaterials (RSB)

VSS are not just defined by their *requirements* but also by corresponding and very distinct formal *process* criteria for verification, marketing, support, revision and governance. ITC Standards Map features details on some (although not all) of these standards system elements in a separate "processes" section for each VSS in the database. It was therefore possible to complement the analysis of VSS requirements with some information on formal VSS processes. The goal was, as a first step, to

---

[4]Lernoud et al. (2018) also use this sample (apart from ETP and RSB) in an ITC-commissioned assessment of "The State of Sustainable Markets 2018".

[5]Sometimes there are several standards operated by one initiative; this analysis focused on the Fairtrade standard for "small producer organizations".

[6]The formal analysis focused on the FSC standard for "forest management".

[7]The formal analysis focused on RSPO "Principles and Criteria".

[8]The formal analysis focused on the GlobalGAP standard for "crops".

assess whether a specific VSS requirement (e.g. "practices promoting healthy/high nutritional value foods", ITC, 2017) or process criterion *fits under one, several or none of the SDGs.*[9]

The SDGs, by their very nature, are much broader in scope and wording than the detailed requirements and processes formally established by VSS. In order to proceed without too much of causal interpretation, the 169 SDG targets and 244 SDG indicators (IAEG-SDGs, 2017)[10] were used to translate the 2030 Agenda's vision into more technical and narrow terms for the purpose of this chapter (with the disadvantage of some aspects of the original SDGs getting lost). It should still be mentioned that matching VSS requirements and processes with corresponding SDGs remains a subjective exercise. Table 1 demonstrates this for a selected goal (SDG 7—Affordable and Clean Energy), listing all categories of VSS requirements and process criteria from the Standards Map that seem to plausibly match it. The on-paper performance of two selected VSS initiatives (ETP and RSPO) in those categories is presented at the right-hand side of the table, as per the 2017 Standards Map data.[11]

Table 1 illustrates the span of causal interpretation that was considered acceptable for establishing plausible formal VSS-SDG correspondences, with the second to last criterion ("responsible entity for implementation cost") probably being the most debatable. The table also shows that one specific requirement or process criterion could be listed only once per SDG at the maximum (but several times across all 17 SDGs, reflecting their interconnectedness). The total results for each SDG were weighted in order to compensate for the different length and complexity of goals.[12]

Turning to the second step of the analysis, i.e. a weighted average of SDG-related VSS requirements and process criteria across all 16 VSS initiatives for each SDG, it is striking to see that VSS, at least on paper, in some or the other way link to all 17

---

[9]The data used for the latest version of this chapter was retrieved from the Standards Map in July/August 2017. There may thus have been updates to formal standards contents in the meantime that were not considered for this analysis.

[10]It is obvious that SDG indicators are not meant to further specify targets in the sense of a guideline for implementation—the purpose of indicators is to measure progress. In fact, however, an indicator integrates key aspects of a target in one very specific, (comparatively) easy-to-measure parameter. The indicator framework therefore provided additional orientation for matching VSS requirements/process criteria with different SDGs (guiding question: "Would implementation of VSS requirement/process criterion X improve the result of indicator Y?"). In several rounds of testing, targets on their own appeared to be too broad, leaving considerable room for interpretation.

[11]The spreadsheet for all 16 VSS across all 17 SDGs comprises more than 1000 rows.

[12]Some SDGs have very few targets and indicators, whereas others have many. In the latter case, it is easier to find corresponding VSS requirements and process criteria on the Standards Map according to the methodology explained above. This could increase statistical bias (i.e. the more targets/indicators one particular SDG has, the more VSS requirements/process criteria correspond to it). Weighting was applied to reduce such bias, with SDG 7 providing the most extreme example of weighting (coefficient 2.392) as it is the shortest goal in terms of the number of its targets and indicators. Coefficients were determined by dividing the total number of indicators (244) by the number of goals (17); this average was then divided by the number of indicators per SDG to define a weighting coefficient for each SDG, ranging from 0.532 (SDG 3, which has the most indicators) to 2.392 (SDG 7, as explained).

Table 1 Matching of relevant VSS requirements/process criteria from the Standards Map with SDG 7; Checking whether or not (✓/✗) the ETP and RSPO standards include such requirements according to 2017 Standards Map data

SDG 7 Targets (7.X) Indicators (7.X.Y)	*Requirements and process criteria from Standards Map that were considered as matching SDG 7*	*Ethical Tea Partnership (ETP)*	*Roundtable on Sustainable Palm Oil (RSPO)*
SDG 7: Ensure access to affordable, reliable, sustainable and modern energy for all		**Total: 9.0 Weighted: 21.5**	**Total: 6.0 Weighted: 14.4**
7.1. By 2030, ensure universal access to affordable, reliable and modern energy services			
7.1.1. Proportion of population with access to electricity	*Services and benefits to local communities*	✗	✓
	Impact assessment on access to basic services to local communities	✗	✓
7.1.2. Proportion of population with primary reliance on clean fuels and technology	–		
7.2. By 2030, increase substantially the share of renewable energy in the global energy mix			
7.2.1. Renewable energy share in the total final energy consumption	*Energy use and management: general principle*	✓	✓
	Use of non-renewable energies: general principle	✓	✓
	Use of alternative energies including solar, wind etc.	✓	✓
	Use of solar energy	✓	✗
	Use of hydropower energy	✓	✗
	Use of wind energy	✓	✗
	Use of wood-based energy	✓	✗
	Use of biofuels	✓	✓
	Criteria relating to the application of a set of clean production practices	✗	✗
	Criteria related to the storage of energy (incl. fuel, electricity…)	✗	✗

(continued)

Table 1 (continued)

SDG 7 Targets (7.X) Indicators (7.X.Y)	*Requirements and process criteria from Standards Map that were considered as matching SDG 7*	*Ethical Tea Partnership (ETP)*	*Roundtable on Sustainable Palm Oil (RSPO)*
7.3. By 2030, double the global rate of improvement in energy efficiency			
7.3.1. Energy intensity measured in terms of primary energy and GDP	*Reduce use of energy resources*	✓	✗
7.a. By 2030, enhance international cooperation to facilitate access to clean energy research and technology, including renewable energy, energy efficiency and advanced and cleaner fossil-fuel technology, and promote investment in energy infrastructure and clean energy technology			
7.a.1. International financial flows to developing countries in support of clean energy research and development and renewable energy production, including in hybrid systems	*Responsible entity for implementation cost (buyer/retailer or the standard-setting organisation carries co-responsibility) (This criterion was taken from the "processes" section of the Standards Map; all others are "requirements")*	✗	✗
	Criteria related to access to technology and innovation	✗	✗
7.b. By 2030, expand infrastructure and upgrade technology for supplying modern and sustainable energy services for all in developing countries, in particular least developed countries, small island developing States and landlocked developing countries, in accordance with their respective programmes of support			
7.b.1. Investments in energy efficiency as a proportion of GDP and the amount of foreign direct investment in financial transfer for infrastructure and technology to sustainable development services	–		

Source Author's compilation based on UN GA (2015), IAEG-SDGs (2017) and ITC (2017)

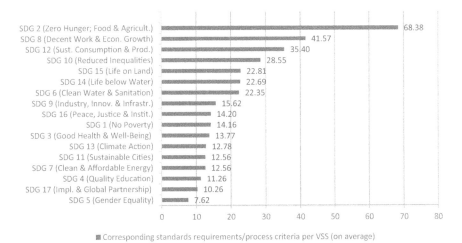

Fig. 1 Average number of standards requirements/process criteria per VSS scheme corresponding to each SDG. *Source* Author

SDGs (Fig. 1), based on an interpretation of 2017 Standards Map data. On average, the 16 schemes comprehend a significant number of requirements and processes corresponding to each of the SDGs, albeit to varying degrees. For instance, on average, 68.38 formal requirements and process criteria per individual VSS are in line with SDG 2 (Zero Hunger; Food Security & Sustainable Agriculture), whereas, on average, only 7.62 requirements/process criteria per VSS correspond to SDG 5 (Gender Equality) according to this formal analysis and as shown in the ranking chart in Fig. 1.

SDG 2 (Zero Hunger; Food Security & Sustainable Agriculture),[13] SDG 8 (Decent Work & Economic Growth) and SDG 12 (Sustainable Consumption & Production) top the ranking, i.e. VSS, on average, list many formal criteria plausibly corresponding to these SDGs (and targets/indicators). This may not come as a surprise as such topics and areas are commonly associated with VSS. SDG 2 comprises relatively broad provisions on productive and sustainable agriculture (targets 2.3, 2.4 and corresponding indicators), which means that many environment-related VSS requirements, e.g. for soil, water and biodiversity conservation as well as for chemicals and waste treatment, plausibly fit under this SDG, along with basic social and economic VSS criteria. However, almost no VSS criteria according to 2017 Standards Map data seem to correspond to the first part of SDG 2, focusing on ending hunger and malnutrition (targets 2.1, 2.2 and corresponding indicators). There are a few VSS out of the sample of 16 that list requirements on "practices promoting healthy/high nutritional value foods" and "avoiding practices endangering food security" (ITC, 2017), but there is nothing beyond this.

---

[13]The full titles of all 17 SDGs can be found in the annex to this chapter.

Regarding SDG 8 (Decent Work & Economic Growth), many VSS on paper require the abolition of forced and child labour and refer to a wide range of labour rights. These were considered as linked to SDG targets 8.7, 8.8 and their respective indicators. A range of formal VSS criteria on resource efficiency were grouped under target 8.4 and its indicator on material footprints (8.4.1), whereas requirements on wages (e.g. "minimum wage"; ITC, 2017) and gender aspects (e.g. "family-friendly policies to increase the labour force participation of women", ibid.) may formally match target 8.5 and related indicators on full/productive employment.

Regarding SDG 12 (Sustainable Consumption & Production), number three in the ranking, several formal VSS process criteria on transparent certification/verification practices and annual reporting were considered to match target 12.7 on sustainable public procurement, as such information may support public procurement decisions, provided that VSS are to play a role in this. Most VSS requirements that seem to correspond well to SDG 12 across the 16 reviewed initiatives, however, focus on resource efficiency as well as on chemicals and waste treatment, matching targets 12.2, 12.4 and related indicators. Several gaps remain, even on paper; there are, for instance, no VSS requirements that can be plausibly linked to target 12.3/indicator 12.3.1 on reducing food loss, according to this formal interpretation of Standards Map data from 2017.

While it may not be surprising to find SDG 14 (Life below Water) and SDG 15 (Life on Land) in the medium to upper range of this ranking based on formal VSS content, one may not have expected rank four for SDG 10 (Reduced Inequalities), given its macro-level scope. SDG 10, however, includes some hints as to how micro-level steps may contribute towards transformative change at a larger scale, if truly implemented. For instance, target 10.3 focuses on "eliminating discriminatory laws, policies and practices" (UN GA, 2015). At the level of VSS, requirements relating to "no discrimination at work (ILO, 111)", "minority rights", "involuntary resettlement, physical displacement and/or economic displacement" (ITC, 2017) and other issues may link to this target and indicator. Requirements regarding the "use of price premium" and formal process criteria on sharing certification and implementation costs as well as on access to finance (free of charge) were grouped under target 10.b/indicator 10.b.1 (development assistance and other financial flows). However, only a few of the 16 VSS initiatives under review include such requirements as per 2017 Standards Map data.

There is a clear decline of potential formal VSS-SDG correspondences in the medium to lower range of the chart. SDG 1 (No Poverty), ranked tenth in this theoretical assessment, covers some of the particularly structural and far-reaching issues on the 2030 Agenda. Target 1.2 as well as the corresponding indicators on multidimensional poverty provides some indication of the kind of VSS contents that may be relevant here, ranging from process criteria specifically targeting vulnerable and minority groups to requirements regarding wages, the "hiring [of] workers from local communities" (ITC, 2017) and the promotion of education as well as medical care services. Many VSS initiatives formally list such requirements according to the data on the Standards Map, but as per 2017 data, there are fewer criteria on average relating to other dimensions of SDG 1, such as disaster risk reduction and resilience of the poor (target 1.5).

Even this formalistic review of VSS, purely based on content analysis, suggests that VSS in their current shape are poorly suited to contribute towards SDG 4 (Quality Education), SDG 5 (Gender Equality), SDG 7 (Affordable & Clean Energy), SDG 11 (Sustainable Cities and Communities), SDG 13 (Climate Action) and SDG 17 (Partnerships for the Goals). Very few formal VSS requirements and processes plausibly link to these fields, according to the assessment of 2017 data from the Standards Map.

Last but not the least, relative standard deviations of 44–58% for SDG 5, SDG 7 and SDG 11 in this formal interpretation of 2017 Standards Map data suggest that some VSS include a larger number of criteria matching these SDGs, whereas other VSS include only a few. Whether or not a VSS initiative has a specific sectoral focus seems to be of low significance in this regard. A comparison between the two forestry VSS under formal review in this section (FSC and PEFC), the two cotton VSS (BCI and CmiA) and the six VSS covering multiple commodities (Fairtrade, IFOAM, SAN/Rainforest Alliance, UTZ Certified, GlobalGAP and ProTerra) produced inconclusive results. Calculations based on this (very small) sample and 2017 Standards Map data suggest that forestry VSS, on average, have the highest number of requirements and process criteria formally corresponding to each of the SDGs, whereas cotton VSS have the lowest. The average numbers for multiple commodity VSS are somewhere in the middle.[14] The chart below (Fig. 2) illustrates this, using the data for multiple commodity VSS as an orientation value (i.e. the ranking follows the descending order of SDG correspondences per multiple commodity VSS).

3 From Paper to Practice: Examining VSS Impacts on the Ground

Even if standards requirements and processes are perfectly in line with the SDGs— which is not always the case, as the previous content analysis has shown—VSS will have anecdotal rather than transformative, and in the worst case, harmful impacts if formal criteria are not properly implemented by producers, processors, manufacturers, traders and/or retailers. All VSS forming part of the formal content analysis in the previous section cover at least the (farm/plantation) level of extraction and production, whereas the processing/manufacturing as well as the trading/retailing levels is covered less frequently, according to Standards Map data from 2017. This in itself might weaken the impact of some initiatives.

Moving beyond the Standards Map sample and turning to VSS impacts in general, it is encouraging to see that, in recent years, VSS impact studies have become more numerous and moved beyond basic facts such as the number of certified producers and the market share of certified products (UNFSS, 2016, p. 2). The socioeconomic

---

[14]The sample for each group, of course, is too small for taking these results at face value.

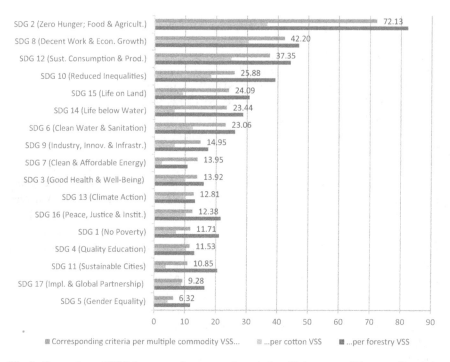

Fig. 2 Comparison of VSS for cotton, forestry products and multiple commodities regarding their average number of requirements/process criteria corresponding to each SDG (for better readability, numbers are only indicated for multiple commodity VSS (upper bar)). *Source* Author

situation of producers and their communities as well as environmental conditions in the production area are increasingly being covered. This is dearly needed for clarity on whether formal VSS requirements and processes are properly and continuously implemented by producers and other entities covered by a scheme so that it has real-life impacts, as mentioned above. A related question is whether VSS adoption as such really leads to higher sales prices and better market access for those who get certified, and whether poorer, vulnerable producers and their workers and communities can benefit from this as well.

An early broad-based impact assessment conducted by the Committee on Sustainability Assessment (COSA) found moderately positive, though sometimes inconclusive, economic, social and environmental impacts of coffee and cocoa certification in 12 countries at the producer and farm level (COSA, 2013, p. 3). The authors note that in most cases the cost of entry and training for VSS were (partly) covered by external partners such as development agencies, NGOs, buyers and traders, which may no longer be the case once larger numbers of producers aspire certification. COSA is a consortium built on partnerships with numerous organisations, ranging from national and international research institutions to VSS initiatives.

A more recent independent literature review on certification in agriculture finds positive effects of VSS adoption for certified producers and their households with regard to prices (plus 14%), sales income (plus 11%) and children's schooling (plus 6%), but negative effects on workers' wages (minus 13%), as well as unclear effects regarding yields, household income, wealth and illness, again at the level of producers and their respective households (Oya, Schaefer, Skalidou, McCosker, & Langer 2017, p. vi). Positive contributions of certification towards "Increased dignity, confidence, control and choice" were found by a Centre for Evaluation/*Centrum für Evaluation* (CEval) study commissioned by Fairtrade on the scheme's poverty reduction impacts, based on six country and sector case studies with comparative data from 2011/12 and 2017/18. There were also moderate contributions to "improved household income, assets and standards of living", "increased environmental sustainability and resilience to climate change", and "enhanced influence and status of small producers" according to this study, but even less significant effects in four other areas such as "improved access to basic services" (Mauthofer, Schneider, Väth, & von Cölln, 2018, p. 124).

A synthesis report on agricultural VSS put together by ISEAL, Rainforest Alliance and WWF for their new Evidensia online platform looks at economic criteria in particular (yield, price, costs and income). Only 13 out of 51 studies in this review focus on net household incomes for certified farms. In 31% of cases, these were higher or significantly higher than for non-certified farms, while in 69% of cases (nine in absolute numbers), there was no significant difference (Evidensia, 2019, p. 18).

Several VSS assessments have focused on potential environmental contributions, such as a recent synthesis report on conservation outcomes, compiled by the Meridian Institute. A section based on seven different studies states that the adoption of certification reduced deforestation rates in some settings, specifically Ethiopia and Colombia as well as primary forests in Indonesia (Komives et al., 2018, p. 4).There was no reported difference between certified and non-certified areas in other settings, however. Impacts on plant diversity were generally found to be positive and impacts on fauna diversity mixed, again based on a very small sample of five studies covering plant and three covering fauna biodiversity (ibid., p. 18).

The clearest positive income and, based on fewer examples, environmental effects seem to relate to the adoption of "organic" standards in farming, as production costs and yields tend to be similar to conventional production (or even more favourable) while sales prices are higher, according to a number of recent impact studies. This leads to higher profits and/or household income for farmers (but not necessarily for their workers, who are not specifically looked at) across different commodity and country samples such as rice from northern India (Eyhorn, van den Berg, Dedock, Maat, & Srivastava, 2018), strawberries from central Brazil (Resende Filho et al., 2017) and tea from northern Vietnam (Doanh, Thuong, & Heo, 2018). As for these three reports, two of them do not specify under what type of scheme organic farms were certified. The India case study of smallholder farmers in hilly Uttarakhand mentions Indian and Swiss standards as well as EU Council Regulation (EC) No. 834/2007, which is about the EU's public organic VSS scheme and has a predominantly agricultural and technical focus. Apart from higher profits for local producers due to less inputs and higher yields and sales prices, this study found that organic management improved soil quality and helped save irrigation water. What is interesting about the Uttarakhand case is the role of one Indian processing company, Nature Bio-Foods Ltd., business partner of Swiss retailer Coop, in providing farmers with organic seeds and biofertiliser at cost prices. The company also paid for participating farmers' third-party certification against the aforementioned organic standards, as well as for additional Fairtrade certification, and purchased the certified paddy for an agreed (Fairtrade) price plus an organic premium of 10–15%.

Without such company engagement, potential transformative impacts of VSS schemes may be hampered by their lack of accessibility for poorer producers, especially smallholders, who are in the most urgent need of livelihood gains but struggle with high certification and implementation costs, among other challenges. In many cases, the bulk of the certification benefits may thus have gone to larger, better-organised producers in regions with higher production capacities, as well as to traders, brands and retailers (UNFSS, 2016, p. 4). What possibly reinforces this pattern is that real price premiums for producers of certified goods still largely depend on external (market) factors, i.e. whether buyers are willing to pay a higher price. What seems to work well for organic farming may work less well for other forms of certification. Only three out of 16 VSS in the sample used in the previous section include a formal internal requirement of price premiums, according to the Standards Map as per 2017 data. Carlson and Palmer (2016, pp. 130–132), focusing on the "less tangible benefits of certification", point to the general unwillingness of powerful retailers to pay a premium to suppliers.

Other work more specifically addresses the social impacts of VSS adoption, such as an independent study by the School of Oriental and African Studies (SOAS), University of London, from 2014 on VSS implementation in Uganda and Ethiopia. It contends that research on Fairtrade standards has so far overly focused on the small farm household using family labour, rather than looking at the plight of seasonal and casual agricultural wage workers (Cramer, Johnston, Oya, & Sender, 2014, pp. 20–22). Considering the scope of other studies, there seems to be a general need to look beyond the level of producers and smallholders to uncover the situation of their workers and/or domestic servants, who may be much worse off. Indeed, the poor wages and labour conditions of workers covered by the SOAS sample did not improve under certification, according to the study (ibid., p. 15).

A growing body of evidence-based academic and NGO research has also pointed to the failures of social auditing, a practice that is part of virtually every VSS scheme, in capturing abuses of the human rights of workers and communities in global value chains.[15] The European Centre for Constitutional and Human Rights (ECCHR, 2018), for instance, comments on the Ali Enterprises fire in a supplier factory in Karachi, Pakistan: "Th[e…] audit failed to notice a range of infractions on the international standards it was upholding (SA 8000) and Pakistani safety standards regulations that would prove fatal, including an illegally constructed floor,

---

[15] See the Business & Human Rights Resource Centre's web portal and blog series on "Beyond Social Auditing" at https://www.business-humanrights.org/en/beyond-social-auditing.

and defunct fire alarm system, as well as the presence of child labour and structural excessive overtime".[16] A research report on forced labour risks in cocoa supply chains in Ghana and tea supply chains in India, based on, *inter alia*, in-depth interviews with more than 120 tea and cocoa workers and a survey of over 1000 tea and cocoa workers, states: "Some of the worst cases of exploitation documented within our research occurred on ethically certified [tea] plantations" (LeBaron, 2018, p. 3).

Auditors, in many cases from a formally independent third-party, certify and verify standards compliance at the supplier level, which is then cited by end-user companies and big brands, but the system is unreliable for a number of reasons. Audit firms may be subject to market pressures and compete for clients, for instance; there is a clear conflict of interest if the cost of certification is met by the entity that is audited, e.g. a supplier farm or factory. A recent Guardian report on migrant worker exploitation at tomato farms in southern Italy quotes an NGO worker arguing that "[w]hen the person being inspected is the same person paying the inspector's fee, 99.9% of the time the inspector will say: 'No, you're not exploiting anyone'" (Jones & Awokoya, 2019). Also, audits may just require "checklist compliance" (Terwindt & Burckhardt, 2018), miss out on contextual factors ranging from building safety to religious discrimination, or proceed without an on-site visit, as alleged in the Ali Enterprises case (ECCHR, 2018). The Guardian report on tomato farming in the Italian south found certification bodies to "perform an arm's-length box-ticking exercise, and [to] rarely visit the farms" (Jones & Awokoya, 2019). There are also accounts of business owners literally cheating on auditors and telling their workers to change working practices while the audit is ongoing (LeBaron, 2018, p. 41).

Engagement with workers, who could point to shortcomings if there were appropriate and safe arrangements for them to speak out, remains low or superficial. For instance, the tea and cocoa research mentioned above found that 95% of surveyed workers on Ghanaian cocoa plantations were unaware whether they were working on a certified site (LeBaron, 2018, p. 42). All this has led critics to argue that "these programs mask significant risks for workers at the bottom and brands atop global supply chains", and that voluntary certification is "part of the problem, not the solution" (WSR Network, 2018, p. 3). The trend of VSS achieving more and more significant market shares in individual commodities such as coffee, cocoa and tea[17] (Lernoud et al., 2018, p. 4) is thus not as good news as it potentially could be.

The growing evidence of human rights risks and abuses going unnoticed by social audits, including VSS certification and verification audits, should also inform the debate on SDG implementation, as SDGs "seek to realise the human rights of all" according to the 2030 Agenda (UN GA 2015, p. 1). A study by the Danish Institute for Human Rights (DIHR) claims that more than 90% of the SDG targets are linked

---

[16]See the Business & Human Rights Resource Centre's coverage of an OECD complaint filed by NGOs against auditing firm RINA, including RINA's response, at https://www.business-humanrights.org/en/ngo-coalition-files-oecd-complaint-with-italian-ncp-against-auditor-rina-for-allegedly-failing-to-detect-safety-labour-abuses-at-ali-enterprises-factory-in-pakistan-incl-co.

[17]According to the 2018 "State of Sustainability Markets" report (Lernoud et al., 2018, p. 4), at least 25.8% of global coffee area, 22.8% of global cocoa area and 13.2% of global tea area are certified.

to core international human rights and labour standards (Filskov & Feiring, 2018, p. 1). VSS content analysis in the previous section has shown that many human and labour rights are explicitly listed as formal VSS requirements. As long as certification and verification audits, however, miss out on rights abuses, the practical value of such requirements remains limited.

Human rights due diligence, as established by the UN Guiding Principles on Business and Human Rights (UNGPs; OHCHR, 2011), has emerged as a central and practicable concept specifying companies' responsibilities in respecting human rights across all their operations and global value chains. Due diligence is about them "assessing actual and potential human rights impacts, integrating and acting upon the findings, tracking responses, and communicating how impacts are addressed" (ibid., p. 17), all in close collaboration with those potentially or actually affected by negative human rights impacts. Another recent discussion paper put forward by the DIHR argues "that the implementation of the UNGPs can be the single-most important contribution by business to the realisation of the SDGs" (Morris, Wrzoncki, & Lysgaard, 2019, p. 9), and thus to real transformations of the status quo.

In order for human rights due diligence to be effective, companies need to internalise due diligence steps rather than outsourcing them to an external scheme. This makes all the more sense as the kind of price and time pressure exerted by many big brands is said to have been driving worker exploitation at the supplier level, e.g. in the garment (HRW, 2019) and food (Jones & Awokoya, 2019) sectors. The Organization for Economic Co-operation and Development's (OECD) Due Diligence Guidance for Responsible Business Conduct, providing practical orientation for companies on how human rights due diligence can be implemented, states that "[p]articipation in an initiative does not shift responsibility from the enterprise to the initiative for adverse impacts that it causes, contributes to or to which it is directly linked" (OECD, 2018, p. 53). Questions of responsibility can become questions of legal liability once human rights due diligence becomes part of binding regulation.[18] Pioneering legislative examples such as the French Duty of Vigilance Law are not limited to human rights as they legally mandate respect for human rights and the environment into business activities (ECCJ, 2017, p. 1), thus having considerable transformative power in line with the SDGs. What role VSS initiatives in their current shape can play in this context is questionable, given their shortcomings in uncovering and mitigating abuse. If they are to play a role in supporting—not replacing—companies' human rights and environmental due diligence, they will, among other steps, have to further align VSS requirements with human rights (and thus with the SDGs, as the two areas are so closely linked), i.e. at least with those expressed in the International Bill of Human Rights and the ILO's core/fundamental Conventions. Most importantly, however, the role of workers and other rights-holders in standards design, governance, implementation and assurance needs to be strengthened.

---

[18] See the Business & Human Rights Resource Centre's web portal and blog series on "Mandatory Due Diligence" at https://www.business-humanrights.org/en/mandatory-due-diligence.

4   Conclusions and Recommendations

To conclude, VSS, in theory, link to the SDGs in many ways, but there are practical constraints regarding their transformative impacts and on-the-ground contributions towards SDG implementation. As long as voluntary certification provides a fig leaf for perpetuated human rights abuse in global value chains that goes unnoticed due to unreliable audits, it is at least in some contexts part of the problem rather than the solution.

At a formal level, a semi-statistical analysis of Standards Map data from 2017 in this chapter pointed to various correspondences between VSS criteria and the 17 SDGs (Fig. 1), suggesting that the detailed requirements of many VSS cover different aspects of the 2030 Agenda. There are areas with less alignment, however, such as poverty reduction, climate change, health as well as gender, where VSS are thin on concrete requirements even on paper. Most of these issues, like many others covered by the SDGs, directly relate to human rights.

Regarding on-the-ground impacts, the increasing number and quality of impact studies is good news. Some of them have been commissioned or co-authored by individual schemes or related organisations, which could pose a credibility problem, but this was not further explored here. Most studies so far have found modest or inconclusive sustainable development impacts in the context of VSS adoption. Improvements of social, environmental and economic indicators may be relatively difficult to measure in some contexts, but there also seems to be an indication that formal requirements are often inadequately implemented by those getting certified, and/or that there is a lack of tangible certification benefits, such as higher sales prices and better market access. What is even more disturbing is the number of documented cases of social audit failure, including in the context of certification. Conditions such as those reported for some cocoa and tea plantations by LeBaron (2018), or in Jones' and Awokoya's (2019) Guardian feature on Italian tomato farms, as well as in many other reports, raise serious doubts as to whether VSS schemes and the audits they require can reliably uncover and mitigate human and labour rights abuses. If these shortcomings cannot be resolved, this will severely hamper the transformative potential and impacts of VSS initiatives, given the mutually reinforcing relationship between human rights and the SDGs.

As VSS seem to be there to stay, however, governments, businesses and civil society should engage with each other, and with standards organisations, to explore and maximise any potential "common good" benefits of certification while mitigating deficiencies and pitfalls and promoting alternatives, including regulation.

- With corporate due diligence on human rights and the environment emerging as the global standard of practice for responsible business conduct in line with human rights obligations and the SDGs, there should be an open an honest debate on what role VSS schemes can—or cannot—play in this context, and whether and how they can be adapted. It is crucial to recognise that prime responsibility for human rights and environmental due diligence across a company's global value chains is with the company, to avoid situations where no one feels—and can be held—accountable. Arguably, many businesses willing to improve respect for human rights and the environment have relied too heavily on external initiatives, including VSS, which then have not always delivered what they (seemed to) promise, especially when it comes to failures in uncovering human rights abuse through certification and verification audits. VSS schemes should state clearly what their limitations are, and companies should be clear about this and internalise human rights and environmental due diligence, effectively integrating it into all their operations rather than outsourcing it. There may be ways in which fundamentally reformed VSS schemes can support—not replace—this, e.g. by helping companies engage with local players and rights-holders, provided that the initiative itself manages to step up its worker engagement and establishes trustful NGO relations on the ground. This includes accessible complaints and grievance mechanisms where whistle-blowers and victims of abuse can speak out without fear of reprisals, including sub-contracted or casual workers and surrounding communities. At a formal level, VSS schemes should further align their requirements with all human rights, which will also strengthen their alignment with the SDGs as there are strong interconnections. At a practical level, they should substantially improve the reliability and independence of certification and verification audits, introduce additional checks, and publish audit results, including negative results. Most importantly, the influence of workers and other local rights-holders in standards design, governance, implementation and assurance needs to be credibly strengthened.

- VSS organisations, academia, civil society and governments could explore opportunities for integrated sustainable development impact monitoring of VSS and SDG implementation attempts, making use of and strengthening current global efforts on statistical capacity and better availability of sustainable development data. The Cape Town Global Action Plan for Sustainable Development Data acknowledges that "[e]ffective planning, follow-up and review of the implementation of the 2030 Agenda for Sustainable Development requires the collection, processing, analysis and dissemination of an unprecedented amount of data and statistics at local, national, regional and global levels and by multiple stakeholders" (HLG-PCCB, 2017, p. 1). Matching SDG monitoring results with data on VSS adoption in a specific region or district may provide cost-efficient opportunities for continuous impact monitoring at an unprecedented scale. For improved development impacts and human rights compliance, the issue of price premiums secured by the standards system (e.g. through a fund supported by end-user companies) is of utmost importance as well as requirements on fair purchasing practices by lead firms and living wages along their value chains that are actually monitored and implemented, including for wage and casual workers in smallholder production. Progress on these and any other human rights- and environment-related matters cannot be left to voluntary initiatives alone, however, but requires effective mandatory due diligence regulation for companies, among other measures.

- Governments should support independent VSS impact assessments and surveys that also look at auditing practices, conducted by leading academics in collaboration with workers and other rights-holders. Governments should also promote "standards for standards" at national and international levels, including mandatory legal requirements, e.g. on audit transparency and auditor liability, to guide and harmonise fundamental reforms of VSS requirements, processes, and most importantly, implementation and assurance. National platforms on sustainability standards, connected to one another through a global "platform of platforms" such as the UN Forum on Sustainability Standards (UNFSS), represent one low-barrier option to bridge coordination gaps, to harmonise the plethora of standards, and to increase local ownership. The Indian government launched such a platform supported by the UNFSS in 2016 already, mandating the autonomous Quality Council of India (QCI) to host its secretariat. Similarly, the Brazilian, Chinese and Mexican governments co-founded sustainbility standards platforms with support from the UNFSS. Platforms should now ensure proper worker and rights-holder engagement and also explore legislative options.

- Considering that the SDGs build on human rights, and that corporate human rights and environmental due diligence potentially represents the single-most important business contribution to sustainable development, governments should promote mandatory due diligence regulation at the national, regional and global (UN) level. Such regulation needs to make clear that prime responsibility for due diligence lies with the company, and that therefore, external initiatives cannot replace but at best support it, if fundamentally reformed.

Annex

Sustainable Development Goals

Goal 1. End poverty in all its forms everywhere
Goal 2. End hunger, achieve food security and improved nutrition and promote sustainable agriculture
Goal 3. Ensure healthy lives and promote well-being for all at all ages
Goal 4. Ensure inclusive and equitable quality education and promote lifelong learning opportunities for all
Goal 5. Achieve gender equality and empower all women and girls
Goal 6. Ensure availability and sustainable management of water and sanitation for all
Goal 7. Ensure access to affordable, reliable, sustainable and modern energy for all
Goal 8. Promote sustained, inclusive and sustainable economic growth, full and productive employment and decent work for all
Goal 9. Build resilient infrastructure, promote inclusive and sustainable industrialisation and foster innovation
Goal 10. Reduce inequality within and among countries
Goal 11. Make cities and human settlements inclusive, safe, resilient and sustainable

Goal 12.   Ensure sustainable consumption and production patterns
Goal 13.   Take urgent action to combat climate change and its impacts*
Goal 14.   Conserve and sustainably use the oceans, seas and marine resources for sustainable development
Goal 15.   Protect, restore and promote sustainable use of terrestrial ecosystems, sustainably manage forests, combat desertification, and halt and reverse land degradation and halt biodiversity loss
Goal 16.   Promote peaceful and inclusive societies for sustainable development, provide access to justice for all and build effective, accountable and inclusive institutions at all levels
Goal 17.   Strengthen the means of implementation and revitalise the global partnership for sustainable development

*Acknowledging that the United Nations Framework Convention on Climate Change is the primary international, intergovernmental forum for negotiating the global response to climate change.

References

Carlson, A., & Palmer, Ch. (2016). A qualitative meta-synthesis of the benefits of eco-labeling in developing countries. *Ecological Economics, 127,* 129–145. https://doi.org/10.1016/j.ecolecon.2016.03.020.

COSA (Committee on Sustainability Assessment). (2013). *The COSA measuring sustainability report: Coffee and cocoa in 12 countries.* Retrieved from http://thecosa.org/wp-content/uploads/2014/01/The-COSA-Measuring-Sustainability-Report.pdf.

Cramer, C., Johnston, D., Oya, C., & Sender, J. (2014). *Fairtrade, employment and poverty reduction in Ethiopia and Uganda.* London: School of Oriental and African Studies (SOAS). Retrieved from http://ftepr.org/wp-content/uploads/FTEPR-Final-Report-19-May-2014-FINAL.pdf.

Doanh, N. K., Thuong, N. T. T., & Heo, Y. (2018). Impact of conversion to organic tea cultivation on household income in the mountainous areas of Northern Vietnam. *Sustainability, 2018*(10), 4475. https://doi.org/10.3390/su10124475.

ECCHR (European Centre for Constitutional and Human Rights). (2018). *OECD complaint against Italian auditor RINA.* Retrieved from https://www.business-humanrights.org/en/ngo-coalition-files-oecd-complaint-with-italian-ncp-against-auditor-rina-for-allegedly-failing-to-detect-safety-labour-abuses-at-ali-enterprises-factory-in-pakistan-incl-co.

ECCJ (European Coalition for Corporate Justice). (2017). *French corporate duty of vigilance law: frequently asked questions.* Brussels: Author. Retrieved from http://corporatejustice.org/documents/publications/french-corporate-duty-of-vigilance-law-faq.pdf.

Evidensia. (2019). *Effects of voluntary sustainability standards on yield, price, costs and income in the agriculture sector.* London: ISEAL Alliance. Retrieved from https://www.evidensia.eco/resources/188/.

Eyhorn, F., van den Berg, M., Dedock, C., Maat, H., & Srivastava, A. (2018). Does organic farming provide a viable alternative for smallholder rice farmers in India? *Sustainability, 2018*(10), 4424. https://doi.org/10.3390/su10124424.

Fairtrade. (2015). *Sustainable development goals and Fairtrade: The case for partnership.* Retrieved from http://www.fairtrade.net/fileadmin/user_upload/content/2009/resources/15-10_Sustainable_Development_Report.pdf.

HLG-PCCB (High-Level Group for Partnership, Coordination and Capacity-Building for Statistics for the 2030 Agenda for Sustainable Development). (2017). *Cape Town global action plan for sustainable development data*. Retrieved January 15, 2017 from http://unstats.un.org/sdgs/files/global-consultation-hlg-1/GAP_HLG-20161021.pdf.

HRW (Human Rights Watch). (2019). Paying for a bus ticket and expecting to fly. In *How apparel brand purchasing practices drive labor abuses*. Retrieved from https://www.hrw.org/sites/def ault/files/report_pdf/wrd0419_web2.pdf.

IAEG-SDGs (Inter-agency Expert Group on SDG Indicators). (2017). *Revised list of global sustainable development goal indicators*. Retrieved from https://unstats.un.org/sdgs/indicators/indicators-list/.

ISEAL (International Social and Environmental Accreditation and Labelling Alliance). (2015). *What is a sustainability standard?* Retrieved from http://www.isealalliance.org/waypoint/what-is-a-sustainability-standard.

ISEAL/WWF (World Wildlife Fund). (2017). *How credible standards can help companies deliver the 2030 agenda*. Retrieved from http://d2ouvy59p0dg6k.cloudfront.net/downloads/wwf_iseal_sdg_2017.pdf.

ITC (International Trade Centre). (2017). *Standards map*. Retrieved from http://standardsmap.org/.

Jones, T., & Awokoya, A. (2019). Are your tinned tomatoes picked by slave labour? *The Guardian*. Retrieved from https://www.theguardian.com/world/2019/jun/20/tomatoes-italy-mafia-migrant-labour-modern-slavery.

Komives, K., Arton, A., Baker, E., Kennedy, E., Longo, C., Newsom, D., …Romero, C. (2018). *How has our understanding of the conservation impacts of voluntary sustainability standards changed since the 2012 publication of "Toward sustainability: The roles and limitations of certification?"* Washington, DC: Meridian Institute. Retrieved from https://merid.org/content/projects/supply_chain_sustainability_research_fund.

LeBaron, G. (2018). *The global business of forced labour*. Report of Findings. Sheffield: SPERI & University of Sheffield. Retrieved from http://globalbusinessofforcedlabour.ac.uk/report/.

Lernoud J., Potts, J., Sampson, G., Schlatter, B., Huppe, G., Voora, V., … Dang, D. (2018*). The state of sustainable markets 2018: Statistics and emerging trends*. Geneva: International Trade Centre (ITC). Retrieved from http://www.intracen.org/uploadedFiles/intracenorg/Content/Public ations/Sustainibility%202018%20layout-FIN-web-v1.pdf.

Mauthofer, T., Schneider, E., Väth, S.J., & von Cölln, F. (2018). *Assessing the impact of Fairtrade on poverty reduction through rural development* (Follow up study). Saarbrücken: CEval. Retrieved from https://www.evidensia.eco/resources/431/.

MKULNV (Ministry for Climate Protection, Environment, Agriculture, Nature and Consumer Protection). (2016). *Sustainability strategy for North Rhine-Westphalia*. Düsseldorf: Author. Retrieved from https://www.nachhaltigkeit.nrw.de/fileadmin/download/sustainability_strategy_for_north_rhine-westphalia.pdf.

Morris, D., Wrzoncki, E., & Lysgaard S. A. (2019). *Responsible business conduct as a cornerstone of the 2030 Agenda—A look at the implications*. Copenhagen: The Danish Institute for Human Rights. Retrieved from https://www.humanrights.dk/sites/humanrights.dk/files/media/dokume nter/udgivelser/hrb_2019/responsible_business_conduct_as_a_cornerstone_of_the_2030_a genda_dihr_2019.pdf.

Filskov, N., & Feiring, B. (2018). *Human Rights and the 2030 agenda for sustainable development: Lessons learned and next steps*. Copenhagen: The Danish Institute for Human Rights. Retrieved from https://www.humanrights.dk/sites/humanrights.dk/files/media/dokumenter/sdg/hr_and_2030_agenda-web_2018.pdf.

OECD (Organisation for Economic Co-operation and Development). (2018). *OECD due diligence guidance for responsible business conduct*. Paris: Author. Retrieved from http://mneguidelines.oecd.org/OECD-Due-Diligence-Guidance-for-Responsible-Business-Conduct.pdf.

OHCHR (Office of the High Commissioner for Human Rights). (2011). *Guiding principles on business and Human Rights*. Geneva: Author. Retrieved from https://www.ohchr.org/documents/publications/GuidingprinciplesBusinesshr_eN.pdf.

Oya, C., Schaefer, F., Skalidou, D., McCosker, C., & Langer, L. (2017). *Effects of certification schemes for agricultural production on socio-economic outcomes in low-and middle-income countries: A systematic review.* London: International Initiative for Impact Evaluation (3IE). Retrieved from https://www.3ieimpact.org/evidence-hub/publications/systematic-review-summaries/effectiveness-agricultural-certification.

Potts, J., Lynch, M., Wilkings, A., Huppé, G., Cunningham, M., &Voora, V. (2014). *The state of sustainability initiatives review 2014: Standards and the green economy: state of sustainability initiatives.* Winnipeg/London: International Institute for Sustainable Development (IISD)/ International Institute for Environment and Development (IIED). Retrieved from https://www.iisd.org/pdf/2014/ssi_2014.pdf.

Resende Filho, M. A., Andow, D. A., Carneiro, R. G., Lorena, D. R., Sujit, E. R., & Alves, R. T. (2017). *Economic and productivity incentives to produce organically in Brazil. Evidence from strawberry production in the Federal District.* Working paper. Retrieved from https://www.researchgate.net/publication/311582588_Economic_and_productivity_incentives_to_produce_organically_in_Brazil_Evidence_from_strawberry_production_in_the_Federal_District.

Scholz, I. (2015). Introduction: A universal agenda for sustainable development and global cooperation. In M. Loewe & N. Rippin (Eds.), *Translating an ambitious vision into global transformation: the 2030 agenda for sustainable development* (pp. 1–9). DIE Discussion Paper 7/2015. Retrieved from http://www.die-gdi.de/uploads/media/DP_7.2015_NEU2_11.pdf.

Terwindt, C. & Burckhardt, G. (2018). *Social audits in the textile industry: How to control the controllers?* Retrieved from https://www.business-humanrights.org/en/social-audits-in-the-textile-industry-how-to-control-the-controllers.

UNFSS (UN Forum on Sustainability Standards). (2016). *Meeting sustainability goals: voluntary sustainability standards and the role of the government.* 2nd Flagship Report. Geneva: Author. Retrieved from https://unfss.files.wordpress.com/2016/09/final_unfss-report_28092016.pdf.

UN GA (United Nations General Assembly). (2015). *Transforming our world: the 2030 Agenda for sustainable development.* New York: Author. Retrieved from http://www.un.org/ga/search/view_doc.asp?symbol=A/RES/70/1&Lang=E.

Verzijden, K. (2017). *A guide to the Dutch sustainable certification jungle in food.* Amsterdam: AXON. Retrieved from https://www.axonlawyers.com/a-guide-to-the-dutch-sustainable-certification-jungle-in-food/.

WSR Network (Worker-Driven Social Responsibility Network). (2018). *Certification ≠ Enforcement.* Retrieved from https://wsr-network.org/wp-content/uploads/2018/08/WSR_Certification%CC%B8Enforcement.pdf.

Chapter 3
The World Trade Organization and Sustainability Standards

Archna Negi

1 Introduction

With the increase in spending power and public awareness about health and environmental concerns on the one hand, and the progressive elimination of quotas and reduction of tariff barriers on the other, the use of standards and technical regulations in international trade has increased exponentially.[1] Goods and services traded across borders need to meet multiple requirements—mandatory or voluntary, international or domestic, public or private, sustainability-targeted or otherwise—before being able to access international markets.

Not all standards are designed with the objective of sustainability in mind; sustainability standards are a type of standards that are increasingly used and accepted, based on the recognition that they serve important social objectives (eg. protection of health and environment) that are otherwise ignored by the private market. Product standards for weights, measures, voltage, quality, etc., have a history dating back to the Industrial Revolution, with initial concerns focused on the objectives of safety and interoperability. Sykes points at the irony of the fact that product standards and regulations, originally created for promoting trade, should be viewed as trade barriers (Sykes, 1995, p. 1). In the 1970s, as social and environmental causes gained in strength, standards were appropriated as instruments to promote sustainability by qualifying the impact of market forces (Sykes, 1995, p. 1; Gale, Ascui, & Lovell, 2017, p. 70). At the same time, scepticism over the role of sustainability standards as protectionist measures led to their being described as "wolves (of protectionism)

---

[1] Robert Baldwin's description of non-tariff barriers has been quoted often, "[t]he lowering of tariffs has, in effect, been like draining a swamp. The lower water level has revealed all the snags and stumps of non-tariff barriers that still have to be cleared away." (cited in Baldwin, 2000, p. 237).

A. Negi (✉)
Centre for International Politics, Organization and Disarmament (CIPOD), School of International Studies, Jawaharlal Nehru University, New Delhi, India
e-mail: archnanegisingh@gmail.com

© The Editor(s) (if applicable) and The Author(s) 2020
A. Negi et al. (eds.), *Sustainability Standards and Global Governance*,
https://doi.org/10.1007/978-981-15-3473-7_3

disguised under sheepskin" (Thorstensen & Vieira, 2016, p. 9). Potential benefits and risks thus accompany the use of sustainability standards in equal measure.

The use of sustainability standards is further complicated by the proliferation of "private standards", i.e. standards initiated and driven by private and non-state actors. Marx, Maertens, Swinnen and Wouters (2012, p. 16) point out that "...while earlier stages in history saw a move from private to public regulation ...what we now see is an opposite movement, back again from public to private". Principal reasons for the turn to private standards include (i) the fact that private standards are an effective means of managing global supply chains, (ii) the fact that standards are viewed by consumers as effective means to attain sustainability objectives (Mavroidis & Robert, 2016, p. 4) and (iii) the fact that private standards can stay safe of legal controls that exist for public standards.

The general legal disciplines that apply to standards apply to sustainability standards as well. Because standards have market access implications, a role for the World Trade Organization (WTO) in regulating and managing their proliferation and application is indisputable. The WTO rules include specific provisions and dedicated legal instruments that address standards. Additionally, the scope and application of these legal provisions have been interpreted by its dispute settlement system (DSS), ordinarily clarifying the rules through judicial elaboration but sometimes resulting in further obfuscation of the existing provisions. The context of voluntary sustainability standards (VSS)—and private standards in particular—is new to the WTO; currently the organization, based on its purist understanding of itself as an inter-governmental entity, does not formally regulate private standards. However, the question of whether it *should* do so has been under discussion for some years, even though no consensus exists around this issue yet. Ambiguity remains over the WTO's role in the context of "private standards", even as they increasingly occupy larger swathes of the landscape of sustainability standards.

The use of sustainability standards has worrisome implications for the "developing countries" in particular, which have, in general, remained wary of the idea of using trade as an instrument to achieve sustainability goals. The developing countries expect the WTO rules to facilitate market access for them and the use of standards—in the setting of which they have very little participation—is perceived as an obstruction to the achievement of this objective. For the "emerging economies", however, there is pressure to undertake measures to ensure that their exports are environment-friendly. The development-related concerns over the use of sustainability and private standards have thus been a core area of debate.

Even while the potentially trade-restrictive impact of standards and technical regulations has been a cause of concern, the WTO has displayed a willingness to recognize that the use of sustainability standards can be complementary to the cause of international trade. The 2005 World Trade Report of the WTO, titled *Exploring the Links Between Trade, Standards and the WTO*, recognized that standard regimes and international trade rules needed to be mutually supportive for an effective trading system (WTO, 2005). A 2017 joint publication of the UN's Food and Agriculture Organization (FAO) and the WTO, titled *Trade and Food Standards*, argued that countries—and developing countries in particular—need to proactively participate in the development of food standards if they wish to be gainers from the benefits of the burgeoning global trade. Roberto Azevedo, the current WTO Director-General, has argued that the alignment of food standards and international trade will not only help ensure food safety but also deliver on the Sustainable Development Goals (SDGs) (FAO & WTO, 2017).[2] In April 2019, the WTO—along with the World Health Organization (WHO) and the Food and Agriculture Organization (FAO)—organized the *International Forum on Food Safety and Trade* at the WTO Headquarters in Geneva, where the role of food standards in ensuring food safety was discussed.[3] This focus on issues of safety and sustainability seems indicative of the in-principle acceptance by the WTO of the fact that international trade is to be conducted within the SDG framework.

This chapter is an overview of the WTO's interface with sustainability standards and is arranged as follows. Section 2 discusses the rules of the WTO that relate to standards in general, points at select judicial interpretations relating to the use of standards and highlights the relevant committees in which discussions on standards take place. Section 3 discusses private standards in particular and analyses the arguments in relation to the nature of the possible engagement of the WTO with them. Section 4 describes the special status of the developing countries in the context of sustainability standards and discusses where the "emerging economies" stand in this regard. Section 5 attempts tentative conclusions.

2   WTO Disciplines on Sustainability Standards

The interface of the WTO with the issue of sustainability standards is viewed below in three contexts: (1) legal provisions; (2) judicial interpretations; and (3) committee structures.

1.   *Legal Provisions and Sustainability Standards*

Regulation of standards arose as a concern for the multilateral trading system (MTS) at the Tokyo Round of the General Agreement on Tariffs and Trade (GATT), which ran through 1973–1979. The Tokyo Round Standards Code[4] recognized the positive contribution that standards could make to international trade and provided for sustainability standards by "recognizing that no country should be prevented from taking measures necessary … for the protection of human, animal or plant life or health, of the environment …" (GATT, 1979, Preamble). Since it was the sole legal document at the time, its coverage was broad and included both regulations and

---

[2]Food safety is closely linked with sustainability as its impacts both the social as well as environmental realms.

[3]*The Future of Food Safety—Transforming Knowledge into Action for People, Economies and the Environment*, https://www.wto.org/english/tratop_e/sps_e/faowhowtoapril19_e.htm.

[4]For a history of the development of the Standards Code, *see* (Thorstensen & Vieira, 2016, pp. 12–13). For a detailed, article-by-article commentary on the Standards Code, *see* (Middleton, 1980).

standards (mandatory and voluntary specifications) applicable to industrial and agricultural goods. The Standards Code was hailed as an "innovative document" as it brought within the normative purview of the MTS an area that till then had not been subjected to multilateral supervision (Middleton, 1980, p. 201).

The Standards Code, however, failed to prevent trade disruptions caused by technical regulations and standards (Marceau & Trachtman, 2002, p. 814). Sykes, in his more cautious assessment of the Code, argues that the Code was effective only in instances where member states were "...determined to pursue formal dispute resolution...the day-to-day process of adopting new standards and regulations...may not have been affected much" (Sykes, 1995. p. 77). There was a felt need to replace the plurilateral Standards Code with a multilateral agreement binding on all parties. Also, with agricultural liberalization brought under the GATT in the Uruguay Round, a need was felt to separately address sanitary and phytosanitary measures (SPMs) relating to agricultural goods (Debroy, 2005, p. 3).

In the 1990s, the use of TBT and SPS measures grew sharply as tariff barriers declined (Thorstensen & Vieira, 2016, p. 13, Figs. 1 and 2). The 1990s also saw the active engagement of civil society organizations in partnering with businesses to "green" global supply chains through sustainability standard-setting in sectors such as organic food and sustainable forestry and fisheries (Gale et al., 2017, p. 65). Two separate agreements were negotiated during the Uruguay Round (1986–1994) to replace the Tokyo Round Standards Code, which formed the basis for the negotiation and adoption of these agreements (WTO & OECD, 2019, p. 20). In distinguishing between the scope of the two WTO agreements, the "type of measure" (all technical regulations, except when they are SPMs) acts as a determinant for the TBT Agreement whereas the "purpose of measure" (any measure—not necessary technical—to protect human, animal or plant life or health) determines the application of the SPS Agreement.[5]

The two agreements of the WTO that deal with the use of environmental and social standards are the *Agreement on Technical Barriers to Trade* (TBT Agreement) and the *Agreement on Sanitary and Phytosanitary Standards* (SPS Agreement). Both agreements regulate the use of certain types of restrictive measures in international trade, allowing their use under permitted circumstances, yet qualifying their use so that international trade is not (or only minimally) adversely impacted. As has been pointed out (Marceau & Trachtman, 2002, p. 815; Thorstensen & Vieira, 2016, p. 15), these agreements represent "... 'interpretation notes' of the rules enshrined in the exceptions of Article XX of GATT".[6]

---

[5] *See* WTO website, *Understanding the WTO Agreement on Sanitary and Phytosanitary Measures*, https://www.wto.org/english/tratop_e/sps_e/spsund_e.htm.

[6] Article XX of the GATT, which sets out the "General Exceptions" to core WTO obligations reads: "Subject to the requirement that such measures are not applied in a manner which would constitute a means of arbitrary or unjustifiable discrimination between countries where the same conditions prevail, or a disguised restriction on international trade, nothing in this Agreement shall be construed to prevent the adoption or enforcement by any contracting party of measures: ... (b) necessary to protect human, animal or plant life or health; ... (g) relating to the conservation of exhaustible

The preamble to the TBT Agreement recognizes that international standards contribute to improved efficiency in international trade and talks of the positive need to encourage the development of international standards. What must be ensured, however, is that technical regulations and standards do not create *unnecessary* obstacles to international trade (WTO, 1994a, Preamble, emphasis added). These agreements thus constitute a "balancing act"—on the one hand, allowing their use for legitimate policy needs of member states, while on the other hand, requiring that their use does not unnecessarily restrict trade (Sampson, 2005, p. 115; Wolfrum, Stoll, & Anja, 2007). The TBT Agreement recognizes and defines three forms of regulatory barriers to trade—technical regulations, standards, and conformity assessment procedures.[7] A core provision of the TBT Agreement mandates member states to ensure that technical regulations do not constitute "unnecessary obstacles to international trade", i.e. are not "more trade-restrictive than necessary to fulfil a legitimate objective...." (WTO, 1994a, Article 2.2). The TBT Agreement also has annexed to it a "Code of Good Practice", which lays out the disciplines for the "preparation, adoption and application of standards" by all standardizing bodies—governmental or non-governmental (WTO, 1994a, Annex 3).

The SPS Agreement, similarly, recognizes the right of members to take sanitary and phytosanitary measures necessary for the protection of human, animal or plant life or health (WTO, 1994b, Article 2.1) provided they ensure that "...any sanitary or phytosanitary measure is applied only to the extent necessary to protect human, animal or plant life or health ... and is not maintained without sufficient scientific evidence..." (WTO, 1994b, Article 2.2). Members are to ensure that their SPMs do not *arbitrarily* or *unjustifiably discriminate* between members and SPMs are not applied so as to constitute a *disguised restriction* on international trade (WTO, 1994b, Article 2.3, emphasis added).

The SPS Agreement promotes the use of international standards developed by international standard-setting bodies and recognizes some—the *Codex Alimentarius* (for food safety), the *World Organisation for Animal Health* (OIE) (for animal health) and the *International Plant Protection Convention* (IPPC) (for plant safety)—whose standards are deemed to be consistent with the requirements of the WTO disciplines [WTO, 1994b: Preamble, Article 3(4)]. "The international standards produced by the "three sisters", while voluntary, provide the basis for harmonization of the SPS measures adopted by WTO members, unless ... there is a scientific justification

---

natural resources if such measures are made effective in conjunction with restrictions on domestic production or consumption..." (GATT, 1947: Article XX).

[7] As defined in the TBT Agreement, a *technical regulation* is "a document which lays down product characteristics or their related processes and production methods, including the applicable administrative provisions, with which compliance is mandatory" (WTO, 1994a, Annex 1:1, emphasis added). A *standard* is "a document approved by a recognized body that provides, for common and repeated use, rules, guidelines or characteristics for products or related processes and production methods, with which compliance is not mandatory" (WTO, 1994a, Annex 1:2, emphasis added). A *conformity assessment procedure* is "any procedure used, directly or indirectly, to determine that relevant requirements in technical regulations or standards are fulfilled" (WTO, 1994a, Annex 1:3, emphasis added).

and based on a risk assessment, a member decides to introduce a measure that would result in a higher level of sanitary or phytosanitary protection" (WTO & OECD, 2019, p. 40). Thus, although member states are free to choose higher levels of protection than international standards, such measures have to be based on a risk assessment carried out by the member state that establishes "sufficient scientific evidence" for the existence of the risk (Sampson, 2005, p. 117). The TBT Agreement similarly requires member states to use "relevant international standards" as a basis for their national regulations and standards but it neither defines "international standards", nor does it list out recognized international standardizing bodies.[8]

Marceau and Trachtman (2002, p. 816), in an exhaustive article comparing the GATT, the TBT Agreement and the SPS Agreement,[9] identify the following disciplines that the TBT and SPS Agreements together encompass: non-discrimination (most favoured nation and national treatment); necessity and proportionality; scientific basis; harmonization (conformity with international standards); mutual recognition and equivalence; internal consistency; permission for precautionary action; and balancing and product/process issues. Besides the TBT and SPS disciplines, some provisions of the General Agreement on Tariffs and Trade (GATT) also apply, in particular, Articles I, III, XI and XX of GATT. In principle, then, the use of standards—for legitimate purposes—is not a problem in the WTO. Problems arise, however, with variant interpretations of what is "legitimate". It is often difficult to distinguish between an intentionally protectionist measure and a non-protectionist measure, with a genuine objective, that incidentally restricts trade (Marceau & Trachtman, 2002, p. 811) and this becomes the key reason for disputes among member states.

2. *Judicial Interpretation and Sustainability Standards*

Judicial interpretations by the WTO panels and Appellate Body (AB) have elaborated upon the content of the legal provisions relating to standards. The WTO website lists 49 disputes that have cited (uptil September 2019) the provisions of the SPS Agreement (spanning measures relating to agricultural products; beef, meat, seafood and poultry products; fruits and vegetables; seeds and oil; bottled water, wood and textiles, biotech products and cigarettes, etc.) and 54 disputes that have cited the provisions of the TBT Agreement in the request for consultations (covering measures relating to gasoline and biodiesel; meat, fisheries and dairy, pharmaceuticals, textiles, tobacco and cigarettes, etc.).[10] Given the close relationship and overlap between the

---

[8]In 2000, in order to elucidate what "relevant international standards" could mean, the TBT Committee adopted a decision laying down the principles based on which international standards should be developed by international standard-setting bodies so as to be considered as "relevant international standards": (i) transparency; (ii) openness (iii) impartiality and consensus; (iv) effectiveness and relevance; (v) coherence; and (vi) the development dimension (WTO & OECD, 2019, pp. 41–42).

[9]For a tabulated comparison of the TBT and SPS Agreements, *see* (Thorstensen & Vieria, 2016, pp. 57–62).

[10]For a complete listing of SPS-related and TBT-related disputes at the WTO, *see* https://www.wto. org/english/tratop_e/dispu_e/dispu_agreements_index_e.htm.

two agreements, very often, a dispute invokes measures of both the TBT and SPS Agreements. However, the panels and Appellate Body dealt substantively with these two agreements in only a few cases as most of the disputes were presumably resolved during the mandatory consultation phase (WTO & OECD, 2019, p. 26).

Emerging interpretations on issues relating to standards can be viewed through the work of the WTO Panels and AB. Several complex TBT- and SPS-related questions that have come up for consideration by the DSS deal with interpretations on "technical regulation", "like product" analysis, objectives fulfilled by a domestic regulation, "least-trade-restrictive" regulations, "process and production methods" (PPMs) "relevant international standard", "precautionary principle", "risk assessment", etc. More specifically, the WTO DSS increasingly engaged with aspects relating to standards that are sought to be implemented through labels. Whether a label is "mandatory" or "voluntary" in effect; what constitutes an "international standard"; whether labels are being used for genuine reasons with the interests of the consumer in mind; what kind of information labels should be expected to carry are all questions that have been addressed. While an exhaustive review of dispute-related interpretations is not possible within the scope of this chapter, some interesting and controversial interpretations are discussed below.

In the 2002 *EC Sardines* case, the importance of Codex Alimentarius harmonized standards was demonstrated. In this case, Peru successfully challenged an EC regulation under which only a species caught in European waters could be marketed as "sardines". As per an international standard set by the Codex Alimentarius Commission, however, a sardine species of the Pacific Ocean could be sold worldwide as "sardines" along with a qualifying phrase such as "Pacific sardines" or "Peruvian sardines". The WTO panel and AB struck down the EC regulation as it was neither based on the Codex standard nor did it demonstrate that the Codex standard was inadequate to fulfil the EC's legitimate objectives relating to "market transparency, consumer protection, and fair competition" (Shaffer & Victor, 2002). The EC had contended in this case that only standards that had been adopted *by consensus* by international bodies could be considered to qualify as "relevant international standards". The AB upheld the panel's finding, stating, "…the definition of a "standard" in … the TBT Agreement … does not require approval by consensus for standards adopted by a "recognized body" of the international standardization community (WTO, 2002, p. 63).

Two interesting interpretations came out of the 2012 *US-Tuna II* dispute. The first related to the characteristic of a measure that helps classify it either as a "standard" or a "regulation". A key characteristic that the WTO has traditionally used to distinguish *standards* from *regulations* is the *voluntary* or *mandatory* nature of the obligations they entail, respectively. However, this distinction was rendered fuzzy in the *US-Tuna II* case. In this case, Mexico challenged a US measure regarding a "dolphin-safe" label as violating the TBT Agreement and claimed that the USA had failed to comply with applicable international standards.[11] Interesting contestations of the *voluntary*

---

[11] The international standard at issue was the 1998 *Agreement on the International Dolphin Conservation Program (AIDCP)*, negotiated among fourteen Eastern Tropical Pacific (ETP) countries, US

versus *mandatory* nature of technical regulations emerged in this dispute. Mexico argued that the US requirements were *mandatory* because the label could be used only when the requirements were met. USA contended that the labelling measure was *voluntary* as it did not require all products to use the label. The panel ruled in favour of Mexico on this point and found that the requirements to grant the label were *mandatory* (WTO, 2011).[12] The AB upheld this view that the US measure was a *mandatory* technical regulation and not a *voluntary* standard, since it imposed legally enforceable conditions that must be met in order to have access to the "dolphin-safe" label;[13] "…the U.S. law effectively prohibits any mention of dolphin safety on cans of tuna that do not meet U.S. regulatory requirements" (Shaffer, 2013, p. 195; WTO, 2012a). This interpretation throws a new light on the traditional distinction that the TBT Agreement has maintained between a *voluntary* "standard" and a *mandatory* "technical regulation" (Trujillo, 2012) and the AB ruling has opened a debate over this distinction.

A second interpretation related to the question of what constitutes an "international standard". Article 2.4 of the TBT Agreement requires that, where international standards exist, WTO member states are to use them as a basis for their regulations. Mexico argued that the USA had failed to comply with international standards, in this case, the 1998 *Agreement on the International Dolphin Conservation Program* (AIDCP). While the panel agreed with Mexico's contention that the AIDCP standard was an international standard and that the USA had failed to base its labelling provisions on it, the AB disagreed with the panel and noted instead that "…under … the TBT Agreement, an international standard must be adopted by "an international

---

and Mexico, which mandated the use of certain equipment and practices to prevent dolphin mortality and injury. The US labelling regime under the 1990 *Dolphin Protection Consumer Information Act* (DPCIA), prohibited the use of labels that tuna products are "dolphin-safe" if tuna are caught by "setting on dolphins" (chasing and encircling dolphins with a net in order to catch tuna) in the ETP. For tuna caught in the ETP, access to the label requires an *additional* certification that "no dolphins were killed or seriously injured" in the process. The labelling of tuna as "dolphin-safe" was not a legal requirement. But Mexican tuna would lose US markets because only tuna that can be labelled as dolphin-safe is preferred (Shaffer, 2013, p. 195). The Mexican tuna fleet was using fishing practices that did not meet the criteria specified in the US law although they complied with the "dolphin-safe" standards agreed upon in the less-stringent AIDCP.

[12]"…*to the extent that they prescribe, in a binding and legally enforceable instrument, the manner in which a dolphin-safe label can be obtained in the United States, and disallow any other use of a dolphin-safe designation, the US tuna labelling measures "regulate" dolphin-safe labelling requirements "in a binding or compulsory fashion". It is not compulsory to meet these requirements and to bear the label, in order to sell tuna on the US market… However, … no tuna product may be labelled dolphin-safe … if it does not meet the conditions set out in the measures, and thus impose a prohibition on the offering for sale in the United States of tuna products bearing a label referring to dolphins and not meeting the requirements that they set out.* (WTO, 2011, p.150, para 7.131).

[13]"*In this case, … the measure at issue sets out a single and legally mandated definition of a "dolphin-safe" tuna product and disallows the use of other labels on tuna products that do not satisfy this definition. In doing so, … the US measure covers the entire field of what "dolphin-safe" means in relation to tuna products. For these reasons, we find that the Panel did not err in characterizing the measure at issue as a "technical regulation" within the meaning of … the TBT Agreement*". (WTO, 2012, p. 80, para 199).

standardizing body" and that the AIDCP did not qualify, since not all WTO members could join it." (Shaffer, 2013, p. 197). In other words, the AB averred that if a state relies on a standard, then the characteristics of the body are salient to an assessment of whether it is a "recognized international standard" (Wijkström & Devin, 2013, p. 1028). The interpretations forwarded in this dispute are especially seen as being problematic as they are likely to endanger market access for developing countries (Trujillo, 2012).

Other than these illustrative cases, there are several others that address various aspects relating to the issue of standards in general and sustainability standards in particular. The application of sustainability standards will remain subject to the interpretations of the WTO DSS, which constitutes a key component of the global governance landscape applicable to sustainability standards (provided, of course, that the WTO DSS itself survives the current crisis it finds itself in).

3. *Committees and Sustainability Standards*

Discussions relating to sustainability standards are also carried out within the relevant committee structures of the WTO. The WTO Committee on Trade and Environment (CTE) has been discussing voluntary sustainability standards (VSS) since many years. In 2001, the CTE received a formal mandate to address "labelling for environmental purposes" under the 2001 Doha Development Agenda (WTO, 2001: Paragraph 32(iii)). The CTE held discussions on the sustainability of palm oil production and trade (including the issue of standards) in May 2019, highlighting the need to ensure that the growth opportunities in this sector are pursued in a way that the environment is safeguarded (WTO, 2019). At the CTE, the developing countries have consistently emphasized their concerns over the rapid proliferation of private standards and the consequent market access difficulties but industrialized member states have maintained that discussion should be limited to public measures.

The TBT and SPS Agreements are supported by their two respective committees— the *Technical Barriers to Trade Committee* and the *Sanitary and Phytosanitary Standards Committee*. Additional to allowing for information exchange and discussion, the committees provide a forum for raising "specific trade concerns" (STCs) relating to draft measures of other members that may obstruct trade. When differences arise between member states over the conformity of national measures relating to SPS and TBT, STCs can be raised and addressed in the committees, preventing differences and frictions from blowing up into full-fledged disputes. It has been pointed out that the conflict resolution contribution of the WTO is grossly undervalued if only the settlement of formal disputes is considered (Horn, Mavroidis, & Wijkström, 2013); the STC mechanism can constitute a viable and effective alternative to the formal DSS (Holzer, 2018). Discussions within the committee structures, however, are outside of the formal negotiation track, even while the outcome of the discussions may feed into the negotiations.

3 WTO and Private Standards

No internationally recognized definition of "private standards" exists as of yet. In order to distinguish between public and private standards, earlier literature asked the question as to whose interests are taken into account in setting a standard, the assumption being that while the former consolidate the interests of all stakeholders (including externalities) in the economy, the latter narrowly pursue profits of private companies (WTO, 2005, pp. 32–33). Such a distinction is based on a narrow definition of "private standards" as it does not take into account the role of non-governmental organizations (NGOs) in setting and implementing standards, expectedly not with a "profit motive". More expansive definitions of "private standards" refer to "…any requirements that are established by non-governmental entities, including wholesale or retail stores, national producer associations, civil society groups, or combinations of them" (Thorstensen, Weissinger, & Sun, 2015, p. 1; Meliado, 2017, p. viii).

In the realm of VSS, in particular, private actors not only act alone to set standards but also interact closely with governments and civil society actors [what Abbot and Snidal (2009) refer to as the "governance triangle"] to form partnerships in order to address sustainability impacts of global value chains (GVCs) (Lambin & Thorlakson, 2018). In fact, the harmonization of public and private standards is advocated as constituting an important strategy for achieving positive welfare gains such as sustainability. The nature of the interaction between public and private standards, it is asserted, will be determined by the legitimacy of the standard (ITC, 2011, p. 10). The subject matter of private standards, which most often relates to food safety, environmental protection, animal welfare, fair trade, labour, human rights, etc.,[14] points to a large overlap between sustainability standards and private standards.

Private standards are a concern because of several reasons. First, private standards add to the already massive proliferation of existing standards that complicate international trade. Starting with sectors such as agriculture, forestry, aquaculture and apparel, private standards are now found in almost all sectors. For suppliers, especially the smaller ones, the "proliferation and increased influence" of private standards is cumbersome (Thorestensen et al., 2015, p. 1). Private standards contribute to further fragmentation in the field of standardization, leading to the possible risk of "standards shopping". Second, the content of private standards is perceived as being much more rigid than public-sector standards and without scientifically established justification. The process of their adoption is seen as lacking in democracy and transparency (Mbengue, 2011).

Third, as per common understanding, private standards are viewed as, by definition, voluntary while public standards can be either mandatory or voluntary (WTO,

---

[14]See examples of private standards listed in Table 1 (Thorstensen & Vieira, 2016, p. 71). Examples of private voluntary standards schemes listed by Mbengue (2011) include "the '*Carrefour Filière Qualité* ' standard, the '*British Retail Consortium Global Standard—Food*', the '*QS Qualitat Sicherheit*', the '*Label Rouge*', the '*Global Food Safety Initiative*', as well as the International Standards Organization (ISO) standards: '*ISO 22000: Food safety management systems*' and '*ISO 22005: Traceability in the feed and food chain*'" (Mbengue, 2011).

2005, p. 33). But private standards may not be as "voluntary" as they are projected to be as they often act as necessary conditions for market access. This is especially the case when they are implicitly endorsed by governments, thereby transforming their voluntary nature to a de facto mandatory one. Marx (2017, pp. 3, 12) questions the relevance of the distinction between public and private standards based on two arguments—(i) private standards are often based on public norms and (ii) when governments back private standards, they become a part of "public" governance. Such "incorporation by reference" is problematic because when a private standard finds government backing, "…the rule becomes mandatory but the process of developing the standard remains private" (Mavroidis & Robert, 2016, p. 14).

Fourth, the legal implications of the use of private standards need to be recognized; since these standards do not fall within the normative purview of the WTO regime, a government could choose to support a private standard to avoid its WTO obligations instead of setting its own public standard which would need to be WTO compliant. This would undermine the structure of the WTO Agreements, which do not recognize private standards unless they are "backed by governments" (Thorstensen and Vieira, 2016, p. 49). Fifth, the developing countries face greater difficulties in dealing with such standards as small-scale producers will bear a greater risk of exclusion from the market if they do not comply with them (Thorestensen et al. 2015, p. 50; Mbengue, 2011).

While the WTO has long discussed the issue of private standards, it has stopped short of bringing private standards within its normative purview. Discussions on private standards have taken place in the committee structures of the WTO, with the SPS Committee discussing the issue since 2005–2006. The issue of private standards caught the limelight when in 2007, Saint Vincent and the Grenadines complained to the WTO about how the proliferation of private standards was posing a challenge for small vulnerable economies, particularly small farmers within them, and argued for application of WTO rules to private standards in order to address the "…confusion, inequity and lack of transparency" that often accompanies them (WTO, 2007a).

This complaint led to the debate gaining strength in the SPS Committee, with member states trying to define "private standard". In 2008, an ad hoc Working Group on private standards was established under the SPS Committee, which came out with a report in 2010 on "Possible Actions for the SPS Committee Regarding SPS-related Private Standards", highlighting the need to define "private standards". In the face of an inability to produce an acceptable definition, an "electronic working group" (E-WG) was set up to continue attempts at definition.[15] The developed countries are against the inclusion of private standards into the purview of the SPS Agreement.

Outside of the committees too, the WTO has discussed the issue of private standards. A joint UNCTAD/WTO informal information session on private standards

---

[15]The E-WG proposal for consideration by the Committee of an SPS-related private standard is: "A written requirement or condition, or a set of written requirements or conditions, related to food safety, or animal or plant life or health that may be used in commercial transactions and that is applied by a non-governmental entity that is not exercising governmental authority" (Mavroidis & Wolfe, 2016, p. 9).

was organized way back in 2007 and in 2008, the Standards and Trade Development Facility (STDF) also held an information session on private standards (WTO, 2007b). The WTO's Public Forum too has, in recent years, discussed private standards multiple times. In September 2016, for instance, a WTO Public Forum session was held under the theme: *Should the Development of Private Standards Be More Transparent?* (WTO, 2016).

Based on their review of the TBT and SPS Committee discussions, Mavroidis and Robert (2016, p. 11) succinctly sum up the current state of play thus: "… both committees perceive the issue, and neither can get past the "public-private" divide, which is partly a north-south debate and partly a transatlantic chasm. … negotiation on the modalities of WTO action is stymied by the absence of agreement on the quintessential element … definition of the term 'private standard'". Clearly, a dominant sense of the inter-governmental nature of the WTO stands in the way of the WTO foraying into the field of private standards. However, analyses suggest that it may be a costly decision to leave out private standards from the purview of the WTO's work. Thorstensen and Vieira (2016, p. 21) suggest that when private standards are backed by governments, they should fall within the scrutiny of the TBT and SPS Agreements. Meliado identifies three reasons for the lack of movement in the WTO over private standards: "(i) lack of clarity as to …the nature of the problem, (ii) fear of agreeing on language that might later be used in WTO disputes and (iii) excessive emphasis placed on the downside of private standards" and offers a "menu of policy options" (Meliado, 2017, p. ix, 32)[16]

Several writings look into the need or otherwise of bringing private standards within the normative purview of the WTO regime (Mavroidis & Robert, 2016; Meliado, 2017; Du, 2018). Mavroidis & Wolfe explicate "…the … line of distinction between what is public, hence subject to WTO rules, and what is private, thus none of its business, still preoccupies the imagination of delegates in Geneva … How reclusive should the WTO allow product standards to be? … even a recluse must abide by certain social norms" (Mavroidis & Robert, 2016, pp. 1, 2–3). Du shares the apprehension that the growth in private standards can have adverse impacts and explores a possible justification for an intergovernmental organization such as the WTO to regulate transnational private standards (Du, 2018, p. 1). Thorstensen and Viera argue in favour of the negotiation of a "meta-regulation" and suggest that the United Nations Forum on Sustainability Standards (UNFSS) could be a good candidate to play the role. For the interim, they suggest that private standards be jointly scrutinized by the TBT and SPS Committees as they fall in the interface of the work areas of the two committees (Thorstensen and Vieira, 2016, p. 65, 102).

---

[16]Meliado's options followed by a SWOT analysis of each (p. 38) are: "(1) Creating a joint SPS–TBT transparency mechanism for private standards; (2) Establishing a public–private crosspollination mechanism under the Agreement on Government Procurement; (3) Launching a work programme on sustainability-related PPPs within the framework of the Trade Facilitation Agreement; and (4) Expanding the work programme of the UNFSS so as to officially include international, regional, and national standards bodies; (5) Using the UN Global Compact to promote transparency and accountability principles" (Meliado, 2017, p. 32).

Mavroidis and Robert (2016, p. 1) do not argue for formally binding or justiciable rules but foresee at least two types of interventions that the WTO could make; (i) it could adopt a "Reference Paper" to encourage its members to apply the rules that apply to standards under the WTO to private standards as well and (ii) as a "meta-regulator", it could effectively ensure transparency in the processes through which private standards are developed and implemented. Mbengue suggests that private standards could either be "imported" into the WTO (member states to develop national standards based on private standards) or WTO rules could be "exported" (WTO to monitor private standards to check their WTO-compliance). A "legalistic" approach would push it to only recognize international standards while a "pragmatic" approach would integrate, through recognition, private standards within the trading system (Mbengue, 2011).

Calls for inclusion aside, as of date, private standards find no mention in the WTO Agreements. However, Article 4.1 of the TBT Agreement is often cited as a relevant provision to address private standards. The text of this Article reads:

> Members ... shall take such reasonable measures as may be available to them to ensure that local government and *non-governmental standardizing bodies* within their territories...accept and comply with this Code of Good Practice. In addition, Members shall not take measures which have the effect of, directly or indirectly, requiring or encouraging such standardizing bodies to act in a manner inconsistent with the Code of Good Practice (WTO 1994a: Art. 4.1, emphasis added).

A similar provision exists in Article 13 of the SPS Agreement, which makes a mention of "non-governmental entities". It has been often asked whether these provisions could be used to allow "private standards" to be treated as "government acts" (Mbengue, 2011). While a GATT panel has held that activities that can be "attributed" to a state should be seen as falling within the ambit of the GATT, the determination of such attribution would be unique to each case. In addition to the private–public relationship at the level of governments, the relationship of private standards and international standards in also not settled. Mbengue points out that international standardization organizations face competition from private standards and describes their confrontation as a hostile one, stating, "...the 'empire' of international standard-setting organisations is ... determined to strike back if the development of private standards goes beyond any normative control" (Mbengue, 2011). Reciprocal information exchange among the two, transparency in their processes and attempts at harmonization could be starting points in promoting coherence between these two types of standards. Given the large overlap between private standards and sustainability standards, the fate of the former—in terms of legal recognition and coverage—will impact the future scope for use of the latter.

4 Sustainability Standards, Developing Countries and Emerging Economies

The history of the multilateral trading system bears out that unlike tariff barriers, non-tariff barriers (NTBs) to trade have proved far more difficult to address. Developing countries, with weaker bargaining power over their terms of trade, are particularly vulnerable to the potentially trade-restrictive implications of NTBs. NTBs are projected as protectionist measures that are likely to be highly disputed (Banerjee, 2006, p. 47; Thorstensen and Vieira, 2016, p. 7). While standards and regulations can perform several vital functions, they can also be used unfairly to become barriers to trade (Saqib, 2003, p. 270).

The politics of the use of standards begins with difficulties in agreeing to the appropriateness of standards. Different actors may hold differing views on the required level and nature of standards imposed. The 1992 *Rio Declaration on Environment and Development* recognized this when it stated, "Environmental standards...should reflect the environmental and developmental context to which they apply. Standards applied by some countries may be inappropriate and of unwarranted economic and social cost to other countries, in particular developing countries". (United Nations, 1992, Principle 11).

For the developing countries in general, market access is impacted by standards, and within the developing countries, especially vulnerable are the small and medium enterprises (SMEs), whose competitiveness in international markets may suffer due to the rise in costs associated with standards (WTO, 2016). Middleton explicates, "The Trade-hampering effects of standards and technical regulations may be … those arising from divergence in the technical specifications and those arising from certification and approval procedures" (Middleton, 1980, p. 203). With regard to voluntary standards, the developing countries face the double burden of acquiring information on standards in an environment of "information-asymmetry" and mobilizing resources to bring process and production methods in line with the requirements of these standards (Wilson, 2002, p. 428). Developing countries are particularly vulnerable to the impact of "conformity assessment procedures" (product testing or plant inspections to ensure compliance with regulations and standards), which are "...vulnerable to non-transparency, delays, arbitrary inspection, and redundant tests...protection by domestic firms" etc. (Saqib, 2003, p. 271).[17] It is in this context that Baldwin warned of the creation of "...a two-tier system of market access with developing nations in the second tier" (Baldwin, 2000, p. 239).

Numerous studies have examined the impact of standards on developing countries in particular (Wilson, 2002, pp. 431–432). Both Saqib's study and Debroy's paper discuss examples of specific measures that are presented as quality or environmental measures but are perceived by Indian exporters to be NTBs (Saqib, 2003; Debroy, 2005; pp. 10–11). A study by Kang and Ramizo (2017, p. 22) shows that the positive

---

[17]Debroy (2005, pp. 8–9) lists out, for example, the list of complaints that India has with relation to standards. These can be seen to be generally reflective of developing country dissatisfaction with standards.

impacts of SPS and TBT measures are limited to the advanced economies while the countries of the South are excluded from the gains of SPS and TBT measures in international trade. A review of literature carried out at the Institute of Development Studies (IDS) in order to test whether standards act as "net barriers" or "net catalysts" to developing country exports showed mixed results: "…standards generally act as a barrier to developing country trade in agriculture, but have a catalytic effect in certain manufacturing sectors … the significance and magnitude of this effect varies across developing countries, sub-sectors and exporting firms … the impact of standards on developing country trade is highly context specific" (Timmis, 2017, p. 4). It must be recognized that accurate quantification of the impact of standards is rarely possible and that perceptions are also key variables to be factored in.

At the WTO, developing countries have remained opposed to the idea of using trade as an instrument to achieve environmental goals because of the potential adverse implications for market access. For the same reason, the developing countries have also harboured suspicions towards the use of standards, fearing their use for protectionist purposes (Banerjee, 2006). "Among the difficulties … identified by the developing countries are the high costs of adaptation, the irrelevance of foreign standards to local conditions, the lack of timely and adequate information and consequent transaction costs, the difficulties in understanding the requirements as well as testing and monitoring them, the perceived lack of scientific data for specific threshold or limiting values, and the uncertainty that arises from rapidly changing requirements in overseas market". (Saqib, 2003, p. 270). Another concern of the developing countries is the use of market access barriers that may result from non-product related production processes and methods (Dutta, Sinha, & Gaur, 2006, p. 348). It has also been pointed out that the logic of using sustainability standards may, in fact, be counter-effective for the developing countries, as standards tend to restrict access to markets that generate additional resources for environmental protection (Dutta et al., 2006, p. 347). The existing provisions and emerging interpretations on standards, therefore, require a thorough analysis for the potential implications they hold for developing country interests.

Both the TBT and the SPS Agreements include special provisions for providing technical assistance to the developing countries but these are not bound to specific commitments by the industrial countries and are inadequate. It is in light of this fact that developing countries have often sought "… a targeted review of the TBT and SPS agreements in light of development needs" (Wilson, 2002, p. 437). The WTO CTE addresses, as part of its mandate, the issue of the impact of environmental standards on market access, in particular for developing countries. The developing countries themselves also need to monitor the emergence of new interpretations relating to the use of standards and strategize to assert their own interests at the WTO DSS (Wilson, 2002, p. 437).

As far as the international standard-setting bodies recognized by the WTO Agreements are concerned, the need for enhancing developing countries' engagement in international standard-setting bodies has been consistently highlighted and developing countries have long argued for a harmonization of standards formulation procedures at the international level (Saqib, 2003, p. 295; Banerjee, 2006, p. 57;

Jansen, 2010). Wilson (2002, pp. 437–438) points out that developing countries should ensure that they are able to influence the development of global standards in ways that accommodate their concerns and he suggests the creation of a "global standards forum". In the context of private standards as well, the lack of factoring in of the special needs of the developing countries in their preparation and application cause them to act as barriers to trade for the developing countries in particular.

> Developing countries … have repeatedly expressed their concern about the way in which international standards are developed and approved in such bodies…Developing countries do not have the institutional capacities to match the developed world in terms of research and technical capacities and as a result their participation is very limited from the point of view of both numbers and effectiveness. As a consequence of the inadequacy of the process, international standards are often inappropriate for use as a basis for domestic regulations in developing countries and these countries face problems when they have to meet regulations in the importing markets developed on the basis of international standards (Banerjee, 2006, p. 63).

Once standards are set and accepted, there emerges the challenge of enabling exporters in the developing countries to meet these standards. A fair participation, in real terms, in the standard-setting bodies coupled with a strengthening of the capabilities to meet standards would contribute to a more balanced impact of standards on the developing countries. Under the Doha Development Agenda, the WTO had instructed its CTE to attend to "(i) the effect of environmental measures on market access, especially in relation to developing countries…(iii) labelling requirements for environmental purposes" (WTO, 2001, Para 32).

The WTO, taking cognizance of the asymmetries that the developing countries face, has set up the *Standards and Trade Development Facility* (STDF)[18]—which describes itself as "…a global partnership that supports developing countries in building their capacity to implement international sanitary and phytosanitary (SPS) standards, guidelines and recommendations as a means to improve their human, animal, and plant health status and ability to gain or maintain access to markets". Its goal is to achieve "increased capacity of developing countries to implement international SPS standards, guidelines and recommendations and hence ability to gain market access".[19] The 2018 Annual Report of the STDF was prepared around the theme *Investing in Safe Trade: Supporting Developing Countries to Meet International Standards*. The actual impact of this well-intentioned innovation awaits assessment.

Most literature on standards in relation to developing countries tends to focus on the developing countries at the receiving end of standards driven by the governments/firms/NGOs located in the Global North. From the perspective of "emerging economies", what needs recognition is also the emergence of standards within the South. It is no longer the case that markets of the South are totally bereft of the imposition of social and environmental accountability through standards (Schouten

---

[18]The STDF is a joint initiative of the FAO, OIE, World Bank, WHO and WTO that was conceived at the Doha Ministerial Conference in November 2001 and formally established in September 2004. See http://www.standardsfacility.org/history.

[19]See STDF website, http://www.standardsfacility.org/vision-and-goal.

& Bitzer, 2015). For instance, based on the International Trade Centre standards map, which contains data on more than 160 standards, Marx's listing of number of VSS per country, lists several emerging economies in the top ten rankings of "highly VSS active"—China (79); Brazil (77); India (72); and Mexico (71) (Marx, 2017, p. 8). The questions that call for attention then are the variations between standards of the Global North and those of the Global South and whether it is an accurate assumption that Southern market standards will necessarily be more inclusive and locally driven and therefore more acceptable (Langford, 2019).

As the WTO becomes more accepting of sustainability standards, the developing countries—and the emerging economies, in particular—will need to adjust to this reality and rethink their stances accordingly. It is often suggested that acceptance and implementation of certain standards may sometimes be in the best interests of the developing countries as "… [e]ffective regulation within their own markets is important for ensuring consumer safety and promoting technical change" (Wilson, 2002, p. 436). One point of view holds that "emerging economies", with larger stakes and shares in global trade, need to undertake effort to make their exports environment-friendly. External pressure to bring about changes may not always be a bad thing. In the case of India, for example, Debroy points out analogies from intellectual property rights and services to state that while initial reaction tended to be negative, the external trigger brought about domestic reforms for the better; the same could be true of standards (Debroy, 2005, p. 14). It is in this context that Grimm, Thomas, Archna, Christoph, & Jorge Perez (2018, p. 46) highlight "the growing pro-active commitment of developing countries to sustainability standards…[and] their efforts in aligning VSS to national priorities…", indicating that it may be time for them to move out of a defensive posturing vis-à-vis sustainability standards.

5   Conclusion

It is important to recognize that standards are not simply technical matters, "… although the considerations of the standard tend to be expressed in rather technical language, behind this façade of engineering jargon, what is actually happening is an economic fight, often of the most savage type imaginable because the stakes are so high" (Federal Trade Commission, quoted in Mattli and Büthe, 2003, p. 1). Taking the argument further, Mattli and Büthe contest the "technical" nature of standards and underscore their "political" nature:

> The study of international standardization raises the kinds of questions familiar to students of international relations, including: Who sets international rules? Do international standards benefit all or are there winners and losers, either in relative or absolute terms? What is the role of power and institutions in international disputes or bargains over standards? What defines power and how does it operate? … First movers set the international standards agenda, and laggards, or second movers, pay the switching costs. (Mattli & Büthe, 2003, pp. 3–4)

The multilateral trading system (WTO, including its GATT years) has evolved over its long history of existence, gathering along newer issues into its fold as required by the changing landscape of international trade. When the GATT became operational in 1948, it focused on free trade and did not take on board issues like standards and regulations. The proliferation of NTBs in international trade caused it to take cognizance of standards by developing rules to govern their use. The WTO stands at a similar crossroads, where it needs to resolve its relationship with private standards in order to clarify the several issues relating to sustainability standards discussed in this chapter. The question of whether or not WTO should regulate private standards will, however, open up larger debates around the appropriateness or otherwise of the WTO regulating "transnational private authority", thereby raising fundamental concerns relating to the very structures of global governance (Du, 2018). With the acceptance of Agenda 2030 and the SDGs as the guiding framework for all international activity, including international trade, global governance frameworks, including the WTO, need to adjust their capabilities to ensure the optimal use of sustainability standards. The real challenge, however, will be to effectively achieve not just the sustainability outcomes of such use but an equitable implementaiton as well that addresses the challenges arising from differential capacities and power asymmetries.

References

Abbott, K. W., & Snidal, D. (2009). Strengthening international regulation through transnational new governance: Overcoming the orchestration deficit. *Vanderbilt Journal of Transnational Law, 42*(2), 501–578.

Baldwin, R. E. (2000). Regulatory protectionism, developing nations, and a two-tier world trade system. In *Brookings trade forum* (pp. 237–280).

Banerjee, P. (2006). SPS-TBT measures: harmonisation and diversification? In: D. Sengupta et al. (Eds.), *Beyond the transition phase of WTO: An Indian perspective on emerging issues* (pp. 47–65). New Delhi: Academic Foundation.

Debroy, B. (2005). *The SPS and TBT agreements—Implications for Indian Policy*. Indian Council for Research on International Economic Relations, Working Paper No. 163.

Du, M. (2018). WTO regulation of transnational private authority in global governance. *International and Comparative Law Quarterly, 67*(4), 1–36.

Dutta, N., Sinha, M., & Gaur, U. (2006). Environmental standards as non-tariff barriers and the problem of market access. In D. Sengupta et al. (Eds.), *Beyond the transition phase of WTO: An Indian perspective on emerging issues* (pp. 347–367). New Delhi: Academic Foundation.

FAO and WTO. (2017). *Trade and food standards*. FAO and WTO. https://www.wto.org/english/news_e/spra_e/spra186_e.htm.

GATT. (1947). *General agreement on tariffs and trade*. https://www.wto.org/english/docs_e/legal_e/gatt47_02_e.htm.

GATT. (1979). *Agreement on technical barriers to trade* (Tokyo Round Standards Code).

Gale, F., Ascui, F., & Lovell, H. (2017). Sensing reality? New monitoring technologies for global sustainability standards. *Global Environmental Politics, 17*(2), 65–83.

Grimm, S., Thomas, F., Archna, N., Christoph, S., & Jorge Perez, P. (2018). Developing countries turn to sustainability standards. In *United Nations forum on sustainability standards. Voluntary sustainability standards, trade and sustainable development* (pp. 39–46) (3rd Flagship Report of the United Nations Forum on Sustainable Development). Geneva: UNFSS.

Holzer, K. (2018). *Addressing tensions and avoiding disputes: Specific trade concerns in the TBT Committee.* WTO Staff Working Papers ERSD-2018-11, WTO Economic Research and Statistics Division.

Horn, H., Mavroidis, P. C., & Wijkström, E. N. (2013). In the shadow of the DSU: Addressing specific trade concerns in the WTO SPS and TBT Committees. *Journal of World Trade, 47*(4), 729–759.

Jansen, M. (2010). Developing countries, standards and the WTO. *The Journal of International Trade & Economic Development, 19*(1), 163–185.

International Trade Centre. (2011). The interplay of public and private standards. *Literature review series on the impacts of private standards—Part III.* Doc. No. MAR-11-215.E.

Kang, J. W., & Ramizo, D. (2017). *Impact of sanitary and phytosanitary measures and technical barriers on international trade.* Munich Personal RePEc Archive (MPRA) Paper No. 82352, https://mpra.ub.uni-muenchen.de/82352/.

Lambin, E. F., & Thorlakson, T. (2018). Sustainability standards: Interactions between private actors, civil society, and governments. *Annual Review of Environment and Resources, 43,* 369–393.

Langford, N. (2019). *Ethical standards in emerging markets: Just how different are they?* Sheffield Political Economy Research Institute, http://speri.dept.shef.ac.uk/2019/08/30/ethical-standards-in-emerging-markets-just-how-different-are-they/.

Mareau, G., & Trachtman, J. P. (2002). The technical barriers to trade agreement, the sanitary and phytosanitary measures agreement, and the general agreement on tariffs and trade: A map of the world trade organization law of domestic regulation of goods. *Journal of World Trade, 36*(5), 811–881.

Marx, A., Maertens, M., Swinnen, J., & Wouters, J. (Eds.). (2012). *Private standards and global governance: Economic, legal and political perspectives.* Cheltenham, UK: Edward Elgar.

Marx, A. (2017). The public-private distinction in global governance: How relevant is it in the case of voluntary sustainability standards? *The Chinese Journal of Global Governance, 3*(1), 1–26.

Mattli, W., & Büthe, T. (2003). Setting international standards: Technological rationality or primacy of power? *World Politics, 56*(1), 1–42.

Mavroidis, P. C., & Robert, W. (2016). *Private standards and the WTO: Reclusive no more.* EUI Working Paper RSCAS 2016/17, Florence: European University Institute.

Mbengue, M. M. (2011). Private standards and WTO Law. *Biores, 5*(1). https://www.ictsd.org/bridges-news/biores/news/private-standards-and-wto-law.

Meliado, F. (2017). *Private standards, trade and sustainable development: Policy options for collective action.* Geneva: ICTSD Issue Paper.

Middleton, R. W. (1980). The GATT standards code. *Journal of World Trade Law,* 201–219.

Sampson, G. P. (2005). *The WTO and sustainable development* (pp. 113–127). Tokyo: United Nations University Press.

Saqib, M. (2003). Technical barriers to trade and the role of Indian standards-setting institutions. In A. Mattoo & R. M. Stern (Eds.), *India and the WTO* (pp. 269–298). Washington D.C.: The World Bank.

Schouten, G., & Bitzer, V. (2015). The emergence of southern standards in agricultural value chains: A new trend in sustainability governance? *Ecological Economics, 120,* 175–184.

Shaffer, G. (2013). United States—Measures concerning the importation, marketing and sale of Tuna and Tuna Products. *The American Journal of International Law, 107*(1), 192–199.

Shaffer, G., & Victor, M. (2002). The EC-sardines case: How North-South NGO-government links benefited Peru. In *Bridges* (Vol. 6(7)), Geneva: ICTSD.

Sykes, A. O. (1995). *Product standards for internationally integrated goods markets.* Washington D.C.: The Brookings Institution.

Thorstensen, V., Weissinger, R., & Sun, X. (2015). *Private standards—Implications for trade, development, and governance, E15 task force on regulatory systems coherence.* Geneva: ICTSD and WEF.

Thorstensen, V., & Vieira, A. C. (2016). *Regulatory barriers to trade: TBT, SPS and sustainability standards.* Sao Paulo: VT Assessoria Consultoria e Treinamento Ltda.

Timmis, H. (2017). *The impact of standards on developing country exports* (K4D Helpdesk Report). Institute of Development Studies, November 23, 2017, https://www.ids.ac.uk/publications/the-impact-of-standards-on-developing-country-exports/.

Trujillo, E. (2012). The Tuna-Dolphin Encore—WTO rules on environmental labeling. *Insights*, 16(7).

United Nations. (1992). *Rio declaration on environment and development.* A/CONF.151/26 (Vol. 1), http://www.jus.uio.no/lm/environmental.development.rio.declaration.1992/portrait.a4.pdf.

Wijkström, E., & Devin, M. (2013). *International standards and the WTO TBT agreement: Improving governance for regulatory alignment.* Staff Working Paper ERSD-2013-06, WTO Economic Research and Statistics Division.

Wilson, J. S. (2002). Standards, regulation, and trade: WTO rules and developing country concerns. In B. Haoekman, A. Matoo, & P. English (Eds.), *Development, trade, and the WTO: A handbook* (pp. 428–438). Washington D.C.: The World Bank.

Wolfrum, R., Stoll, P.-T., & Anja, S.-F. (Eds.) (2007). *WTO—Technical barriers and SPS measures, Max Planck commentaries on World Trade Law* (Vol. 3). Leiden: Martinus Nijhoff Publishers.

World Trade Organization. (1994a). *Agreement on technical barriers to trade.* https://www.wto.org/english/docs_e/legal_e/17-tbt.pdf.

World Trade Organization. (1994b). *Agreement on the application of sanitary and phytosanitary measures.* https://www.wto.org/english/tratop_e/sps_e/spsagr_e.htm.

World Trade Organization. (2001). *Doha WTO ministerial: Ministerial declaration.* WT/MIN(01)/DEC/1, November 20, 2001.

World Trade Organization. (2002). *European communities—Trade description of sardines* (Report of the Appellate Body, WT/DS231/AB/R), September 26, 2002.

World Trade Organization. (2005). *Exploring the links between trade, standards and the WTO*, 2005 (World Trade Report). file:///C:/Users/HOME/Downloads/world_trade_report05_e(1).pdf.

World Trade Organization. (2007a). *Private industry standards: Communication from Saint Vincent and the Grenadines*, G/SPS/GEN/766, Committee on Sanitary and Phytosanitary Measures, February 28, 2007.

World Trade Organization. (2007b). *Joint UNCTAD/WTO informal information session on private standards*, Sanitary and Phytosanitary Measures: Events, 25 June 2007, https://www.wto.org/english/tratop_e/sps_e/private_standards_june07_e/private_standards_june07_e.htm.

World Trade Organization. (2011). *US measures concerning the importation, marketing and sale of Tuna and Tuna products* (Report of the Panel, WT/DS381/R) September 15, 2011.

World Trade Organization. (2012a). *US measures concerning the importation, marketing and sale of Tuna and Tuna products* (Report of the Appellate Body, WT/DS381/AB/R) June 13, 2012.

World Trade Organization. (2012b). (World trade report) *Trade and public policies: A closer look at non-tariff measures in the 21st Century.* https://www.wto.org/english/res_e/publications_e/wtr12_e.htm.

World Trade Organization. (2016). *Sustainability standards: Effects for developing countries' SME Trade.* WTO Public Forum, September 29, 2016, https://www.wto.org/english/forums_e/public_forum16_e/wrksesions_e/session100_e.htm.

World Trade Organization. (2019). *WTO Members consider sustainability of palm oil trade and production, news item*, May 15, 2019. https://www.wto.org/english/news_e/news19_e/envir_15may19_e.htm.

World Trade Organization and Organization for Economic Cooperation and Development. (2019). *Facilitating trade through regulatory cooperation: The case of the WTO's TBT/SPS agreements and committees.* https://www.wto.org/english/res_e/publications_e/tbtsps19_e.htm.

Chapter 4
Towards Greening Trade? Environmental Provisions in Emerging Markets' Preferential Trade Agreements

Axel Berger, Dominique Blümer, Clara Brandi, and Manjiao Chi

1 Introduction

The recently adopted Sustainable Development Goals (SDGs) of the United Nation's Agenda 2030 underscore the significance of reconciling economic, social and environmental objectives. Transforming our economic activity such that it is consistent with environmental sustainability is dependent not only on global environmental rules, but also hinges on the right regulatory framework for the world economy.

One important forum for regulating global economic activities is the World Trade Organization (WTO), responsible for providing, monitoring and enforcing rules for international trade flows. However, multilateral trade negotiations under the roof of the WTO have been sluggish over the last years and countries increasingly resort to bilateral or regional preferential trade agreements (PTAs) to negotiate trade rules. PTAs have not only become more numerous, they also have become bigger, covering larger volumes of world trade, and they have become deeper as contracting parties go beyond the reduction of tariffs and have started negotiating issues such as services, investment, intellectual property rights and standards. Due to their increasing role in shaping global trade rules, PTAs potentially can be used as leverage for promoting environmental issues as well as other sustainability concerns in the global economy. Moreover, strong environmental provisions in PTAs may provide a context that is conducive to the effective implementation and use of standards and regulations that

---

This chapter draws from the authors' previously published work Berger, Brandi, Bruhn, and Chi (2017) and portions have been re-used here with permission from copyright owner.

A. Berger (✉) · D. Blümer · C. Brandi
German Development Institute/Deutsches Institut für Entwicklungspolitik (DIE), Bonn, Germany
e-mail: axel.berger@die-gdi.de

M. Chi
Law School, University of International, Business and Economics (UIBE), Beijing, China

Center for Global Cooperation Research, University of Duisburg-Essen, Duisburg, Germany

seek to address sustainability challenges. For instance, environmental provisions in PTAs might boost the uptake of industry—and product-specific public regulation or private standards in a given market, including voluntary sustainability standards (VSS).[1]

The EU and the USA already seem to promote 'high-standard' PTAs to set a precedent and shape globalization in their interest, presumably also with the aim to avoid 'unfair' competition and environmental dumping from emerging markets that can take advantage of lower levels of environmental and labour standards to keep production cost low (Steinberg, 1997). The argument is based on the assumption that emerging markets have less interest in higher environmental and labour standards and would be cautious to promote them through their trade policies. However, there is little systematic evidence about the prevalence of environmental standards in emerging markets' trade policies and their PTAs in particular. This chapter aims to address this question by assessing environmental provisions in emerging market PTAs and thus contribute to current policy debates about the 'green' design of trade policy. We aim to complement the existing literature at the interface of trade and environmental governance and investigate how different countries drive and/or react to the trend of entangling trade and environmental issues. While the EU and USA are seen as pioneers in including environmental matters in PTAs, we will explore whether emerging markets follow this trend and 'go green' or whether they refrain from doing so—and what this implies for leveraging environmental standards for the global economy. We thereby seek to contribute to the emerging literature on the design of PTAs and their non-trade dimensions (Baccini, Dür, & Elsig, 2016; Dür, Baccini, & Elsig, 2014; Gray, 2014; Kim, 2012; Kucik, 2012; Postnikov & Basti-aens, 2014) as well as to the growing literature on the role of rising powers like China and other emerging economies in global governance (Gray & Murphy, 2013; Kahler, 2013; Kennedy & Cheng, 2012; Stephen, 2014; Wang & French, 2014).

We conduct our analysis on the basis of our original data set mapping environmental provisions in emerging market PTAs. Our findings show that the PTAs of emerging markets incorporate more and more environmental provisions over time and that they tend to include more environmental content when they have been negotiated and signed with OECD countries, which in turn suggests that OECD countries can still be considered as rule-makers and emerging markets still largely as rules-takers in the context under consideration.

The remainder of the chapter is structured as follows. Section 2 provides an overview of the existing literature on the nexus between trade and the environment, with a focus on environmental provisions in trade agreements. Section 3 outlines the methodology for generating and analysing the data used in this chapter. In Sect. 4, we provide a bird's eye view of the different dimensions of environmental provisions in emerging market PTAs, as well as their development over time and in relation to partner countries. In Sect. 5, we zoom into specific country cases, namely China, India, Indonesia, Brazil and Mexico, to explore in more detail their stance towards

---

[1]So far, there is not much data available on the uptake of private standards by country, by sector and by year. For first insights, see Marx, Sharma, and Bécault (2015) and the data provided by ITC.

'green' trade rules. Section 6 concludes and discusses what our findings might imply for shaping environmental standards for the world economy.

2 Background and Related Literature

The relationship between international trade and the environment has been the subject of debate for a long time (for example, Birdsall & Wheeler, 1993; Cole & Elliot, 2003; Copeland & Taylor, 1995; Levinson & Taylor, 2008). Critics have argued that trade liberalization stands in conflict with environmental objectives while others have pointed to the potential of international trade to contribute to addressing environmental concerns. In general, the literature on trade and the environment distinguishes three effects (Copeland & Taylor, 1994; for empirical results, see Cole & Elliot, 2003; John & Pecchenino, 1994; Managi, Hibiki, & Tsurumi, 2009; Selden & Song, 1994; Stokey, 1998). First, economic integration increases economic activity which results in higher environmental pressure (scale effect). However, if environmental quality is a normal good, then the increased income should lead to a higher demand for high environmental standards and the adoption of new technologies (technique effect). Finally, trade liberalization may affect the distribution of pollution-intensive activities, shifting them where preferences to adopt clean technologies are lowest. As a consequence, pollution intensities in high-income countries may decrease, while developing countries shoulder most of the environmental burden (composition effect). Indeed, recent research unveils that much of the carbon embodied in the developed world's consumption of goods is imported from the developing world, rather than being produced at home (Peters, 2008; Peters & Hertwich, 2008). Other concerns relate to the impact of invasive species or transportation on the environment (Colyer, 2011). Moreover, there is a discussion on whether trade liberalization provokes a 'race to the bottom' where countries keep environmental standards low in order to retain their low-cost competitive advantage over other countries in global value chains (Sheldon, 2006). Irrespective of its direction, the bottom line is that there is a clear link between international trade and the environment—supporting the current trend towards regulating certain components of both areas jointly. But while scholars have long discussed the relationship between international trade and the environment, they have tended to overlook the potential implications of the design of trade policy for achieving environmental protection.

Even though the Marrakesh Agreement establishing the WTO names environmental protection and sustainable development explicitly as objectives of the organization (Johnson, 2015), its main aim remains trade liberalization. As a consequence, environmental issues mostly show up as exceptions to articles concerning liberalization. More precisely, under certain circumstances, it is permitted to restrict trade liberalization in order to avoid adverse effects on the environment. Such clauses are contained already in GATT Article XX, GATS Article XIV, as well as the Agreement on Agriculture (AoA), Agreement on Trade-Related Aspects of Intellectual Property

Rights (TRIPS), Sanitary and Phytosanitary Standards Agreement (SPS) and Agreement on Technical Barriers to Trade (TBT). The idea behind these clauses is that committing to trade liberalization should neither lead to a deterioration of environmental standards nor hinder environmental protection. However, a country applying trade-distorting measures has to prove that a removal would indeed harm the environment. While this might not be easy to do, it is meant to prevent protectionism under the veil of environmental concerns.

Beyond such 'do no harm' clauses, efforts in the WTO include the liberalization of environmental goods and services, the removal of subsidies on fossil fuels and sustainable fisheries, among others. However, as with many other policy areas, the success of reform at the multilateral level is limited (George, 2014). As a consequence, countries aiming to proceed on the agenda fall back upon negotiations at the plurilateral level (as in the case with e-commerce, investment and environmental goods) or at the bilateral/regional level in the form of PTAs.

Since the WTO has not made much progress with respect to environmental issues up to now, looking at developments at the bilateral/regional level is the natural next step. Throughout the last two decades, the number of PTAs that incorporate non-trade issues such as human rights and labour standards has risen notably (Hafner-Burton, 2009; Kim, 2012; Postnikov & Bastiaens, 2014). The same is true for the extent of environmental content included in PTAs (Morin, Dür, & Lechner, 2018). Our research contributes to the emerging literature on the design of PTAs, their implementation and their non-trade implications (Baccini et al., 2016; Dür et al., 2014; Gray, 2014; Kim, 2012; Kucik, 2012; Morin, Blümer, Brandi, & Berger 2019; Postnikov & Bastiaens, 2014).

While the relationship between international trade and the environment has been the subject of scholarly research, until recently, scholars have often disregarded the role of PTA design. The empirical literature on environmental provisions in PTAs is still quite small, but gives important first insights. Jinnah and Morgera (2013) compare environmental provisions in three EU and 11 US trade agreements since the mid-2000s by coding their scope and legal dimension. They find that environmental rules in PTAs have successively moved from reproducing the environmental exemptions stipulated in the GATT to references to Multilateral Environmental Agreements (MEAs) and full stand-alone environmental chapters that address enforcement and implementation issues. Moreover, they classify the EU and US approaches to addressing environmental issues in PTAs as cooperative and confrontational, respectively. This is in line with the overview on PTAs and the environment given by Anuradha (2011) and with the methodology of Bastiaens and Postnikov (2014) who differentiate in their empirical analysis between sanctions (US) and dialogue (EU) as enforcement mechanisms used for environmental provisions in PTAs. Based on a comprehensive and fine-grained dataset, Morin et al. (2018) argue that democracies facing import competition and countries which care about environmental protection are more likely to include environmental provisions in their PTAs. Morin et al. (2019) investigate the diffusion of environmental provisions and show that provisions that have been integrated in intercontinental agreements are more likely to be picked up in future agreements.

Empirical research suggests that the total number of provisions covered in PTAs is highest for PTAs between developed and developing countries (subsequently referred to as 'North–South' for convenience) (WTO, 2011). In general, developing countries—among each other—seem to prefer shallow agreements that only cover 1–2 substantive provisions on average, focussing on the elimination of tariffs (Bruhn, 2014). A possible explanation for the greater depth of North–South agreements is the bargaining power of developed countries that offer valuable market access in return for concessions regarding PTA content. If this pattern also holds for environmental rules, this would suggest that developing and emerging countries are reluctant to regulate environmental issues in PTAs among each other, but are more likely to agree to environmental content when negotiating with more developed partners.

Covering environmental issues within the international trading system can entail both advantages and disadvantages for different country groups; compared to the relatively toothless international environmental law, the WTO possesses an enforcement mechanism—namely the dispute settlement body—that it makes use of to settle inter-country conflicts. This dispute settlement body has also been used for disputes on trade-related environmental issues (Johnson, 2015). Equally, many PTAs possess enforcement mechanisms for environmental rules. On the one hand, this can be seen as an advantage since the availability of sanctions requires more commitment to agreements on environmental issues and increases their enforceability. On the other hand, some countries are concerned that the principle of 'common but differentiated responsibilities' meant to adapt developing country commitments to their capacities is undermined by drawing on agreements that are based on reciprocity (Jinnah & Morgera, 2013). Moreover, it is far from clear whether developing countries are able to meet high environmental standards. Their inability to do so could then be used by more developed countries to prohibit market access to goods that do not meet these standards ('green protectionism').

It is equally uncertain whether incorporating environmental provisions in the WTO and in PTAs actually has positive environmental effects. According to a survey in OECD countries, a main objective of 'green' PTAs is to prevent the relaxation of environmental standards which may result in a race to the bottom as a side effect of competition for trade and investment (George, 2014). Overall, the (scarce) empirical evidence is rather inconclusive. Gallagher (2004) states that in Mexico, the environment in terms of soil erosion, municipal solid waste and urban air and water pollution deteriorated after its accession to NAFTA, without claiming a causal relationship between trade liberalization and environmental degradation. Baghdadi, Martinez-Zarzoso, and Zitouna (2013) find a convergence of emissions levels and an overall reduction for country pairs that have signed a PTA with environmental provisions. Bastiaens and Postnikov (2014) show that PTAs including sanctions improve environmental performance measured on the basis of the Environmental Performance Index (EPI),[2] so do PTAs based on environmental cooperation when paired with a strong

---

[2] The EPI is an aggregation of both environmental health and ecosystem vitality measures including air quality, water and sanitation, health, water resources, agriculture, forests, fisheries, biodiversity and habitat, and climate and energy.

civil society in partner states. One could also imagine that countries having agreed to environmental standards at the bilateral/regional level are more inclined to also commit to multilateral environmental agreements. However, much more research is needed to clearly establish the links between trade rules, environmental governance and environmental performance. In the following discussion, we contribute to filling the gaps in the literature and focus on the take-up of environmental content in PTAs in emerging market PTAs.

This chapter puts the spotlight on environmental provisions of emerging markets' PTAs and thereby adds to the emerging research on the content and design of PTAs and their non-trade dimensions. It also contributes to the literature on the implications of rising powers like China and other emerging economies for the future of global governance (Gray & Murphy, 2013; Kahler, 2013; Stephen, 2014), i.e. to what extent emerging economies are rule-makers or rule-takers in the world economy and when and under which conditions they are willing take over global responsibility (Berger, 2013; Kennedy & Cheng, 2012; Wang & French, 2014).

3   Measuring Environmental Provisions in PTAs

PTAs have been largely treated as 'black boxes' in the literature, meaning that most econometric analyses have not taken their contents and thus their heterogeneity into account. This shortcoming is important to address, in particular in light of the fact that PTAs are becoming deeper and are covering more issue areas beyond the mere elimination of tariffs (Horn, Mavroidis, & Sapir, 2010). Some recent studies and projects have tried to remedy this situation by developing comprehensive data sets and providing numerical data measuring the variance of PTA design (Dür et al., 2014; Horn et al., 2010; Kohl, Brakman, & Garretsen, 2013). These databases, however, have the ambition to capture a large number of policy areas and therefore do not go into the details of a specific issue area. Environmental issues are therefore covered in a very general way in these databases ignoring the details on the variation of 'green' provisions.

We developed a new dataset mapping environmental provisions in PTAs to fill this gap in the literature. The dataset comprises detailed data on the design of environmental provisions along nine dimensions:

1. **Reference to environmental goals in the preamble or other chapters**: PTAs that cover environmental aspects in their main text often also include preambular language that highlights the intention of the contracting parties to protect the environment.
2. **Environmental exceptions**: PTAs often include a general exception clause that is modelled on GATT Article XX and specifies that actions by the contracting parties 'necessary to protect human, animal or plant life or health' are not inconsistent with the trade-related obligations of the treaty. In addition to these general

exceptions, some PTAs include specific environmental exceptions in certain chapters, such as the investment chapter.

3. **References to multilateral environmental agreements**: some countries use PTAs to refer to MEAs such as the Montreal Protocol for the Protection of the Ozone Layer or the Washington Convention on International Trade in Endangered Species of Wild Fauna and Flora (CITES). References to MEAs include, among others, commitments by the contracting parties to ratify or implement those agreements. At times, the MEAs are even made an integral part of the PTA.

4. **Inclusion of a whole chapter on environment or sustainable development**: some recent PTAs include a dedicated chapter on the environment or sustainable development where the parties specify their commitment to the protection of the environment.

5. **Obligations to uphold environmental law**: some PTAs include clauses that prevent the contracting parties from increasing trade and investment flows by weakening domestic environmental laws and regulations.

6. **Incorporation of the right to regulate in environmental matters**: with this set of provisions, the contracting parties want to preserve their right to go beyond the existing level of environmental protection by introducing new regulation in the area of the environment.

7. **Cooperation in environmental matters**: PTAs at times include provisions that state the objective that the contracting parties cooperate on environmental issues, sometimes creating institutions such as intergovernmental committees.

8. **Transparency in environmental matters**: some PTAs require the contracting parties to provide public access to relevant information on environmental policies and policy-making processes.

9. **Public participation in environmental matters**: often in connection with the prior dimension PTAs include provisions specifying how the public can participate in environmental policy-making processes.

For the purpose of this chapter, we have coded and analysed all full free trade agreements and customs unions established by the emerging markets—China (13), India (10), Indonesia (7), Brazil (4) and Mexico (16). The full list of agreements is provided in Annex. The coding scheme that was used to analyse environmental provisions in emerging market PTAs draws on the broad conceptualization of environmental provisions in PTAs provided by OECD (2007). The codebook has been tested on a smaller set of PTAs signed by various countries (not only emerging markets) to ensure general validity and has been revised accordingly. On the basis of the final version of the codebook, each text of emerging market PTAs was manually coded by two independent persons. In case of differences, a third person coded the respective treaty.

In order to compare the different agreements to each other, we have calculated an additive indicator ranging from 0 to 9, which captures the presence of the nine

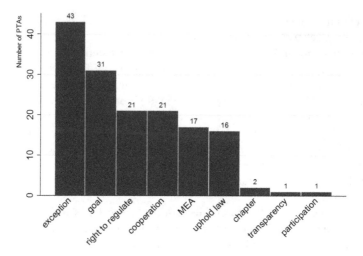

Fig. 1 Distribution of environmental dimensions across emerging markets' PTAs. *Source* Authors

environmental dimensions in the PTA. The higher the indicator, the more the dimensions covered in the respective agreement.[3] In the subsequent section, we use this indicator to analyse 48 emerging market PTAs signed by China, India, Indonesia, Brazil and Mexico.

4   Emerging Markets: A Bird's Eye View

In what follows, we provide a bird's eye view of environmental provisions in emerging market PTAs before we zoom into specific country cases in the subsequent section. Figure 1 illustrates how often the nine dimensions specified above occur in the PTAs of emerging markets. Almost all of the agreements coded ($\approx$ 90%) include environmental exceptions. These exceptions, based on GATT Article XX, allow countries to violate the rules of the PTA if this is 'necessary to protect human, animal or plant life'. However, according to GATT Article XX, measures aimed at protecting human, animal or plant life have to be applied in a non-discriminatory manner and should not be used as 'disguised restriction' on trade. This important qualification may be the reason why the dispute settlement body of the WTO has often tended to rule in favour of trade liberalization rather than environmental protection. It remains to be seen which role environmental exceptions play in the context of PTAs.

---

[3]We emphasize that this indicator only captures the *quantity* of environmental content, while not taking into account the *quality* and strength of different provisions (e.g. there is no weighting of different dimensions). We acknowledge that this generates only a rough picture of environmental issues in PTAs, but it is nevertheless a good initial instrument to study the environmental content in PTAs over time and across partners.

Importantly, in the context of PTAs, signatories often go beyond the inclusion of exceptions modelled on the rules of the WTO and include other environment-related clauses. Roughly two-thirds of the agreements coded also include references to environmental goals. Most agreements signed by emerging markets (75%) contain provisions that emphasize the countries' commitment to environmental protection and sustainable development already in the preamble. While these provisions are not of substantive nature (i.e. they do not imply any substantive rights or obligations in environmental matters to the parties), they may have an impact on how the PTA is interpreted in dispute settlement. References to MEAs, intended to renew the commitments already made elsewhere, are also frequently found in emerging market PTAs.

An important part of the debate on standards in the international trading system is focused on how international agreements interfere with domestic environmental law. Many critics are concerned about PTAs lowering environmental standards or limiting the right to pass new environmental legislation. As can be seen in Fig. 1, 16 emerging market PTAs oblige the parties to maintain, i.e. not lower, existing standards and 21 even explicitly stress the countries' right to regulate in environmental matters, this amounts to one third and 44% of the PTAs, respectively.

While cooperation in environmental matters is quite commonly encouraged in PTAs, transparency and public participation hardly occur at all. An exception is an agreement between the EU and Mexico of 1997, which includes a provision on public participation, as well as the agreement between Switzerland and China signed in 2013, which includes a whole chapter on environment. Notably, both of these agreements are signed with industrialized/OECD countries. Another PTA that has a full chapter on environment is the one between China and Korea, signed in 2015.

While the indicator can in principle range from 0 to 9, none of the emerging market agreements reaches the highest score. The annex to this chapter lists all PTAs from the lowest to the highest number of environmental dimensions covered. The 'greenest' agreements, achieving an indicator of 7, are the PTAs between China-Switzerland and China-Korea. Three agreements do not mention any environmental matters, namely China–Macao 2003, China–Hong Kong 2003 and India–Bangladesh 2006.

Table 1 gives the summary statistics for the variable of interest. On average, the 48 emerging market agreements score a 3.19, meaning that roughly three of the dimensions stated above are included in their PTAs. However, there is quite some variation between the agreements, as indicated by the standard deviation of 1.89. In the subsequent paragraphs, we use our original data to shed light on where this variation comes from.

Table 1 Descriptive statistics

Variable	Obs.	Mean	Std. dev.	Min	Max
Number of environmental dimensions covered	48	3.19	1.89	0	7

Source Authors

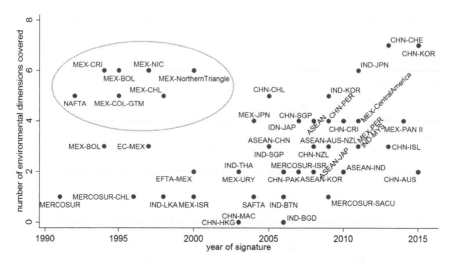

Fig. 2 Environmental dimensions in PTAs over time. *Source* Authors

Figure 2 illustrates the temporal variation of the indicators in emerging market PTAs. At first glance, we cannot identify a clear time trend, although it seems that PTAs include more environmental content after the year 2000. An interesting observation is that Mexico has very early on signed PTAs with significant environmental content. It is likely that this development was initiated by the conclusion of NAFTA, signed in 1992 and entered into force in 1994, which was the first PTA that addressed environmental issues in a more comprehensive way. When Mexico is excluded from the sample of emerging markets, we see a clear upward trend of the indicator over time. This indicates that the aggregate picture masks significant trends at the country level which will be further investigated in Sect. 5.

Another explanation for the variation in the indicator could be found in the type of partner country, as suggested in Sect. 2. Based on our calculations for emerging market PTAs, Fig. 3 illustrates that the indicator is slightly higher when emerging markets sign the agreement with an OECD country.[4] This finding is even more pronounced when excluding Mexico's agreements, which seems to be a special case (as explained above). We could interpret this finding as OECD countries pushing for more environmental content in PTAs and imposing them on emerging markets with lower bargaining power.

---

[4]OECD status at time of PTA signature.

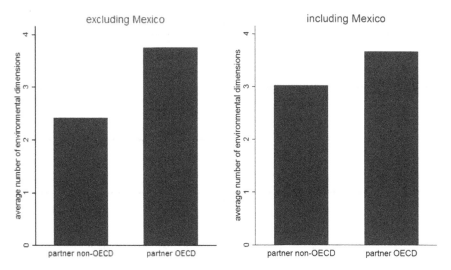

Fig. 3 Average environmental dimensions by status of partner country. *Source* Authors

5 Emerging Markets: Zooming In

5.1 China

China has been a latecomer in negotiating PTAs, starting to negotiate them only after its accession to the WTO (Berger, 2013). While the first two PTAs concluded by China did not include environmental provisions,[5] all subsequent agreements did include environmental provisions, though to varying degrees. Some PTAs incorporate a stand-alone environmental clause or a chapter; others incorporate environmental provisions of various types, such as the clause of general exceptions.

Two general trends may be identified from the provisions of Chinese PTAs. First, while earlier PTAs contain few or no environmental provisions, more recent PTAs incorporate more. Second, environmental provisions are more frequently seen in Chinese PTAs concluded with more developed partners, since those appear to have stronger policy-making aspirations on environmental protection and sustainable investment. Such trends can be witnessed by the fact that China–Switzerland PTA contains multiple environmental provisions and that the China–Korea PTA includes a chapter on the environment. China experienced rapid economic growth in the past decades. Yet, the environmental pollution in China deteriorated in the meantime.

---

[5]The absence of environmental provisions in the China-Macao and China-Hong Kong PTAs may be explained by the fact that these PTAs are not truly meant to be 'international' agreements. They are aimed at promoting trade liberalization between the different legal jurisdictions of China. Thus, it is understandable that they exclude certain issues, especially sensitive ones such as environmental issues, from the PTAs.

One may conclude that environmental concerns have become an important consideration in China's PTA-making nowadays, partly to help address the environmental challenge. China has sped up its efforts in concluding PTAs recently, and the Belt and Road Initiative (BRI) newly proposed by China would inevitably necessitate the conclusion of more PTAs with the countries involved. It remains to be seen to what extent environmental issues will also feature in China's future South–South PTAs, where China can be expected to be the rule-maker.

5.2 India

India embarked on the path of economic liberalization in the early 1990s. While first initiating national reforms, India has subsequently, slowly but steadily, removed barriers to international trade and foreign direct investment throughout the last two decades (UNCTAD, 2012). Even though India is carefully embracing liberalization, the country takes the position that trade and investment agreements, be it under the roof of the WTO or within bilateral and regional PTAs, should not be mingled with issues not directly related to trade, such as human rights or the environment—rather, these topics should be discussed in other international fora (ICTSD, 2010). In a 2001 press release, India voiced concern that 'environment was being used as some sort of a Trojan horse to provide legitimacy to protectionist trends' on the part of industrialized countries (Government of India, 2001). Similar concerns remain until today. Besides colliding interests in the strength of intellectual property rights protection, India's reluctance to include environmental provisions in the EU-India PTA was a contentious issue during the negotiations and later one of the reasons for the temporary suspension of the negotiations (Khandekar, 2011; Singh, 2015).

However, experts argue that India, in order to be attractive and credible as a partner in global value chains, may need to rethink its strategy. Recent regional trade deals—the Comprehensive and Progressive Agreement for Trans-Pacific Partnership (CPTPP) being of particular importance in this context—regulate not only trade but also many behind-the-border issue areas such as investment, intellectual property rights and the environment. Indian producers will have to adjust to these new standards if they wish to participate in the production networks governed by these agreements (Meltzer, 2015).

In fact, despite the strong national narrative of separating trade from environmental issues, the data shows that the case of India reflects the global trend of PTAs becoming greener over time, the agreements with the largest environmental content being those with South Korea and Japan, signed in 2009 and 2011, respectively. South Korea and Japan both have a higher level of economic development and play a significant role in Asian and global production networks. However, so far none of India's PTAs includes a whole chapter on trade and the environment or sustainable development. Whether India's stance towards mixing trade and environmental matters has and will become more reconciliatory therefore remains an open question. In any case, the negotiations for the PTA between the EU and India, resumed in January 2016 (Suneja, 2015), will require a discussion about this topic—the outcome could be an indication on India's future direction of trade policy.

5.3 Indonesia

Indonesia has been a long-standing participant in the multilateral trading regime and is a founding member of the Association of Southeast Asian Nations (ASEAN). In fact, Indonesia concluded all its PTAs—with the exception of the bilateral agreement with Japan in 2007—as a member of ASEAN. The adoption of liberal trade and investment policies at the end of the 1990s in Indonesia and across the South Asian region can be attributed to a variety of factors, most importantly the increasing competitive pressure from China, the Asian economic crisis as well as the conclusion of important regional integration initiatives in North America (NAFTA) and the EU (single market). Liberal economic policies at the national level were accompanied by a wave of PTAs signed at the end of the 2000s.

While negotiated within a rather short period of time, Indonesian PTAs display a relatively high variation in terms of the coverage of environmental issues. The two most comprehensive agreements in this regard are the 2007 bilateral agreement with Japan and the ASEAN Free Trade Area concluded in 2010, covering four environmental dimensions. The ASEAN agreements with Korea, Japan and India, on the other hand, only cover two dimensions. All PTAs concluded by Indonesia include an environmental exception modelled on GATT Art. XX and most PTAs include provisions on cooperation. Compared to North American and European PTAs, none of the Indonesian agreements included an environment chapter or provisions on cooperation and participation in environmental matters. This restraint to include comprehensive environmental provisions is not only characteristic for Indonesian or ASEAN PTAs, but also for other Asian industrialized countries like Japan (Yanai, 2014). Indonesia is currently negotiating a PTA with the EU and has been considering an accession to the CPTPP. It is therefore likely that Indonesia will come under pressure to sign up to more comprehensive environmental provisions in the near future.

5.4 Brazil

Brazil considers the WTO to be the main arena where the most pressing issues in international trade should be discussed (Fishlow, 2004; WTO, 2013). Brazil has focused strongly on the multilateral trade liberalization track and has not put much emphasis on PTAs so far. Indeed, Brazil remains among the most closed economies as measured by the share of exports and imports in GDP. One explanation for the country's limited openness to trade is that Brazil has strongly relied on domestic value chain integration rather than participation in global production networks (Canuto, Fleischhaker, & Schellekens, 2015).

The limited number of PTAs signed by Brazil illustrates the reluctance to open up and the lack of focus on bilateral and regional trade agreements. Brazil, however, is part of Mercosur (Southern Common Market), the Latin American regional bloc established in 1991, which also includes Argentina, Paraguay, Uruguay and Venezuela as full members. Mercosur is Brazil's main preferential agreement in terms of value of trade (WTO, 2013). As member of Mercosur, Brazil has signed a number of PTAs.

Whereas the founding treaty for Mercosur did not include any provisions on labour or environmental rights, the subsequent developments that occurred in Mercosur in the 1990s brought about a recognition of these rights (Giupponi, 2014). Still, analyses of the environmental components in the Mercosur agreement indicate that they are weak (Hochstetler, 2003). At the same time, Mercosur does include rather elaborate provisions on cooperation for the implementation of MEAs (OECD, 2007, p. 5). The PTAs Brazil signed as a member of Mercosur, do not include many environmental provisions, let alone a whole chapter on trade and environment or sustainable development.

It is likely, however, also in light of the possible end of the multilateral Doha Round as well as the proliferation of PTAs around the world and the recent rise of mega-regional trade agreements, that Brazil will review its prevailing trade strategy where efforts have so far focused on multilateral rather than bilateral or regional negotiations (Canuto, 2015). Negotiations with the European Union on a free trade agreement with Mercosur were relaunched and a number of new PTA negotiations have been initiated. It remains an open question which stance Brazil will take towards environmental provisions in its upcoming PTAs, both in the context of Mercosur and beyond.

5.5 Mexico

Mexico's free trade policy has been influenced heavily by its participation in the North American Free Trade Agreement (NAFTA). Subsequently, Mexico has been one of the most active emerging markets with respect to the negotiation of PTAs. The coverage of environmental provisions in Mexican PTAs displays a peculiar pattern distinct from other emerging markets. While environmental provisions got more numerous over time in other emerging economies' PTAs, Mexico experienced a reverse trend. Mexico's early and comprehensive commitment to environmental provisions stems from its membership in the NAFTA which, at the time, was the most comprehensive PTA and covered five of the nine dimensions of our data set. Beyond the environmental provisions included in the main text, the three NAFTA member countries also signed an environmental side agreement on environmental cooperation which triggered a number of legal measures and increased the level of cooperation on environmental matters in North America (Gallagher, 2009).

NAFTA included references to environmental protection in the preamble, a GATT Article XX-type environmental exception, references to MEAs, commitments to uphold environmental laws and provisions on the right to regulate in environmental matters. Mexico's experience with NAFTA had repercussion for the PTAs it concluded in the years following the landmark agreement. The PTAs Mexico negotiated during the 1990s with other developing countries such as Costa Rica (1994), Bolivia (1995), Colombia and Guatemala (1995), Nicaragua (1997) and Chile (1998) included similar commitments on the environment as NAFTA and in some cases even incorporated provisions on cooperation in the main text. In other words, towards other developing countries Mexico acted as a rule-maker transferring its experience gained in negotiations with the USA. The PTA Mexico signed with the EU in 1997, on the other hand, included less comprehensive commitments on environmental protection than Mexico's agreements with its NAFTA partners and other developing countries. The same is true for two subsequent PTAs Mexico concluded with industrialized countries. The PTAs with the countries of the European Free Trade Association (EFTA) and Israel included even fewer environmental provisions than the agreement with the EU.

While Mexico's treaty-making practice during the 1990s was to a large extent influenced by NAFTA, the influence of this landmark deal decreased after the turn of the century. The environmental commitments in Mexican PTAs negotiated with industrialized and developing countries after 2000 were more diverse and less ambitious compared to those of the 1990s. The atypical development with regard to the inclusion of environmental provisions in Mexican PTAs can, therefore, be mainly attributed to the impact of NAFTA.

6 Conclusion

The coverage of non-economic commitments in PTAs has received comparatively little attention in the academic literature. In this chapter, we have addressed this gap by making use of a novel dataset including nine dimensions of environmental commitments in PTAs: reference to environmental goals in the preamble or other chapters, environmental exceptions, references to MEAs, inclusion of a whole chapter on environment or sustainable development, obligations to uphold environmental law, incorporation of the right to regulate in environmental matters, cooperation in environmental matters, transparency in environmental matters and public participation in environmental matters.

With regard to the PTAs of emerging markets, there are two main conclusions. First, in the aggregate, the PTAs of emerging markets have become greener over time. Second, their PTAs tend to include more environmental content when signed with OECD countries. This, in turn, indicates that OECD countries are still rule-makers and emerging markets still largely rules-takers with regard to environmental provisions in trade agreements.

However, the general patterns mask some heterogeneity at the country level. China's recent PTAs indicate that the country is already embarking on a path towards agreements with more environmental content. India is still very reluctant to combine trade and non-trade issues in the same agreement, but things seem to have started moving as well. Indonesia is mostly negotiating PTAs with weak environmental content as a member of ASEAN, but has signed a 'greener' agreement with Japan. Brazil is not very active in the conclusion of PTAs in general and the agreements signed through its membership in Mercosur are rather weak in terms of environmental content. Mexico, as a consequence of NAFTA, signed relatively 'green' agreements early on, but its PTAs show more variation in recent years. Both the rise of comprehensive mega-regional agreements and the expansion of global value chains are likely to further shape the future of the trend towards incorporating environmental provisions in trade agreements.

Our findings show that environmental considerations play an increasingly important role in trade—both the spread of voluntary sustainability standards (e.g. Brandi, 2016; Fiorini et al., 2018; Marx et al., 2015) and public regulation that seeks to address sustainability concerns for a specific sector or product, as discussed in other chapters in this book, are an expression of this. More research is needed in order to provide a more detailed picture of the interlinkages between international trade and the environment, both in emerging economies and beyond. More particularly, there is a need for more research on the diffusion of environmental provisions in PTAs, the relation between environmental provisions in PTAs and the uptake and effective implementation of public regulation as well as private standards that contribute to tackling environmental concerns and types of sustainability challenges.

Acknowledgements This paper was developed as part of the DIE research project "Research for a Climate Smart and Just Transformation (Klimalog)" funded by the German Federal Ministry for Economic Cooperation and Development (BMZ) and has previously been published as a DIE discussion paper. We cordially thank our research assistants Martina Holzer, David Schuhler and Janina Sturm for their excellent support.

Annex

Name of agreement	Year of signature	Year of entry into force	Partner country[a]	Number of environmental dimensions covered
China-Hong Kong	2003	2003	Non-OECD	0
India-Bangladesh	2006	2006	Non-OECD	0
China-Macao	2003	2003	Non-OECD	0
MERCOSUR	1991	1991	Non-OECD	1
South Asian Free Trade Agreement (SAFTA)	2004	2006	Non-OECD	1
India-Sri Lanka	1998	2000	Non-OECD	1

(continued)

(continued)

Name of agreement	Year of signature	Year of entry into force	Partner country[a]	Number of environmental dimensions covered
India-Bhutan	2006	2006	Non-OECD	1
MERCOSUR-SACU	2009	2008	Non-OECD	1
MERCOSUR-Chile	1996	1996	Non-OECD	1
Mexico-Israel	2000	2000	Non-OECD	1
India-Thailand	2003	2003	Non-OECD	2
China-Pakistan	2006	2007	Non-OECD	2
EFTA-Mexico	2000	2001	OECD	2
ASEAN-Korea	2007	2006	Non-OECD	2
ASEAN-India	2010	2009	Non-OECD	2
MERCOSUR-Israel	2007	2010	Non-OECD	2
Mexico-Uruguay	2003	2004	Non-OECD	2
ASEAN-Japan	2008	2009	OECD	2
China-Australia	2015	2015	OECD	2
China-Iceland	2013	2014	OECD	3
India-Singapore	2005	2005	Non-OECD	3
China-New Zealand	2008	2008	OECD	3
Mexico-Peru	2011	2012	Non-OECD	3
ASEAN-China	2005	2004	Non-OECD	3
EC-Mexico	1997	2000	OECD	3
India-Malaysia	2011	2011	Non-OECD	3
Mexico-Bolivia	1994	1995	Non-OECD	3
ASEAN-Australia-New Zealand	2009	2009	OECD	3
China-Singapore	2008	2009	Non-OECD	4
China-Costa Rica	2010	2011	Non-OECD	4
Mexico-Panama II	2014	2015	Non-OECD	4
Mexico-Central America	2011	2013	Non-OECD	4
Indonesia-Japan	2007	2008	OECD	4
Mexico-Japan	2004	2005	OECD	4
ASEAN	2009	2010	Non-OECD	4
China-Peru	2009	2009	Non-OECD	4
NAFTA	1992	1994	OECD	5
China-Chile	2005	2006	Non-OECD	5
Mexico-Colombia-Guatemala (G3)	1995	1994	Non-OECD	5

(continued)

(continued)

Name of agreement	Year of signature	Year of entry into force	Partner country[a]	Number of environmental dimensions covered
Mexico-Chile	1998	1999	Non-OECD	5
India-South Korea	2009	2010	Non-OECD	5
Mexico-Nicaragua	1997	1998	Non-OECD	6
Mexico-Northern Triangle	2000	2001	Non-OECD	6
Mexico-Bolivia	1995	1994	Non-OECD	6
India-Japan	2011	2011	OECD	6
Mexico-Costa Rica	1994	1995	Non-OECD	6
China-Switzerland	2013	2013	OECD	7
China-Korea	2015	2015	Non-OECD	7

[a]OECD status at year of signature

References

Anuradha, R. V. (2011). Environment. In J.-P. Chauffour & J.-C. Maur (Eds.), *Preferential trade agreement policies for development: A handbook*. Washington, DC: The World Bank.

Baccini, L., Dür, A., & Elsig, M. (2016). The politics of trade agreement design: Revisiting the depth–flexibility nexus. *International Studies Quarterly, 59*(4).

Baghdadi, L., Martinez-Zarzoso, I., & Zitouna, H. (2013). Are RTA agreements with environmental provisions reducing emissions? *Journal of International Economics, 90*(2), 378–390.

Bastiaens, I., & Postnikov, E. (2014). Environmental provisions in EU and US trade agreements and regulatory change in the developing world. In *8th Annual Conference on the Political Economy of International Organizations*, February 12–14, 2015.

Berger, A. (2013). Investment rules in Chinese PTIAs—A partial 'NAFTA-ization'. In R. Hofmann, S. Schill, & C. Tams (Eds.), *Preferential trade and investment agreements: From recalibration to reintegration* (pp. 297–333). Baden-Baden: Nomos.

Berger, A., Brandi, C., Bruhn, D., & Chi, M. (2017). *Towards "greening" trade? Tracking environmental provisions in the preferential trade agreements of emerging markets* (Discussion Paper). Bonn: Deutsches Institut für Entwicklungspolitik. Available at https://www.die-gdi.de/uploads/media/DP_2.2017.pdf.

Birdsall, N., & Wheeler, D. (1993). Trade policy and industrial pollution in Latin America: Where are the pollution havens? *Journal of Environment and Development, 2*(1).

Brandi, C. (2016). Sustainability standards and sustainable development: Synergies and trade-offs of transnational governance. *Sustainable Development*. Online first.

Bruhn, D. (2014). *Global value chains and deep preferential trade agreements: Promoting trade at the cost of domestic policy autonomy?* (Discussion Paper 23/2014). Bonn: German Development Institute/Deutsches Institut für Entwicklungspolitik (DIE).

Canuto, O. (2015). Are mega-trade agreements a threat to Brazil? *Economic Monitor*. http://www.economonitor.com/blog/2015/02/are-mega-trade-agreements-a-threat-to-brazil/.

Canuto, O., Fleischhaker, C., & Schellekens, P. (2015). *The curious case of Brazil's closedness to trade*. VoxEU. http://www.voxeu.org/article/brazil-s-closedness-trade.

Cole, M. A., & Elliot, R. J. R. (2003). Determining the trade-environment composition effect: The role of capital, labor and environmental regulations. *Journal of Environmental Economics and Management, 46*(3), 363–383.

Colyer, D. (2011). *Green trade agreements*. London: Palgrave Macmillan.

Copeland, B. R., & Taylor, M. S. (1994). North-south trade and the environment. *The Quarterly Journal of Economics, 109*(3), 755–787.

Copeland, B., & Taylor, M. S. (1995). Trade and transboundary pollution. *The American Economic Review, 85*(4).

Dür, A., Baccini, L., & Elsig, M. (2014). The design of international trade agreements: Introducing a new dataset. *Review of International Organization, 9,* 353–375.

Fiorini, M., Hoekman, B., Jansen, M., Schleifer, P., Solleder, O., Taimasova, R., & Wozniak, J. (2018). Institutional design of voluntary sustainability standards systems: Evidence from a new database. *Development Policy Review*.

Fishlow, A. (2004). Brazil: FTA or FTAA or WTO? In J. J. Schott (Ed.), *Free trade agreements: US strategies and priorities*. Washington, DC: Peterson Institute for International Economics.

Gallagher, K. P. (2004). *Free trade and the environment: Mexico, NAFTA and beyond*. Stanford, CA: Stanford University Press.

Gallagher, K. P. (2009). NAFTA and the environment: Lessons from Mexico and beyond. In K. P. Gallagher, E. D. Peters, & T. A. Wise (Eds.), *The future of North American trade policy: Lessons from NAFTA*. Boston: Boston University.

George, C. (2014). *Environment and regional trade agreements: Emerging trends and policy drivers* (OECD Trade and Environment Working Papers 2014/02).

Giupponi, M. B. O. (2014). Free trade and labour and environmental standards in MERCOSUR. *Colombia Internacional,* 67–97.

Government of India. (2001, September 5). India reaffirms position on WTO issues at Mexico meet. *Press Release*. Government of India, Ministry of Commerce and Industry, Department of Commerce. Available online http://commerce.nic.in/PressRelease/pressrelease_detail.asp?id=674.

Gray, J. (2014). Domestic capacity and the implementation gap in regional trade agreements. *Comparative Political Studies*.

Gray, K., & Murphy, C. N. (2013). Introduction: Rising powers and the future of global governance. *Third World Quarterly, 34*(2), 183–193.

Hafner-Burton, E. M. (2009). *Forced to be good: Why trade agreements boost human rights*. Ithaca: Cornell University Press.

Hochstetler, K. (2003). Fading green? Environmental politics in the Mercosur free trade agreement. *Latin American Politics and Society, 45*(4), 1–32.

Horn, H., Mavroidis, P. C., & Sapir, A. (2010). Beyond the WTO? An anatomy of EU and US preferential trade agreements. *The World Economy, 33*(11), 1565–1588.

ICTSD. (2010, February 24). *Indian official says trade and environment should not mix*. Available online http://www.ictsd.org/bridges-news/bridges/news/indian-official-says-trade-and-environment-should-not-mix.

Jinnah, S., & Morgera, E. (2013). Environmental provisions in American and EU free trade agreements: A preliminary comparison and research agenda. *Review of European, Comparative & International Environmental Law, 22*(3), 324–339.

John, A., & Pecchenino, R. (1994). An overlapping generations model of growth and the environment. *The Economic Journal,* 1393–1410.

Johnson, T. (2015). Information revelation and structural supremacy: The World Trade Organization's incorporation of environmental policy. *The Review of International Organizations,* 1–23.

Kahler, M. (2013). Rising powers and global governance: Negotiating change in a resilient status quo. *International Affairs, 89*(3), 711–729.

Kennedy, S., & Cheng, S. (2012). *From rule takers to rule makers: The growing role of Chinese in global governance*.

Khandekar, G. (2011, August). *The EU and India: A loveless arranged marriage* (FRIDE Policy Brief 90). Available online http://fride.org/download/PB_90_EU_and_India.pdf.

Kim, M. (2012). Ex ante due diligence: Formation of PTAs and protection of labor rights. *International Studies Quarterly, 56*(4), 704–719.

Kohl, T., Brakman, S., & Garretsen, H. (2013). *Do trade agreements stimulate international trade differently? Evidence from 296 trade agreements* (CESIFO Working Paper No. 4243).

Kucik, J. (2012). The domestic politics of institutional design: Producer preferences over trade agreement rules. *Economics and Politics, 24*(2), 95–118.

Levinson, A., & Taylor, M. S. (2008). Unmasking the pollution haven effect. *International Economic Review, 49*(1), 223–254.

Managi, S., Hibiki, A., & Tsurumi, T. (2009). Does trade openness improve environmental quality? *Journal of Environmental Economics and Management, 58*(3), 346–363.

Marx, A., Sharma, A., & Bécault, E. (2015). *Voluntary sustainability standards. An overview.* Available online https://ees.kuleuven.be/klimos/papers/marx_2015_voluntary_sustainability_standards.pdf.

Meltzer, J. P. (2015). *For Modi's India, a new trade policy.* Brookings India. Available online http://www.brookings.in/in-focus/for-modis-india-a-new-trade-policy/.

Morin, J.-F., Blümer, D., Brandi, C., & Berger, A. (2019). Kick-starting diffusion: Explaining the varying frequency of PTAs' environmental clauses by their initial conditions. *The World Economy.* https://doi.org/10.1111/twec.12822.

Morin, J.-F., Dür, A., & Lechner, L. (2018). Mapping the trade and environment nexus: Insights from a new data set. *Global Environmental Politics, 18*(1), 122–139.

OECD. (2007). *Environment and regional trade agreements.* Paris: OECD.

Peters, G. P. (2008). From production-based to consumption-based national emission inventories. *Ecological Economics, 65*(1), 13–23.

Peters, G. P., & Hertwich, E. G. (2008). CO_2 embodied in international trade with implications for global climate policy. *Environmental Science and Technology, 42*(5), 1401–1407.

Postnikov, E., & Bastiaens, I. (2014). Does dialogue work? The effectiveness of labor standards in EU preferential trade agreements. *Journal of European Public Policy, 21*(6), 923–940.

Selden, T. M., & Song, D. (1994). Environmental quality and development: Is there a kuznets curve for air pollution emissions? *Journal of Environmental Economics and Management, 27*(2), 147–162.

Sheldon, I. (2006). Trade and environmental policy: A race to the bottom? *Journal of Agricultural Economics, 57,* 365–392.

Singh, K. (2015, October 12). *India-EU FTA: Time for a fundamental rethink?* Global Research, Centre for Research on Globalization. Available online http://www.globalresearch.ca/india-eu-fta-time-for-a-fundamental-rethink/5481631.

Steinberg, R. H. (1997). Trade-environment negotiations in the EU, NAFTA, and WTO: Regional trajectories of rule development. *American Journal of International Law, 91*(2), 231–267.

Stephen, M. D. (2014). Rising powers, global capitalism and liberal global governance: A historical materialist account of the BRICs challenge. *European Journal of International Relations, 20*(4), 912–938.

Stokey, N. L. (1998). Are there limits to growth? *International Economic Review,* 1–31.

Suneja, K. (2015, December 4). India and European Union to resume talks on free-trade agreement in January. *The Economic Times.* Available online http://articles.economictimes.indiatimes.com/2015-12-04/news/68771101_1_india-eu-28-nation-bloc-the-eu.

UNCTAD. (2012). *Twenty years of India's liberalization: Experiences and lessons* (R. Banga & A. Das, Eds.). United Nations Conference on Trade and Development. Available online http://unctad.org/en/PublicationsLibrary/osg2012d1_en.pdf.

Wang, H., & French, E. (2014). China in global economic governance. *Asian Economic Policy Review, 9*(2), 254–271.

WTO. (2011). *The WTO and preferential trade agreements: From co-existence to coherence.* Geneva: WTO.

WTO. (2013). *Trade policy review Brazil*. Geneva: WTO.

Yanai, A. (2014). *Environmental provisions in Japanese regional trade agreements with developing countries* (IDE Discussion Paper No 467).

Chapter 5
Corporate Social Responsibility: The Interface Between the Private Sector and Sustainability Standards

Jorge Antonio Pérez-Pineda

1 Introduction

The last two decades of the last century were marked by several economic crises that started in the mid-1970s and resulted in a change from closed and protected economies to an open and export-oriented view. This new model was applied by several economies—developed and developing—and was understood in the terminology of 'neoliberalism' or the 'Washington Consensus' (Williamson, 1990). This change of paradigm sped up the globalization process in the 1980s and the 1990s, as it implied the liberalization of trade, finance, technological change, and the internationalization of firm activity (WTO, 1998). Among other things, it resulted in a rise in the number of free trade agreements, a consolidation of regional integration processes, and a renewed multilateral impetus signified by the rebirth of the General Agreement on Tariffs and Trade (GATT) as the World Trade Organization (WTO) in 1995. This changing landscape had two significant implications for the concerns about the private sector.[1] In the 1980s, the main concern was around the adverse effects of firm activity, technological changes and a new environmental agenda. In the 1990s, concern was focused on the increasing competition among countries (developed and developing) and the role of governments in promoting good environmental policies for transnational corporations (TNCs) (Dunning, 2005; Fischer, 1999, p. 79).

---

[1] As has been pointed out in many sources, the 'private sector' can be broadly understood, including not only large enterprises or firms of many sizes, but also chambers of commerce, firm associations, philanthropic foundations, worker-owned cooperatives, self-employed etc. (CCIC, 2001, p. 4; Pingeot, 2014, p. 17). In this chapter, by 'private sector' we mean mainly transnational companies since they are closely associated with global standards and regulations, However, it must be said that some small-medium-micro enterprises, and other private firms may also adopt, directly or indirectly, the same kind of norms and regulations.

J. A. Pérez-Pineda (✉)
Faculty of Economics and Business, Universidad Anáhuac México, Estado de México, Mexico
e-mail: japerpe@yahoo.com

© The Editor(s) (if applicable) and The Author(s) 2020   83
A. Negi et al. (eds.), *Sustainability Standards and Global Governance*,
https://doi.org/10.1007/978-981-15-3473-7_5

In this period, as Dunning (2005) states, intergovernmental organizations such as the United Nations (UN) became more and more concerned about how the activities of governments, international organizations and TNCs could jointly contribute towards reaching social objectives and strengthening the benefits of Foreign Direct Investment (FDI) and globalization in recipient countries. Perhaps the most significant manifestation of such concern was the launch of the Global Compact by the UN in the year 2000 to support the development agenda as articulated in the Millennium Development Goals (MDGs).

Nowadays, the role of the private sector in the context of globalization, international cooperation and global governance is well recognized and the private sector is also a part of the current debates around sustainability (Rio + 20, green economy, green growth) and development [MDGs as well as the Sustainable Development Goals (SDGs)], which bring these two strands of discussion together. In reflecting economic, environmental and social goals, standards play an important role in a broadened sustainable development agenda as they provide a common ground for different actors formally and informally linked to global governance.

The aim of this chapter is to review the role of the private sector at the beginning of the current century and to link it with the debate over social and environmental standards and regulations in the context of global governance. The chapter seeks to address the following guiding questions: what context best explains the current use of social and environmental standards and regulations by the private sector?; what conceptual approaches can help understand the current use of standards and regulations by this actor?; and what are the policy implications and trends around norms and standards for the international debates and the relevant actors?

The chapter is divided into two sections that cover the first two questions. In the first, the context is reviewed, and in the second, the framework of Corporate Social Responsibility (CSR) as an interface of the private sector with standards and norms is discussed. Finally, some concluding remarks relating to policy implications are presented.

2   The Relevance of the Private Sector

To understand the role of the private sector in the current use of social and environmental standards and regulations, we need to understand the context and evolution of this relationship. It is well recognized that firms bring positive outcomes for society, particularly through FDI and related effects on employment, technology transfer, balance of payments, market development and spillover effects. However, it is equally well-known that firms may bring negative impacts, also related to FDI, such as unemployment, delocalization of investment, low wages, pollution, and depletion of resources (Aziz, Lerche, & Lerche, 1995; Dunning, 1992; Stiglitz & Charlton, 2005).

Dunning (2005) identifies the evolution of TNCs and their influence at the global level, as well as some of the global initiatives to regulate them:

- In the 1970s, the main concern was focused on the role of FDI in recipient countries and on the negative effects of TNCs. This opened the door to the first initiatives to regulate firm activity through guides, codes of conduct and multilateral agreements, such as the OECD Guidelines for Multinational Enterprises, or the Tripartite Declaration of Principles concerning the Multinational Enterprises of the International Labor Organization (ILO).
- The 1980s were influenced by a deep technological change, trade openness and the new approach of 'sustainable development'. This context facilitated a change of economic model towards a market-oriented approach, resulting in the strengthening of the private sector vis-à-vis state power.
- By the 1990s, the international agenda started to get involved more closely with the private sector in order to make globalization and the effects of trade and investment a more balanced process, given the emergence of strong middle-income countries such as the BRICS (Brazil, Russia, India, China, South Africa) and the competitive environment created as a result.
- In the post-2000 phase, the context shows a clear and close involvement of the private sector with the international agenda, particularly oriented to a sustainable approach. Some of the most relevant initiatives in this period include the UN Global Compact that sought to incorporate the principles of human rights, labour standards, environment and anti-corruption in firm activity, and some other initiatives such as the 'Guiding Principles on Business and Human Rights', developed by John Ruggie in his role as the UN Secretary-General's Special Representative on Business and Human Rights and endorsed by the UN Human Rights Council in 2011.

As Schäfer, Beer, Zenker, and Fernandes (2006) and Elkington (1998) point out, since the 1990s, there has been a big movement, where the private sector has benefitted from the change in the economic model that has increased the volumes of trade and investment around the word. This expansion of firm activity has provided more profits to enterprises, more political power through lobbying, and more capacity to mobilize support for their processes worldwide. Such an expansion of the businesses implies a new division of labour at the international level and an expansion in the value chain of the firm. In this context, governments, civil society and different stakeholders demand more transparency, ethics and accountability from the private sector in its activities.

On similar lines, Dembinski (2003, p. 39) identifies three main issues where we can weigh the current relevance of the private sector at the international level: the aggregate weight of the non-financial enterprises in the world economy, comparing their weight with the poorest countries, and considering categories such as the 'very big enterprises' as forces of globalization. Based on this proposal, the relevance of such categories is examined in Fig. 1 and Table 1.

In order to demonstrate the current weight of the private sector compared with that of the public sector, a couple of examples may be cited; first, the comparison of FDI flows from the North to the South and the public flows of official development

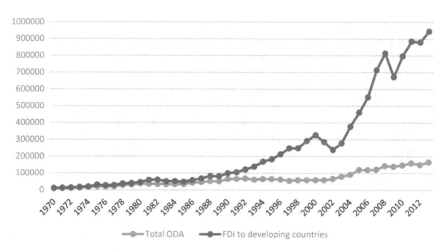

Fig. 1 ODA versus FDI flows, 1970–2013 (millions USD, current). *Source* For FDI, UNCTAD statistics, http://unctadstat.unctad.org, and for ODA, OECD statistics, http://stats.oecd.org

assistance (ODA) in recent years. As is clearly seen, private flows have overtaken the public flows, pointing at the new strength of the private sector (Fig. 1).

A second example compares the richest TNCs—or multinational enterprises (MNEs)—of the world by foreign assets (Table 1) against the gross domestic product (GDP) of some poor and low-income countries.[2] It is clear that the value of some non-financial TNCs—from developed and developing countries—is many times superior to the GDP of some countries, showing the economic power that firms have acquired as compared to countries (on the lines of Dembinski). For instance, the GDP of Samoa is roughly 964 times smaller than the foreign assets of General Electric and roughly 131 times smaller than those of Hutchison Whampoa Limited.

In addition, it should not be forgotten that firms cause increasing damage to the environment as part of their economic activity and patterns of consumption. The climate change consequences of firm activity have been widely documented since a couple of decades by the United Nations Environment Programme (UNEP), by the Intergovernmental Panel on Climate Change (IPCC)[3] and by the Stern Review. Such a landscape requires a clear response from the public and private sector to strengthen social and environmental standards and regulations. One framework that facilitates the analysis of sustainable development, in the context of the relationship among different actors, such as the private sector, is the framework of 'global governance'.

---

[2] A list of the poorest countries was considered to illustrate the magnitude of difference in the value of some of the biggest non-financial TNCs against the income of some developing countries' GDP. This can help illustrate the distance in economic value from firms to countries. This comparison may not be so relevant if we select developed countries or middle-income countries. Data is based on World Bank statistics.

[3] Some recommended readings on this include the Climate Change Reports from the IPCC, https://www.ipcc.ch/, and the Emissions Gap Report published by UNEP, http://web.unep.org/climatechange/cop21/publications.

Table 1 TNCs versus poor countries

Country	GDP 2010 (USD current)	Non financial TNCs from developed countries	Foreign assets (USD)	% of foreign assets on GDP	Non financial TNCs from developing and transition countries	Foreign assets (USD)	% of foreign assets on GDP
Tuvalu	$31,824,701	General Electric	$551,585,000,000	17,332	Hutchison Whampoa Limited	$75,446,865,839	2371
Kiribati	$150,431,114	Royal Dutch Shell	$271,627,000,000	1806	CITIC Group	$53,251,006,926	354
Santo Tome y Principe	$201,037,917	BP	$243,950,000,000	1213	Vale SA	$49,176,198,337	245
Comoros	$543,376,206	Vodafone	$224,449,000,000	413	Cemex S.A.B. de C.V.	$36,415,927,699	67
Samoa	$572,160,378	Toyota	$211,153,000,000	369	Petronas—Petroliam Nasional Bhd	$35,511,000,000	62

Source World Development Indicators Data Bank, World Bank: https://databank.worldbank.org. All data are for the year 2017

Authors such as Rosenau (1995), Finkelstein (1995), Dingwerth and Pattberg (2006) are representatives of different approaches to this framework and most of them build upon the definition provided by the Commission on Global Governance that defined global governance as:

> ... the sum of the many ways in which individuals and institutions, public and private, manage their common affairs [...] At the global level, governance has been viewed primarily as intergovernmental relationships, but it must now be understood as also involving non-governmental organizations (NGOs), citizens' movements, multinational corporations, and the global capital market. (1995, pp. 1–2)

As per Dingwerth and Pattberg (2006, p. 189), global governance can be understood in two different ways. The first is as an analytical concept to explain the contemporary reality and the second as a normative view on how political institutions should react given the diminished strength of governments. Most importantly, 'global governance is conceived to include systems of rule at all levels of human activity—from the family to the international organization—in which the pursuit of goals through the exercise of control has transnational repercussions' (Rosenau, 1995, p. 13). It is useful to conduct the analysis of social and environmental standards and regulations for the private sector using the concept of global governance as a framework of reference. As Levi-Faur points out, '... scholars of global governance tend to focus on standards and soft norms' (Levi-Faur, 2011, p. 3).

The negative effects of firm activity on the environment started to be recognized as a serious concern at the end of the 1970s and the beginning of the 1980s. Examples of the multifarious problems included depletion of the ozone layer, the rational use of natural resources (forests, oil, water, etc.), and ecological disasters (oil spills, chemicals, nuclear energy disasters). The international regimes on environment, sustainable development and climate change have become a relevant pathway to bring firms to be more accountable to the needs of the planet (dimensions related to the sustainable development approach). Some of the most relevant developments in this context include:

- Creation of the United Nations Environment Programme (UNEP) in 1972
- Adoption of the Montreal Protocol on Substances that Deplete the Ozone Layer in 1987
- Brundtland Report that conceptualized 'sustainable development' in 1987
- Earth Summit in Rio de Janeiro that introduced the Agenda 21 in 1992
- Kyoto Protocol in 1997
- Johannesburg Summit in 2002
- Rio + 20 in 2012
- SDGs and the 2030 Agenda in 2015.

Concerns regarding the effects of firm activity would not be so significant if the influence of such activity were not so deep. What is needed is an approach that can help firms align their work with social and environmental standards and norms relating to the current agenda (Bruce Hall & Biersteker, 2002). The CSR framework can act as a bridge to facilitate this linkage.

3 The Corporate Social Responsibility Interface

In this section, the relevance of two relationships is examined—the linkages of social and environmental norms, standards and regulations with the private sector, and the linkages of the sustainable development approach with the CSR framework. These links seem to point to the same set of solutions to create new rules for different stakeholders to align their activities with the new sustainable development agenda based on the SDGs to be achieved by 2030.

First, when we refer to the private sector and link it with norms, regulations and standards, following ITC (2011, p. 1), we must consider the framework of public rules within which producers, exporters and buyers operate, as well as its growing interplay with private rules. Possible categories of research as identified by the ITC include:

- private standards in global value chains
- private standards' impacts on producers and exporters
- public and private standards interplay
- public standards' benefits for producers and exporters.

There is also a possibility of differentiating between public and private standards in the following ways (ITC, 2011, p. 1), even though there are overlaps:

- Private standards tend to include requirements related to wider social and environmental aspects of production, e.g. working and living conditions at the farm/factory or even community level.
- Public standards may focus on narrower aspects such as product and food safety as well as quality, but they also go beyond to address environmental (and worker) protection, for instance.

Büthe and Mattli further explain the differences between norms, standards and regulations, to appreciate their utility, in the following sense:

> Like norms and regulations, standards are instruments of governance. But standards differ from most social norms in that they are more explicit. At the same time, standards differ from governmental regulations in that the use of, or compliance with, a standard is not mandatory. Only if a standard becomes the technical basis for a law or regulation – which often and increasingly occurs – does it become legally binding. (2010, p. 455)

On the same lines, the above-mentioned authors (Büthe & Mattli, 2011), quoted by the ITC (2011, pp. 5–6) propose the following typology of standards, whether public or private:

- public non-market-based standards and norms developed by international organizations or domestic regulators (such as ILO labour standards)
- public market-based standards established by competing public regulatory agencies of individual states or regional and multilateral standard-setting bodies (such as Codex Alimentarius)
- non-market-based private standards set up by major private bodies (such as ISO 26,000, ISO 14,000, etc.)

Fig. 2 What to regulate or standardize? *Source* Levi-Faur (2011, p. 9)

- market-based private standards developed by firms, NGOs, academia, industry associations, etc. (such as Fairtrade).

Once we can differentiate between public and private rules at the global or local level, a key question is 'what to regulate?', particularly by the private sector. Levi-Faur (2011) proposes that not only the private sector (market), but also the society (civil) or governmental actors (state), as regulators, can be categorized in eight ways in any governance system (Fig. 2). If we place the private sector at the core of the figure, we see through the diagram how firms create value for their different stakeholders, and by extension, the possibility of identifying what are the main aspects to be regulated. Figure 3, taken from the Stakeholder Theory (Freeman, Harrison, Wicks, Parmar, & De Colle, 2010), illustrates this relationship between the firm and the value creation for others.

As part of the stakeholder theory, CSR becomes a helpful tool to develop social and environmental standards and regulations under the sustainable development approach. In addition, as Nuñez (2003, p. 5) points out, most of the CSR aspects are already included to some extent in the international standards[4] relating to new concerns such as environmental protection. To contextualize briefly, CSR can be

---

[4]In this case, the reference is to standards related to human rights or labour issues, which have had a longer tradition within the UN and ILO. The Global Compact incorporates these two fields, plus

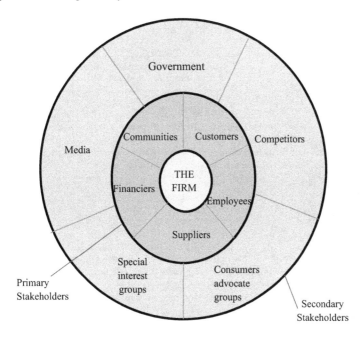

Fig. 3 Whom to regulate or apply standards to? *Source* Freeman et al. (2010, p. 24)

understood in its classical definition as '... the economic, legal, ethical, and discretionary expectations that society has of organizations at a given point in time' (Carroll, 1979, p. 500; Carroll, 2008). While linking it with sustainable development, it has been proposed that the most accurate definition of CSR must incorporate not only dimensions of analysis like those identified by Carroll, but also incorporate the concerns of the different stakeholders of the firm (primary and secondary), at least in four main areas: government (states and public administration), society (consumers, NGOs and citizens), market (industries and competition) and nature (the environment) (Elkington, 1998; Nuñez, 2003; Raufflet, Lozano, Barrera, & García de la Torre, 2012).

The main theoretical frameworks that can be used to understand CSR include: the economic approach (Friedman [1962] 2002), the social performance theory (Carroll, 1979), the stakeholder theory (based on an ethical view) and the corporate citizenship approach (Melé, 2008, pp. 48–49; Mutz, 2008). Similarly, many initiatives related to norms and standards that incorporate different concerns around sustainable development can be identified. It is important to note that such initiatives under CSR go beyond many of the norms and standards with a social and environmental focus as they also include economic and financial dimensions.

Nuñez (2003) proposes a three-level classification of initiatives of CSR—global, regional and national—to guide the private sector under a sustainable development

---

two more contemporary concerns—environment and corruption. This is an example of international standards and principles for the private sector in the global governance context.

Table 2 CSR initiatives

Global level

Global Indexes DJSI, FTSE 4 Good	Norms and technical standards ISO 14,000, AA1000, SA800

Principles and global guidelines

Caux principles for business, Sullivan principles, Equator principles (Banking), OCDE guidelines, Global Reporting Initiative, Global Compact, ICGN, Boston College, UNCHR Human Rights Code of Conduct for Companies, Consumers Int. Business Charter, ILO principles, Universal declaration of human rights

Regional level

WBCSD   EMPRESA

National level

Local initiatives through local institutions related to private sector, chambers of commerce, private foundations related to WBCSD (such as CEADS en Argentina, CESPEDES in Mexico, CEBDS BCSD Brazil, among others), and to EMPRESA (such as CBSR in Canada, Instituto Ethos Brazil, Acción Empresa Chile, CEMEFI Mexico, among others)

Source Nuñez (2003, p. 17)

approach through norms, standards, principles, guides, codes of conduct, global indexes, and reports (Table 2). Table 2 can be complemented with later initiatives such as the ISO 26,000 on social responsibility for organizations, the Extractive Industries Transparency Initiative (EITI) and its standard, or, at the local level in the Mexican case, the Sustainable IPC for the Mexican Stock Exchange and initiatives such as the ESR emblem provided by the Mexican Center for Philanthropy (CEMEFI) (Pérez, 2011).

To illustrate the interface between the private sector, and social and environmental standards and regulations, through CSR, three key institutions in México are considered—The Mexican Center for Philanthropy (CEMEFI), The Global Compact Mexican Chapter (GCMC), and the Caux Round Table Mexican Chapter (CAUX)—as examples of the influence of CSR strengthening standards, norms and regulations locally. The main findings are listed in the Annex, and can be summarized as follows:

1. There is a perception that CSR is influencing the strengthening of standards at value chain level, however, it seems this influence is limited to reputational rather than strategic considerations. Even then, some local institutions are promoting international initiatives around social and environmental norms and standards, such as the SR10 from IQNet adopted by the Mexican private sector.
2. Related to the current state of social and environmental standards and regulations in México, new alternatives have been emerging lately. On the government side, institutions such as the Mexican Ministry of Labour (STPS), the National Institute for Women (INMUJERES), or the National Council to Prevent Discrimination

(CONAPRED) have launched, in the last few years, initiatives such as the Norm NMX-R-025-SCFI-2015 against discrimination and labour inequality. From civil society and the international community, alternatives such as the certification of family-friendly enterprises (EFR) and the GCMC have emerged. A direct relationship can be perceived between each component of CSR and the local implementation of international standards and norms that cover all those areas, such as SA 8000 or ISO 9000 and some others. However, the coverage is still low, as Global Compact figures show (Annex).

3. Finally, relating to broader initiatives or national platforms such as the ones promoted by the United Nations Forum on Sustainability Standards (UNFSS), there is a lack of knowledge of such work at the level of local stakeholders. However, local institutions such as the Ministry of Environment and Natural Resources (SEMARNAT) have been working on the launch of labels and certifications on responsible consumption. The 2030 Agenda is likely to influence the implementation of social and environmental standards to attain the SDGs.

It is perceived, in general, that given the SDGs and the increasing involvement of the private sector in the sustainable development agenda, many other initiatives will appear at this interface, such as the Emerging Market Multinationals Network for Sustainability, the movement around impact investment linked, among others, with the International Finance Corporation (IFC) of the World Bank Group, the work of the UN around the promotion of the Global Compact, development agencies such as the Deutsche Gesellschaft für Internationale Zusammenarbeit (GIZ) and their work promoting business models for sustainable development, or the efforts around business and development carried out by the World Business Council for Social Development (WBCSD), the UNDP, the OECD or the International Institute for Sustainable Development (IISD).

As a concluding example in this context, we can consider a given ministry related to any environmental topic (water, forest, seas, lakes, etc.) in any developing country or emerging economy. Its technical department may manage a pool of contractors that can contribute, with their technology, to improve certain aspects regulated by this ministry (water filters, pipes, paper and packing materials, renewable energy technology, etc.). In collaboration with the international cooperation department, which also interacts with development agencies and engages in global debates, such pool of firms could increasingly be filtered based on general (or specific) norms and standards adopted by the international community in the labour and environmental areas. Applying the CSR approach, requirements that can be imposed include: that the firm belongs to the Global Compact; that the firm produces an Annual Sustainability Report that has been certified by the Global Reporting Initiative (GRI); or that the firm has achieved a local or international standard or certificate, such as the ISO 14,000 family, ISO 26,000, or in the Mexican case, the NOM-120-SSA1-1994 on health and sanitation practices in the processing of food, alcoholic and non-alcoholic beverages etc.

4 Conclusions

The main aim of the chapter was to underline the relevance of the private sector in the context of social and environmental norms, standards and regulations in the world economy. In particular, the chapter sought to show that in the current situation, the evolution of the private sector must take place in a way in which, through the creation of certain norms and standards, the goals of the private sector can be aligned with the goals of society in order to guarantee sustainable development.

It was shown that the main activities of a firm along many of its processes (production, distribution and consumption) intersect with relevant aspects of the sustainability approach, i.e. to take care of the economy, of the society and of the environment. In this context, corporate social responsibility appears to be a framework that can help integrate the use of social and environmental standards into firm activity in the context of global governance, promoted both by public and private initiatives. This needs to be done not only for the sake of the local environment, but for the provision of global public goods. The 2030 Agenda can be an opportunity to promote the convergence of social and environmental standards and regulations with CSR, with the aim of better aligning the private sector's and other actors' activities with the SDGs. The Mexican experience shown here briefly can work as an example of how such convergence is in fact happening and contributing to the 2030 goals.

Acknowledgements I appreciate the feedback for this work from Johannes Blankenbach from the German Development Institute/*Deutsches Institut für Entwicklungspolitik* (DIE), Bonn and Archna Negi from the Jawaharlal Nehru University, New Delhi, and all the colleagues from the MGG network that attended the workshops of the project 'Social and Environmental Standards and Regulations for the World Economy'. At the same time, I appreciate the time and inputs provided by Lorena Cortes from CEMEFI, Marco Pérez Ruíz from the United Nations Global Compact Network Mexico, and Walter Zehle from Caux Round Table Mexican Chapter for the interviews provided. The current text was developed between 2015 and 2016—at the beginning of the 2030 Agenda—and therefore focuses on the Mexican developments in the context of sustainability standards in that period.

Annex

Apart from literature, this chapter builds upon interviews on the relationship between CSR and social and environmental standards and regulations in Mexico with three experts from key local institutions:

- Ms. Lorena Cortes (LC), Head of Research at the Mexican Centre for Philanthropy (CEMEFI)
- Marco Pérez (MP), Coordinator of the Global Compact's Mexican Chapter (GCMC)
- Walter Zehle (WZ), Representative of the Mexican Chapter of the Caux Round Table (CAUX).

The interviews focused on three main aspects:

- Question 1—What is the role of CSR in the strengthening of standards in Mexico?
- Question 2—What is the current state of social and environmental standards and regulations in Mexico?
- Question 3—Is there any progress on the configuration of a national platform on (private) sustainability standards like the one recently launched in India? (*Note: The Mexican National Platform on Voluntary Sustainability Standards was subsequently launched in April 2018*).

The following table summarizes the main findings of the interviews:

	Q1	Q2	Q3
LC	• CSR is currently influencing the strengthening of standards in Mexico, particularly at the value chain level • Defining a common concept of CSR and establishing its link with standards is still difficult • In many sectors such as agriculture or construction, there is a debate on the implications for corporations and their collaborators if CSR is implemented in those sectors. Small and medium-sized enterprises (SMEs) implement international standards as they are obliged to comply with the international benchmarks of multinational corporations in order to be accepted as part of their value chains • There is still the feeling that CSR standards can only be complied with by big corporations and not by local and small companies	• It is possible to identify a number of initiatives driven by different actors, but particularly the Mexican government through the Ministry of Labour (*Secretaría del Trabajo y Prevision Social*—STPS), has been recently promoting different labelling initiatives linked to the value chain of different sectors, e.g. for: – family-friendly enterprises (DEFR) (https://www.gob.mx/stps/articulos/distintivo-empresa-familiarmente-responsable-efr?idiom=es) – enterprises promoting inclusive labour (Gilberto Rincón Gallardo), and – farms free of child labour (DEALTI) https://www.gob.mx/stps/articulos/convocatoria-a-empresas-para-obtener-distintivos-en-materia-de-inclusion-laboral-y-contra-el-trabajo-infantil • Another example is the recent creation of the NMX-R-025-SCFI-2015 norm against discrimination and equal labour, developed by three governmental institutions: INMUJERES, CONAPRED and STPS (http://www.gob.mx/inmujeres/acciones-y-programas/norma-mexicana-nmx-r-025-scfi-2015-en-igualdad-laboral-y-no-discriminacion) • Finally, the private Fundación Más Familia awards the EFR certification to family-friendly enterprises based on CSR principles. It is a management model with presence in more than 20 countries and three core areas: family and labour conciliation, support for equal opportunities, inclusiveness. The levels of engagement are: firms, municipalities, education, social economy, franchises, micro-entities, global (http://www.masfamilia.org/iniciativa-efr/que-es)	The interviewee had no information regarding this question

(continued)

(continued)

	Q1	Q2	Q3
MP	The general opinion is that currently, CSR is still limited more to philanthropy and voluntary services rather than to sustainable business strategies. In practice, there is not yet an alignment between CSR and standards. CSR for many Mexican firms (mostly SMEs) still is a means and not an end	Although the number of norms has grown in the recent years, the challenge is still too big, because firms use them very little. Even though the Global Compact (GC) is one of the biggest movements worldwide related to CSR and some social and environmental standards, the number of firms engaged in the GC at country level (around 781 organizations and among them around 530 firms) is still low considering that there are almost five million firms in Mexico (The country has the third biggest GC network in the world, and the first in the Latin-American region. At global level, the GC accounts for 9000 firms and 3000 non-businesses https://www.unglobalcompact.org/what-is-gc/participants). There is a need to align initiatives such as GC, Global Reporting Initiative, etc.	The interviewee had no information regarding the specificities of social and environmental standards However, there was a perception that the 2030 Agenda and the SDGs offer new potentials for standards and indicators development as well as for their alignment with these global goals
WZ	The CSR movement has influenced many local institutions and initiatives around standards and norms, for example: • Under ISO 26,000, IQNet (The International Certification Network) developed the SR10 certificate, an international standard on responsible and sustainable management that is supported and operated in Mexico by the Instituto Mexicano de Normalización y Certificación A.C. (IMNC) and by the Asociación de Normalización y Certificación A.C. (ANCE). (Private, independent multisectoral organizations that support the industry). Another case is the 'Etica y Valores' award presented by the Confederation of Industrial Chambers of Mexico (CONCAMIN) since around 15 years	There is a big influence of international standards on local standards and norms. In the case of CSR, for each CSR topic we can identify a particular standard, some of them international (e.g. SA 8000, ISO 9000 and many environmental standards) but at the same time referred to in Mexican laws and standards. For this reason, it does not seem clear why to consider the creation of (new) standards when most of the international standards are represented in local laws, norms or standards	There are no clear initiatives in this regard; however, the government will launch standards and norms relating to CSR (e.g. on responsible consumption) through institutions such as the Ministry of Environment and Natural Resources (SEMARNAT). These are intended to complement regulations in promoting sustainability

References

Aziz, A. S., Lerche, O. C., Jr., & Lerche, O. C., III. (1995). *Concepts of international politics in global perspective*. Englewood Cliffs, NJ: Prentice Hall.

Bruce Hall, R., & Biersteker, T. J. (2002). *The emergence of private authority in global governance*. Cambridge: Cambridge University Press.

Büthe, T., & Mattli, W. (2010). Standards for global markets: Domestic and international institutions for setting international product standards. In H. Enderlein, S. Wälti, & M. Zürn (Eds.), *Handbook on multi-level governance* (pp. 455–476). Cheltenham: Edward Elgar.

Büthe, T., & Mattli, W. (2011). *The new global rulers: The privatization of regulation in the world economy*. Princeton, NJ: Princeton University Press.

Carroll, A. (1979). A three-dimensional conceptual model of corporate performance. *Academy of Management Review, 4*(4), 497–505.

Carroll, A. (2008). A history of corporate social responsibility: Concepts and practices. In A. Crane, A. McWilliams, D. Matten, J. Moon, & D. Siegel (Eds.), *The Oxford handbook of corporate social responsibility*. Oxford: Oxford University Press.

CCIC. (2001). *Bridges or walls?: Making our choices on private sector engagement*. A Deliberation Guide For Action Against Poverty. Ottawa, Ontario: Canadian Council for International Cooperation.

Commission on Global Governance. (1995). *Our global neighbourhood* (Report of the Commission on Global Governance). Oxford: Oxford University Press.

Dembinski, P. (2003). Economic power and social responsibility of very big enterprises: Facts and challenges. In *UNCTAD 2004, disclosure of the impact of corporations on society: Current trends and issues*.

Dingwerth, K., & Pattberg, P. (2006). Global governance as a perspective on world politics. *Global Governance, 12*(2), 185–203.

Dunning, J. H. (1992). *Multinational enterprises and the global economy*. Wokingham: Addison-Wesley.

Dunning, J. H. (2005). The United Nations and transnational corporations: A personal assessment. In L. Cuyvers & F. De Beule (Eds.), *Transnational corporations and economic development, from internationalization to globalization* (pp. 1–37). Basingstoke: Palgrave Macmillan.

Elkington, J. (1998). *Cannibals with forks: The triple bottom line of the 21st century business*. Stony Creek: The New Society Publishers.

Finkelstein, L. (1995). What is global governance? *Global Governance, 1*(3), 367–372.

Fischer, S. (1999). ABCDE: Past ten years, next ten years. In B. Pleskovic & J. E. Stiglitz (Eds.), *Annual World Bank Conference on Development Economics 1998* (pp. 77–86). Washington, DC: The World Bank.

Freeman, R. E., Harrison, J., Wicks, A. C., Parmar, B. L., & De Colle, S. (2010). *Stakeholder theory, the state of the art*. Cambridge: Cambridge University Press.

Friedman, M. ([1962] 2002). *Capitalism and freedom* (Fortieth Anniversary ed.). Chicago: The University of Chicago Press.

ITC. (2011). *The interplay of public and private standards: Literature review series on the impacts of private standards—Part III*. Geneva: International Trade Center.

Levi-Faur, D. (2011). Regulation and regulatory governance. In D. Levi-Faur (Ed.), *Handbook on the politics of regulation* (pp. 3–21). Northampton, MA: Edward Elgar.

Melé, D. (2008). Corporate social responsibility theories. In A. Crane, A. McWilliams, D. Matten, J. Moon, & D. Siegel (Eds.), *The Oxford handbook of corporate social responsibility* (pp. 47–82). Oxford: Oxford University Press.

Mutz, G. (2008). CSR and CC: Social responsibility and corporate citizenship. In ICEP & CODESPA, *Business and poverty, innovative strategies for global CSR* (pp. 107–111). España: ICEP Austria, Fundación Codespa.

Nuñez, G. (2003). *La responsabilidad social corporativa en un marco de desarrollo sotenible*. CEPAL, GTZ, serie medio ambiente y desarrollo 72.

Pérez, J. A. (2011). *La responsabilidad social mexicana, actores y temas*. México: Instituto Mora, Universidad Anahuac, Red Puentes.

Pingeot, L. (2014). *La influencia empresarial en el proceso post-2015*. Madrid: Editorial Plataforma 2015 y más.

Raufflet, E., Lozano, J. F., Barrera, E., & García de la Torre, C. (2012). *Responsabilidad Social Empresarial*. México: Pearson.

Rosenau, J. N. (1995). Governance in the twenty-first century. *Global Governance, 1,* 13–43.

Schäfer, H., Beer, J., Zenker, J., & Fernandes, P. (2006). *Who is who in corporate social responsibility rating?* Gütersloh, Germany: Bertelsmann Foundation.

Stiglitz, J. & Charlton, A. (2005). *Fair trade for all: How trade can promote development*. Oxford: Oxford University Press.

Williamson, J. (1990). *Latin American adjustment: How much has happened?* Washington, DC: Institute for International Economics.

WTO. (1998). *Annual report 1998*. Geneva: World Trade Organization.

Chapter 6
Advances in Sustainability Reporting: What Is Missing?

Ana Carolina Mendes dos Santos, Ayuni Larissa Mendes Sena, and Vana Tércia Silva de Freitas

1 Introduction

Social and environmental global challenges have generated pressure on companies to be more proactive in social and environmental responsibility. Because of their political and economic influence and the impact of their activities, corporations have an important role to play in sustainable development. A growing number of companies—especially large and midsized ones—understand the need to address sustainability issues and go beyond short-term gains if they want to survive in the long run, because their reputation among stakeholders and market value varies depending on their involvement with social and environmental issues, as shown by KPMG (2011). As corporate social responsibility (CSR) emerges as a new business paradigm, sustainability reporting (SR) is increasingly recognized globally as an important instrument of transparency and accountability, contributing to companies' efforts to achieve sustainability.

Although we recognize the importance of disclosing information, we go further. In our understanding, more than being an end in itself, SR must play the most important role of serving as an instrument to monitor companies' activities regarding social and environmental impacts—and as an instrument of good governance. One can naturally expect governments and civil society organizations to play a principal role in this process of holding companies responsible for their activities. However, one may question the level of seriousness with which the process of SR is taken and whether this tool is utilized to its full potential. We argue that stakeholder involvement is the

A. C. M. dos Santos · V. T. S. de Freitas (✉)
Ministry of Environment, Brasília, Brazil
e-mail: vana.freitas@mma.gov.br

A. L. M. Sena
Brazilian Institute of the Environment and Renewable Natural Resources (IBAMA), Brasília, Brazil

© The Editor(s) (if applicable) and The Author(s) 2020
A. Negi et al. (eds.), *Sustainability Standards and Global Governance*,
https://doi.org/10.1007/978-981-15-3473-7_6

99

missing link that needs to be strengthened in order to make SR a strong instrument of good governance for sustainability.

After a brief historical description of the evolution of SR and an analysis of the concepts of sustainability standards and good governance found in literature, we discuss the potential of SR as an instrument for strengthening corporate social and environmental standards. In doing so, and based on some case studies also found in the literature, we identify what we believe is a condition for using this tool to its full potential—stakeholder involvement, or more specifically, government and civil society use of information disclosed to influence companies' actions. Special focus is given to the Group of Friends of Paragraph 47 (GoF47), a voluntary group of national governments that are in the forefront of the discussions on SR and the necessary legal framework to promote disclosure about sustainability-related information. We conclude the paper with a discussion of some elements that we believe can directly affect the use of SR—i.e. governance processes that lead to improvements in reporting practices and corporate policies—and finally, we provide some recommendations to policymakers and civil society organizations in order to promote a more effective use of SR.

2 Historical Background and State of the Art

From a historical perspective, the development of SR has witnessed several shifts. In the 1970s, traditional financial reporting was complemented by supplementary social information. In the 1980s, with the launch of the first principles of SR by the Coalition for Environmentally Responsible Economies (CERES), reporting increasingly began to include the social and environmental dimension, usually in a joint report published alongside the traditional financial report (Hahn & Kühnen, 2013). Today, the Global Reporting Initiative (GRI) is the most used guide for SR due to the broad acceptance of its principles and indicators. More than 5000 organizations comply with it—over 80 per cent of the world's 250 largest corporations across more than 90 countries (GRI, 2014). The well-known GRI Guidelines have recently been transformed into a "set of modular, interrelated GRI Sustainability Reporting Standards (GRI Standards)", mainly to improve the structure and format of contents (GRI, 2017).

Widespread acceptance of SR has stimulated many individual and collective efforts towards developing and exchanging best practices and guidance in this area, such as the UN Global Compact, Ethos Institute for Business and Social Responsibility, ISO 26000, GRI, UN Environment Programme (UNEP) and Organization for Economic Cooperation and Development (OECD) Guidelines for Multinational Enterprises, which contribute to increased compliance levels among countries and sectors.

Although SR is basically a voluntary process, there is a growing tendency to make it mandatory, as shown in the recent Directive 2014/95/EU of the European Parliament on disclosure of non-financial and diversity information by certain large undertakings and groups. Other countries leading in the use of SR have also

Table 1 Sustainability reporting and current national policies in GoF47 member countries (*Argentina, Austria, Colombia, Norway and Switzerland did not participate in the study*)

Country	National policy on SR
South Africa	Mandatory for listed companies (since 2010)
Brazil	Mandatory for the electricity sector (distributors, transmitters, permit holders and generating companies (since 2006)
Denmark	Mandatory for listed companies and state-owned companies and any other exceeding at least two of the following: (a) balance sheet total of EUR 19.2 million; (b) net revenue of EUR 38.3 million; (c) more than 250 full-time employees (since 2009)
France	Mandatory for listed companies and for non-listed companies from December 2011, as follows: (a) from 31 December 2011, for non-listed companies with over 5000 employees and a turnover or total balance sheet above EUR 1 billion; (b) from 31 December 2012, for non-listed companies over 2000 employees and a turnover or total balance sheet above EUR 400 million; (c) from 31 December 2013, for non-listed companies over 500 employees and a turnover or total balance sheet above EUR 100 million
Chile	Mandatory for state-owned companies and voluntary for listed companies under the "comply or explain" approach (under implementation)

Source Authors' compilation based on UNEP and GoF47 (2015)

adhered to mandatory approaches (Table 1). The general trends in the practice of SR have demonstrated the importance of integrating it with traditional financial reports, providing a more holistic view of companies' policies. The so-called integrated sustainability reports have gained popularity among different sectors and stakeholders based on the recognition that efficient investments are necessary to make sustainable transformation appealing.

A recent initiative is the GoF47, founded in 2012 by the governments of South Africa, Brazil, Denmark and France, later enlarged to include Argentina, Austria, Chile, Colombia, Norway and Switzerland, while other countries have expressed interest to join (Morocco, Sri Lanka and Vietnam). UNEP and GRI support this group, whose name comes from Paragraph 47 of the final document "The Future We Want" of the 2012 United Nations Conference on Sustainable Development (Rio + 20), in which governments pledged to encourage companies to consider integrating sustainability information in their periodic reports.

The special feature of this group is its government-led nature. It aims at pushing forward the discussions about SR, promoting the practice globally and developing and exchanging best practices and policy guidance in this area. GoF47 is dedicated to strengthening an international culture of corporate transparency and accountability as key elements of a well-functioning economy that enhance the private sector's contribution to sustainable development. The group believes that the widespread practice of SR has the potential to contribute to the assessment of sustainability impacts by the corporate sector and to encourage sustainable business practices.

In 2014, in its Position Paper,[1] GoF47 committed to advancing the implementation of Paragraph 47 and strongly recommended that SR should be retained within the framework of the 2030 (then "post-2015") Agenda on Sustainable Development. Considering that monitoring and accountability frameworks are crucial for the implementation of the 2030 Agenda, the group has been acting as a global player in promoting SR as a tool to generate data and measure progress and companies' contribution towards the Sustainable Development Goals (SDGs).

In this sense, one of the most remarkable results of GoF47 was the strong participation of its member countries during the negotiations to build and maintain target 12.6 ("Encourage companies, especially large and transnational companies, to adopt sustainable practices and to integrate sustainability information into their reporting cycle") in the SDGs document, showing an evolution from a recommendation (Paragraph 47) to a global development goal (SDG 12).

Based on previous experiences at the national level of some leading member countries (Table 1), GoF47 encourages policymakers to consider a combination of mandatory and voluntary policies, striking a balance between the strong need for standardization and comparability (typical of mandatory reporting) and the desire to allow flexibility and innovation in SR (characteristic of the voluntary approach), as is the case for listed and non-listed companies on stock market sustainability indexes (UNEP & GoF47, 2015). More recently, with the support of UNEP, GoF47 country members from Latin America and the Caribbean region—especially Argentina, Brazil, Chile and Colombia—have been engaging in regional projects in order to enhance governmental capacities to manage information from CSR—promoting a follow-up approach in CSR policies, encouraging comparability of current reporting procedures and targeting better alignment of corporate activities to SDGs (SDG 12.6).

Table 1 shows some GoF47 member countries and their current policies on SR. According to UNEP and GoF47 (2015), in 2013, 45 countries had sustainability reporting-related policies in place—an increase of 26 countries since 2006. This rapid growth demonstrates a strong recognition of the positive role of SR and its importance in addressing society's needs for transparency. Notwithstanding this, most of the cases and discussions still centre on the issue of promoting the adoption of SR. There is little focus on how SR is really changing companies' performance or improving social and environmental standards. Once reports are published, it is also important to see who is assessing them and what end they are serving.

3   Concept and Principles of Sustainability Reporting

Sustainability standards can be understood as "a set of criteria defining good social and environmental practices (...), bringing about better production practices and

---

[1]GoF47 Position Paper was an internal document to endorse a position, as a group, to present to the Permanent Missions of New York at the 11th Open Working Group.

driving long-term sustainability improvements" (ISEAL, 2015). This means that in an interconnected world, there are certain minimum expectations for any activity to consider potential social and environmental impacts and to ensure that adverse social and environmental risks and impacts are avoided, minimized, mitigated and managed.

Based on this definition, SR can be understood as a standard (there are many international SR standards: UN Global Compact, Ethos Institute for Business and Social Responsibility, ISO 26000, GRI, UNEP and OECD guidelines), but—at the same time—as an instrument of change. We argue that the most import role of SR is to serve as an instrument to improve corporate social and environmental behaviour in the wider sense; therefore, the exact SR standard or methodology applied is not the focus of this chapter. Although in order to be effective, the adopted methodology must be easy to understand, focused on important issues and able to generate easy to compare corporate results (Mohin, 2014).

By requiring companies to report their performance according to the most advanced methodologies, SR criteria may provide a basis for good business practices, i.e. the common rules that should be followed in order to achieve sustainability. Reporting practices result in a long-term learning and improvement process in which companies have the opportunity to review their internal procedures, public relations, resource use, production efficiency and social and environmental impacts, which, aligned with CSR policies, can lead to more responsible business.

We view SR as a set of principles and practices—the act and process of reporting performance—rather than a specific document or methodology (Fig. 1). This is why we prefer the term sustainability *reporting* rather than *report*. Applying a broader understanding of SR allows for discussions and policies that may foster the adoption of reporting practices by other institutions, such as small and medium enterprises,

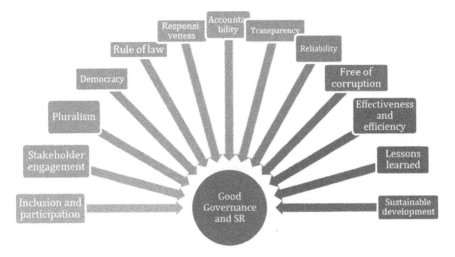

Fig. 1 Common principles and practices of good governance and sustainability reporting. *Source* Authors

governmental institutions and civil society organizations, since their engagement with SR requires adaptation in order to make it more attractive, simple and cost efficient. In this sense, we understand SR more as a practice than a report, embracing the principles of good governance. Reporting methodology should be understood as a means towards standardization, which at the same time needs to be adapted to specific contexts and institutions.

Even though there are still bottlenecks to be overcome in terms of indicator comprehension and use (Moneva, Archel & Correa, 2006; Azcárate, Carrasco & Fernández, 2011; Camargos, Jannuzzi & Gavira, 2014), SR practices have shown significant improvements (KPMG, 2013). This suggests that the focus can now shift to a broader discussion about whether companies follow all means to be accountable, transparent and inclusive towards broader stakeholders such as the government and civil society, which tend to face more difficulties in appropriating SR, as shown in this paper.

Although the term governance—usually related to the "process of governing"—has a variety of definitions, depending on the context and the objectives that are pursued (Guisselquist, 2012), principles of good governance seem to be well agreed upon. We argue that they overlap to a large extent with principles and practices of SR as illustrated in Fig. 1. In the context of sustainability standards for the economy, good governance also requires a strong commitment to sustainable development (Sachs, 2015) or what some call governance for sustainability (Bosselmann, Engel & Taylor, 2008).

SR, as we see it, has a high potential to promote good governance schemes as well as social and environmental standards, given its emphasis on transparency and accountability criteria required for an active participation of various actors. Moreover, SR boosts commitments to institutional learning and transformation processes through data collection and information disclosure.

4 Stakeholder Involvement: The Missing Link

If we recognize that one of the most important roles of SR is to provide information to stakeholders in a way that they can monitor social and environmental impacts of companies' activities, it is important to understand how those stakeholders effectively use SR as an instrument of change. This requires an active participation of those actors that are most closely concerned with the social and environmental impacts of corporate activity—government and civil society (especially environmental and human rights-oriented NGOs and consumer organizations). Business groups (investors, shareholders, etc.)—profit stakeholders—show more interest in sustainability information that has an added value for the direct assessment of a company's value now and in the future.

Nonetheless, evidence on how these stakeholders use SR—understood as "assessing the reports with the aim of making a decision or taking an action"—rarely appears either in the literature or in practitioners' experience. The 2008 KPMG

Sustainability study on the perspective of report readers (KPMG, 2008) and, later, the GRI study about how different stakeholder groups use sustainability data (GRI, 2015) are some of the few in-depth and global studies undertaken in this field, which reveal that SR is not used to its full potential.

The quality of SR has been especially criticized by academics. Garcia & Lima (2019) point out that the quality aspects usually presented in the reports are limited to adherence to disclosure protocols, with little follow-up regarding the accuracy and usefulness of the reported information, the balancing of positive and negative aspects and the possibility of comparability of performance from one period to another.

During this research, we identified that governments and civil society representatives do not appropriate information disclosed through SR as much as other actors closely related to companies—such as investors, shareholders and labour unions—do. This underutilization of sustainability data is particularly noted in the case of governments. Although always recognized as an important stakeholder group in promoting CSR, they are not well equipped to use SR optimally. The ineffective and weak impact of governments on SR is the result of state inability (financial and personnel) to monitor and enforce, and to downsize traditional command-control roles while promoting market forces to encourage better behaviour in industry and civil society (Mai-Lan, 2012). This imposes more and more responsibility on civil society and citizens to fulfil governments' roles.

An interesting case is the use of data by state and local governments of North America (the city of Seattle, Washington; Municipality of Hamilton-Wentworth, Ontario; and the province of British Columbia) studied by Maclaren (2014); they began to adopt sustainability as a goal in their plans and other planning activities:

> Urban sustainability reports include a range of information about environmental, economic, and social conditions and policies in the local community and use that information to make judgments about whether the community is making progress towards sustainability. Evidence of positive progress is important for justifying past expenditures on sustainability initiatives. Evidence of lack of sustainability can provide ammunition for community groups in local government, other levels of government, or the private sector. Individuals in the community can use sustainability reports to educate themselves about sustainability trends and evaluate how their own actions may improve sustainability. (Maclaren, 2014, p. 368)

Our research revealed that, in principle, there is no difference between countries that are part of the GoF47 and those who are not in terms of the use of SR and also in terms of reporting practices by governmental institutions, as shown in Table 1 and in the cases described above.

Literature shows sparse evidence pointing to civil society use of information available from SR, suggesting that these are rather timid approaches in, at times, precarious situations. Yakovleva and Vazquez-Brust (2012) examine the conceptualization of CSR in the context of multinational mining enterprises in Argentina, presenting the main conflicts with local communities, the organization and strategies adopted by them and the main results achieved.

On the other hand, in 2012, the International Movement of People Affected by Vale Company[2] launched a document called Vale Unsustainability Report, which uses the same structure as the company's SR to show independent counter-data about the reality of workers, affected communities and environmental impacts, countering information released in the company's reports and advertising campaigns. The second version of the Vale Unsustainability Report was launched in April 2015, which gathered information on more than thirty cases of conflict involving the entire production chain of the company in different countries such as Canada, Chile, Indonesia, Peru and Mozambique. The Vale Unsustainability Report represents a counterbalance to corporate governance and represents a more proactive example of civil society's use of SR. Its effectiveness relies on the capacity to affect the company's image and, consequently, to threaten profitability. Even though changes are not yet documented, this strategy will most likely affect not only the company's actions, but also the way SR is carried out (Adams & Whelan, 2009).

It is to be expected that the reports contain only what has been done. Unfortunately, practice shows a different reality. According to Moneva et al. (2006), some organizations that label themselves as GRI reporters do not behave in a responsible way concerning sustainability questions. This means that if SR is not used and checked by specific stakeholders, one can expect neither a guaranteed quality of reports nor improvements in corporate activities. A representative example comes from Vale Company—the second largest mining company in the world. Despite all its marketing concerning sustainability, and the publication of SR since 2006 on a voluntary basis, its 2016 and 2017 reports do not disclose information concerning effluents and wastes (topic of GRI-306), since this topic was not considered material, i.e. relevant to be included in the report (Garcia & Lima, 2019). Again, despite the mining dam accident in Mariana in 2015, Vale Sustainability Reports still offer superficial information about dam risks and ways to mitigate them. The extent to which these facts influence government or civil society's ability to monitor company's activities is still unknown, but one can expect that SR could help stakeholders investigate and take actions towards environmental risks and problems, such as in the recent accident in Brumadinho in 2019.

Fernandez-Feijoo, Romero and Ruiz (2014) demonstrated that the pressure by some stakeholder groups (consumers, clients, employees and environment) has increased the quality and transparency of reports, and Quaak, Aalbers and Goedee (2007) observed a similar effect with large breweries in the Netherlands, although not on a regular basis. These results do not show how stakeholders appropriate information disclosed in reports to claim better corporate governance but rather, how powerful their participation is in promoting better governance.

We could say that to be completely able to improve social and environmental standards, SR needs to be increasingly used by people who are interested in such improvements. Stakeholders' participation is the missing link between SR practices

---

[2]The International Coordination of People Affected by Vale is a result of network cooperation between stakeholders directly affected by Vale activities in mentioned countries. Vale is a global mining company with headquarters in Brazil and is a leading producer of iron and nickel.

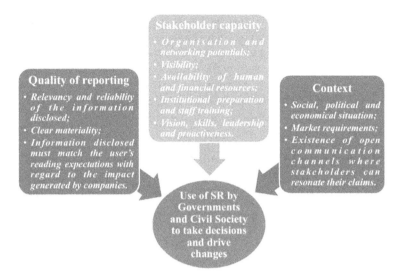

Fig. 2 Factors that directly affect the use of SR and, in turn, the governance processes leading towards improvements in reporting practices and corporate policies. *Source* Authors

and social and environmental improvement. According to UNEP (2015), there is a need for better collaborative reporting to transform SR from the current one-way, broadcast-type format to a more multi-directional, dynamic, ongoing exchange with all relevant stakeholders.

Unfortunately, participation in most cases is wanting. Stakeholders do not get involved or do not use SR for many reasons: complexity and length of the reports, making them inaccessible to most people, lack of a report's visibility, lack of human or financial resources, lack of relevance or reliability of the information disclosed, absence of an open communication channel with the company. Figure 2 illustrates the three factors or elements that we believe directly affect the use of SR by governments and civil society, and the governance process that leads to better CSR.

We argue in this chapter that discussions at the national and international levels still focus on the technical implementation of SR practices in a business environment, while neglecting the broader role of stakeholders such as the government and civil society. If we want SR to become a strong instrument of assessing companies' activities or performance in relation to sustainability issues, a particular challenge lies in providing those stakeholders with the conditions for better use of disclosed information. At the same time, there is need for starting a discussion at the international level to simplify corporate sustainability reports in order to generate meaningful and comparable data. For instance, even though the GRI is the most accepted and used methodology, its use of about 90 key performance indicators and a myriad of measurements renders its comprehension and comparability between companies difficult, if not impossible, for most people.

In order to achieve sustainability in business as well as better coordination between companies, governments and civil society on issues of standards and regulation, we believe that GoF47 and other leading international initiatives should engage in a post-SR debate, i.e. how to transform SR into better governance. Such a discussion would involve the elements presented in Fig. 2 through an ongoing dialogue with different stakeholders, especially the public sector and civil society.

5 Conclusion and Policy Recommendations

SR is an important instrument of transparency and accountability; it demonstrates companies' efforts to achieve sustainability and it has been increasingly adopted and fostered. We are not only witnessing a steady increase in reporting companies globally, but also in SR-related policies at the national level. Significant improvement in the implementation of SR polices worldwide is evident, which means there is no turning back in the process—SR is here to stay

In this chapter, we argue that the most important role of SR is to provide information to stakeholders in such a way that they can monitor social and environmental impacts of companies' activities and, as a consequence, to serve as an instrument to improve corporate social and environmental behaviour. But we also recognize that this requires the active participation of those actors most concerned with social and environmental impacts of corporate activities. Literature has shown that SR has not been fully and effectively utilized by stakeholders from government and civil society, who should be the most interested parties in ensuring that companies' activities do not result in negative social and environmental impacts. Stakeholders' participation, in this sense, is the missing link between SR practices and social and environmental improvements. The present study identified the sparseness of registered cases on the use of SR, which demonstrates that the debate needs to move forward. Discussions on SR both at the national and international levels are still more concentrated on implementing and strengthening SR policies. Despite the recent advances in reporting practices, the focus remains on stimulating companies to disclose sustainability information, rather than on the effective use of the information so provided. We believe that GoF47 has a great potential in leading this advanced debate.

By analysing a few cited cases, we could identify a group of elements that directly affect the use of SR and, in particular, the results achieved by stakeholders making use of the information disclosed. This is an interesting aspect to be addressed by national and international entities in future discussions on SR if we want to foster the use of SR as an instrument of change. Finally, we recommend a set of actions to governments and civil society to make better use of SR (Table 2), since we believe it has a big potential to improve governance models that favour the emergence of social and environmental standards for the world economy. But this can only be achieved if key stakeholders participate in this process and make use of SR to take decisions and action.

Table 2 List of recommendations to policymakers and civil society organizations to promote a better use of sustainability reports

Government	Civil society
• Develop legislation with minimum requirement of social and environmental standards for public and private companies to report on their performance, considering different challenges faced by companies of different sizes in different sectors • Set clear results to be achieved in SR policies and create institutional conditions to make effective use of the reports • Establish an ongoing multi-stakeholder dialogue • Make use of up-to-date technologies and social media • Create mechanisms to stimulate and reward best practices on SR • Lead by example and publish information about own sustainability performance	• Use reports to urge companies to improve CSR and governments to improve national policies • Consolidate, strengthen and expand the discussion arena on SR in order to qualify the proposals of civil society representatives • Rank and disseminate best practices of companies that produce and disclose their sustainability reports according to socio-environmental standards • Since civil society organizations are generally non-profit entities, it is important that they lead by example and publish financial and non-financial information • Work in partnership with governments in order to strengthen capacities and to monitor social and environmental impacts of companies' activities • Raise consumer awareness to encourage responsible consumption on the basis of SR

Source Authors

References

Adams, C. A., & Whelan, G. (2009). Conceptualising future change in corporate sustainability reporting. *Accounting, Auditing & Accountability Journal, 22*(1), 118–143.

Azcárate, F., Carrasco, F., & Fernández, M. (2011). The role of integrated indicators in exhibiting business contribution to sustainable development: a survey of sustainability reporting initiatives. *Spanish Accounting Review, 14*(1), 213–240.

Bosselmann, K., Engel, R., & Taylor, P. (2008). *Governance for sustainability—Issues, challenges, successes* (IUCN Environmental Policy and Law Paper 070). Gland: International Union for Conservation of Nature (IUCN). Retrieved from http://www.iucn.org/about/work/programmes/environmental_law/elp_resources/elp_res_publications/?uPubsID=3559.

Camargos, M. R., Jannuzzi, G. M., & Gavira, M. O. (2014). Analysis of the sustainability reporting initiatives of electric utilities in Brazil. *Industrija, 42*(1), 127–147.

Fernandez-Feijoo, B., Romero, S., & Ruiz, S. (2014). Effect of stakeholders' pressure on transparency of sustainability reports within the GRI framework. *Journal of Business Ethics, 122*(1), 53–63.

Garcia, S., & Lima, F. G. (2019). A Vale emBrumadinho: a queminteressa a sustentabilidade das empresas? *Jornal da USP*. Retrieved from https://jornal.usp.br/artigos/a-vale-em-brumadinho-a-quem-interessa-a-sustentabilidade-das-empresas/.

GRI (2014). *Forward thinking future focus: GRI 2013–2014*. Amsterdam: Author. Retrieved from https://www.globalreporting.org/resourcelibrary/GRI-CombinedReport-2013-2014-forward-thinking-future-focus.pdf.

GRI (2015). *Informing decisions, driving change: The role of data in a sustainable future*. Amsterdam: Author. Retrieved from https://www.globalreporting.org/resourcelibrary/Informing-decisions,-driving-change-The-role-of-data-in-a-sustainable-future.pdf.

GRI (2017). *Transition to standards.* Retrieved from https://www.globalreporting.org/information/g4/transition-to-standards/Pages/default.aspx.

Guisselquist, R. M. (2012). *Good governance as a concept, and why this matters for development policy* (Working Paper 2012/30). Helsinki: World Institute for Development Economics Research of the United Nations University (UNU-WIDER).

Hahn, R., & Kühnen, M. (2013). Determinants of sustainability reporting: A review of results, trends, theory, and opportunities in an expanding field of research. *Journal of Cleaner Production, 59,* 5–21.

ISEAL Alliance (2015). *What is a sustainability standard.* Retrieved from http://www.isealalliance.org/waypoint/what-is-a-sustainability-standard.

KPMG (2008). *KPMG international survey on corporate responsibility reporting 2008.* Amstelveen: Author. Retrieved from https://www.kpmg.com/EU/en/Documents/KPMG_International_survey_Corporate_responsibility_Survey_Reporting_2008.pdf.

KPMG (2011). *KPMG international survey of corporate responsibility reporting 2013.* Amstelveen: Author. Retrieved from https://www.kpmg.com/PT/pt/IssuesAndInsights/Documents/corporate-responsibility2011.pdf.

KPMG (2013). The *KPMG survey of corporate responsibility reporting 2013.* Amstelveen: Author. Retrieved from http://www.kpmg.com/Global/en/IssuesAndInsights/ArticlesPublications/corporate-responsibility/Documents/kpmg-survey-of-corporate-responsibility-reporting-2013.pdf.

Maclaren, V. W. (2014). Urban sustainability reporting from Journal of the American planning association (1996). In S. M. Wheeler & T. Beatley (Eds.), *The sustainable urban development reader* (3rd ed., pp. 367–374). New York, NY: Routledge.

Mai-Lan, H. (2012). *Literature review on voluntary social and environmental standards and governance.* Oakland, CA: Pacific Institute. Retrieved from http://pacinst.org/wp-content/uploads/2013/06/pacinst-standards-and-public-governance-lit-review-sept-2012.pdf.

Mohin, T. (2014). Are sustainability reports driving change or just "losing the signal"? *The Guardian.* Retrieved from https://www.theguardian.com/sustainable-business/2014/sep/11/corporate-responsibility-reporting-transparency-toxic-emissions-labeling-change.

Moneva, J. M., Archel, P., & Correa, C. (2006). GRI and the camouflaging of corporate unsustainability. *Accounting Forum, 30*(2), 121–137.

Quaak, L., Aalbers, T., & Goedee, J. (2007). Transparency of corporate social responsibility in Dutch breweries. *Journal of Business Ethics, 76*(3), 293–308.

Sachs, J. D. (2015). *The age of sustainable development.* New York, NY: Columbia University Press.

UNEP (2015). Raising the bar – Advancing Environmental Disclosure in Sustainability Reporting. Paris: Author. Retrieved from http://www.unep.org/resourceefficiency/Business/SustainableandResponsibleBusiness/CorporateSustainabilityReporting/MERITAS/RaisingtheBar/tabid/106 0852/Default.aspx.

UNEP & Group of Friends of Paragraph 47. *Evaluating National Policies on Corporate Sustainability Reporting,* 2015. Paris: UNEP. Retrieved from http://wedocs.unep.org/handle/20.500.11822/9435.

Yakovleva, N., & Vazquez-Brust, D. A. (2012). Stakeholder perspectives on CSR of mining MNCs in Argentina. *Journal of Business Ethics, 106*(2), 191–211.

Chapter 7
The Impact of Global Labour Standards on Export Performance

Kuntala Bandyopadhyay

1 Introduction

Labour interests in high-standards countries argue that low labour standards are an unfair source of comparative advantage, and that increasing imports from low-standards countries will have an adverse impact on wages and working conditions in high-standards countries, thus leading to a race to the bottom of standards. Low-standards countries fear that the imposition of high labour standards upon them is just a form of disguised protectionism and is equally unfair since it will erode their competitiveness, which is largely based on low labour costs. There exists extensive literature on the potential impact of labour standards on trade (Anderson, 1996; Brown, 2000; Dion, Lanoie, & Laplante, 1997; Krueger, 1996; Mah, 1997; Maskus, 1997; Sengerberger & Campbell, 1994; Srinivasan, 1998; Stephenson, 1997; White, 1996). The objective of this chapter is to empirically investigate the effects of labour standards on the export performance of a country. If the popular views on the issue of trade and labour standards are correct, one should expect low-standards countries to enjoy a better export performance, *ceteris paribus*. This chapter also discusses the ways in which the emerging economies and the public and private sectors within them are likely to emerge as setters of standards that affect producers and consumers across the world. The structure of the chapter is as follows: Sect. 2 is an overview of emerging economies and their participation in global standards setting, Sects. 3 and 4 discuss the data, empirical analysis and results and Sect. 5 concludes.

K. Bandyopadhyay (✉)
Indian Council for Research on International Economic Relations (ICRIER), New Delhi, India
e-mail: kbandyopadhyay@icrier.res.in

© The Editor(s) (if applicable) and The Author(s) 2020

A. Negi et al. (eds.), *Sustainability Standards and Global Governance*,
https://doi.org/10.1007/978-981-15-3473-7_7

2   Emerging Economies and Global Standards

Weiss and Thakur (2006) have defined global governance as "the complex of formal
and informal institutions, mechanisms, relationships, and processes between and
among states, markets, citizens and organizations, both inter- and non-governmental,
through which collective interests on the global plane are articulated, duties, obligations and privileges are established, and differences are mediated through educated
professionals". In other words, "global governance" can be identified as a move
towards the political co-ordination of transnational actors aimed at negotiating
responses to transnational issues or problems. With economic liberalization, global
governance is increasingly relevant for achieving sustainable development. Global
standards are one of the most important tools for this governance. They aim to develop
a set of common principles and standards for propriety, integrity and transparency
in international business and finance.

There is a growing recognition that the rise of the emerging economies will
change the contours of global governance. Many commentators suggest that this is
a transformative moment in global history and these economies will bring about
structural changes in global production, trade and aid relationships (Brautigam,
2009; Henderson, 2008; Kaplinsky & Messner, 2008; Power, Giles, & Tan-Mullins,
2012; Yeung, 2009). How these countries might influence the "rules of the game"
that pertain to international trade, particularly those relating to process standards
associated with labour conditions and environmental impacts will be interesting to
observe. The fundamental questions are, as Nadvi (2014) puts it, "(i) are the emerging
economies moving from being "standard-takers" to becoming "standard-makers"?
and (ii) if so, what kinds of standards will be shaped by the emerging economies and
what will be the implications of those standards for the overall trajectory of global
labour and environmental standards?"

Before we start looking for answers to the above questions, it will be useful
to identify the emerging economies. The definitions of "emerging economies" are
multiple and continually evolving. Initially, in the early 1980s, the fast growing and
export oriented Asian and Latin American economies were named the "newly indus-
trializing economies" (NIE). But by the 1990s, most developing countries adopted
globalization/liberalization; therefore, a broader term "emerging market economies"
was introduced. Along with the Asian and Latin American countries, this group
included countries from Africa and West Asia. In the beginning of the 2000s, Brazil,
Russia, India, China and South Africa (BRICS) were identified as the new drivers
of global economic growth (O'Neill, 2001). But since other large economies have
embarked on a similar growth path, some other terminologies have been coined to
include them, e.g. Mexico, Indonesia, Nigeria, Turkey and South Africa (MINTS),
Next Eleven (Bangladesh, Egypt, Indonesia, Iran, Mexico, Nigeria, Pakistan, Philippines, South Korea, Turkey, and Vietnam), Colombia, Indonesia, Vietnam, Egypt,
Turkey and South Africa (CIVETS). There are no common criteria for the classification of these countries. Different sources list different countries in their list of
emerging economies. Some authors have tried to provide a categorization of such

powers using criteria of growth, intermediate income, institutional transformations and economic opening. According to Nadvi (2014), the following six factors make the 'emerging economies' different from other developing countries:

- strong economic growth since the 1990s
- significant participation in global trade
- a large domestic market
- strong state involvement in the economy
- availability of local private and public capital for investment
- growing space for civil society in public-private discourse.

How these emerging economies will affect the global standards making process will depend mainly on two factors: (i) what are their preferences and how they wish to (if they wish at all) to participate in the process. (ii) whether they have the *capacity* to influence the global standards making process. Increasing economic weight may not be enough; appropriate strategy may prove equally important. Nadvi (2014) has identified the main processes and channels through which the emerging economies can engage with the global standards setting process.

2.1   Via Supply-Side Participation

Two most important phenomena of the global economy in the past two decades have been the shift in geography of global production and the increasing fragmentation of production across borders. The presence of the emerging economies in global value chains (GVCs) is rising (Lee & Gereffi, 2015). The production of goods and services is increasingly carried out wherever the necessary skills and materials are available at competitive cost and quality (OECD, 2013). The share of richer countries in total value added that was generated in all manufacturing GVCs declined from 74% in 1995 to 56% in 2008; the share of Japan and East Asian NIEs dropped from 21 to 11%; emerging economies' share of value added in manufacturing increased by 18%. Half of this increase can be accrued to China. China's global share rose from 4 to 13%. Brazil, Russia, India and Mexico also increased their global share. During this period, 42 million manufacturing jobs were added in China, 20 million in India, 6 million in Brazil and 2 million in Mexico (Timmer, Erumban, Los, Stehrer, & de Vries, 2014). This shifting pattern was exacerbated by the 2008–2009 global recession. The major brunt of this recession was borne by the developed countries, whereas large emerging economies such as China, India and Brazil suffered relatively less. In 2005–2010, the merchandise imports of the European Union and the USA increased only by 27 and 14%, respectively, while emerging economies expanded their merchandise imports much faster: Brazil (147%), India (129%), China (111%) and South Africa (51%) (WTO, 2011). The import growth in emerging economies is also driven by rising demand for intermediate goods and raw materials because manufacturing GVCs are concentrated in those economies, as discussed above (Kaplinsky, Terheggen, & Tijaja, 2011).

This phenomenon is already impacting trade and investment patterns and policies, and it has also triggered concerns about standards. In a world dominated by GVCs, protecting final consumers through appropriate quality standards and on the supply side protecting the interests of the labourers by enforcing occupational safety and health becomes complicated. The richer countries have already faced challenges over the governance of labour and environmental standards. The insertion of emerging economies in the global value chains is expected to change the standards making process. But to predict exactly how it will change requires more evidence-based research. It has also to be borne in mind that the emerging economies are not only suppliers in these value chains but also they are increasingly becoming organizers and value chain leading firms. Now, it remains to be seen if the emerging economy firms face the same pressure that western firms have been facing to address the issue of labour and environmental standards and if so, how they tackle it.

2.2   Via Demand-Side Participation

Not only in the production process but also on the consumption side, the emerging economies have emerged as major consumers in the global market. During the recent global recession, markets shifted from Europe and North America towards the East and the Global South. The fact that a significant proportion of the global middle class is located in the emerging economies will have significant consequence on the process of global standards (Guarín & Knorringa, 2014). The implications of this will depend upon the behaviour patterns of global consumers. Western consumers have already shown their sensitivity towards health and safety criteria, and quality of labour and environmental conditions of the production process. Whether the emerging economies' consumers' behaviour will converge and create a "global consumer culture" where social and environmental impacts, along with price and quality, impact consumption decisions (Alden, Steenkamp, & Batra, 1999), remains to be seen. As Elliott and Freeman (2001) put it:

> The *sine qua non* of activist efforts to improve labour standards around the world is that consumers care about the conditions of the workers who make the items they consume. If consumers do not care or do not associate the conditions with their consumption, human rights vigilantes could not pressure firms to improve working conditions. (Elliott & Freeman, 2001, p. 48)

There is evidence that this has happened in the developed world. Organized consumer pressure and effective state action have been able to improve working conditions of labourers (Trumbull, 2006). But Guarín and Knorringa (2014) claim that none of these conditions can be assumed for the emerging economies for various reasons. First, organized consumer mobilization is still relatively weak in these countries and the presence of NGO and other civil societies is not significant. Kaplinsky and Farooki (2010) share a similar perspective. The fact that developing and emerging economies have relatively low incomes and weak state institutions will prevent them from developing private standards and they will continue to demand cheap undifferentiated commodities.

2.3 Via Civil Society and State and Private Actors

The other channels through which emerging economies can impact global standards are state, private actors and civil society bodies. Studies like Bartley (2007) and O'Rourke (2003) found that civil society has emerged as one of the most effective proponents of strong labour and environmental standards. In many western developed economies, these work as a primary stakeholder in negotiating labour, health and safety and environmental standards. But it is still not certain whether the same thing will happen in the emerging economies. To what extent civil societies in the emerging economies will be able to perform an active role is yet to be seen.

While much of the recent agenda on labour, environmental and social standards in production has been driven by private actors (private firms and NGOs), the importance of state in global governance is increasing. The state provides the regulatory framework, promulgating laws and ensuring their judicial enforcement, under which labour and environmental considerations are structured. It will be interesting to see how the governments of the emerging economies address these issues.

3 Empirical Analysis

3.1 Description of Data

For the econometric analysis, I estimate the effect of labour standards on the export of manufacturing goods. The intention is to see if there is any significant effect of stricter labour standards on exports and also to check if this effect is different across countries at different levels of economic growth. Following the specifications in Dehejia and Samy (2008), my dependent variable in the econometric analysis is *lexm*, which is log of exports of manufacturing goods as a percentage of merchandise export. The data for *lexm* was collected from the World Development Indicators data set of the World Bank. The control variables of this analysis are *lpop* and *lenroll*. The *lpop* variable is the log of working age population to land ratio of a country. The *lenroll* variable is the lagged measure of log of gross enrolment in secondary education based on secondary education duration in each country. This is considered as a proxy of the human capital stock in a country. Although average years of education as computed by Barro-Lee are a better measure of human capital, their data set is on a five-yearly basis. A yearly estimate of average years of education is available only for EU countries. Since for my purpose, I require yearly data, I have used the log of gross enrolment in secondary education lagged based on secondary education duration in each country.

The purpose of taking lagged measure of this variable is that any change in gross enrolment in secondary education will have an impact on the stock of human capital only after the cohort passes out at the end of secondary education. There are some obvious problems with using this as a measure for human capital. It does not take into account that many students will actually not complete their secondary education. Despite this problem, it has been used previously in the literature as proxy of human capital. Both *lpop* and *lenroll* are proxy for the determinants of comparative advantage and they are expected to have a positive relation with *lexm*. The data for *lpop* and *lenroll* were collected from the World Development Indicators data set of the World Bank as well. Labour standards are our main dependent variable. To measure labour standards, I have first looked at whether ILO labour conventions have been ratified or not. There are eight basic labour conventions (Table 1). The variable of interest is "fundamental", which is an index measuring the number of conventions that have been ratified or not. If a country has not ratified any of these conventions, its score is 0, while if it has ratified all, its score becomes 8.

For labour standards, I looked at different sources and used different types of measurements. The first set of variables describes whether the countries have ratified the eight core ILO conventions namely:

- C87—Freedom of Association and Protection of the Right to Organize Convention, 1948
- C98—Right to Organize and Collective Bargaining Convention, 1949
- C100—Equal Remuneration Convention, 1951
- C111—Discrimination (Employment and Occupation) Convention, 1958
- C29—Forced Labour Convention, 1930
- C105—Abolition of Forced Labour Convention, 1957
- C138—Minimum Age Convention, 1973
- C182—Worst Forms of Child Labour Convention, 1999

This data is collected from the ILOLEX data set of the ILO. I first created four variables, namely free_asso, disc, forced_lab and child_lab. If any of the core conventions are ratified in a country, it takes value 1 in that country and otherwise 0. free_asso is C87 + C98 and measures out of two core conventions regarding free association of labour how many have been ratified. It can take values 0, 1 or 2. If neither C87 nor C98 is ratified, *free_asso* is 0 and if both are ratified, then *free_asso* is 2. If only 1 of the 2 is ratified, then *free_asso* is 1. Similarly, *disc* = C100 + C111, *forced_lab* = C29 + C105 and *child_lab* = C138 + C182. Then, there is another variable which is *fundamental* and it measures how many of all 8 fundamental labour conventions have been ratified by a country. It takes value from 0 to 8 and it is the sum of *free_asso, disc, forced_lab and child_lab*.

Besides using these variables measuring how many of the labour conventions have been ratified, I also look at actual measures of labour standards. Ratification does not mean that labour standards have actually been made stricter. So I have considered other variables and indices that measure actual condition of labour rights. The primary reason being that ratification of a labour convention does not imply that it is actually being implemented. The other variables that I look at are *linj, lstrike, lunion* and *lhou*.

Table 1 Core conventions of ILO

Freedom of association		Forced labour		Discrimination		Child labour	
C087	C098	C029	C105	C100	C111	C138	C182
Freedom of Association and Protection of the Right to Organize Convention, 1948	Right to Organize and Collective Bargaining Convention, 1949	Forced Labour Convention, 1973	Abolition of Forced Labour Convention, 1957	Equal Remuneration Convention, 1951	Discrimination (Employment and Occupation) Convention, 1958	Minimum Age Convention, 1973	Worst Forms of Child Labour Convention, 1999

Source Author's compilation

These variables have been constructed following Dehejia and Samy (2008) and the source is the ILO database LABORSTA. The *linj* variable is the log of the number of fatal injuries in the manufacturing sector per 100,000 employees. It is an indicator of the safety of labour at the workplace. The *lstrike* variable measures the number of strikes and lockouts in the manufacturing sector in a year. While the *lunion* variable is the log of trade union density in the manufacturing sector of a country. Both these variables express the extent to which labourers are free to associate and organize themselves and to what extent they are able to express their concerns and opinions. The *lhou* variable that I use is the log of average hours actually worked in a week for the manufacturing sector. The *lhou* variable is a proxy of the extent to which labourers have rights and are not overworked and exploited.

Along with these variables that indicate the actual condition of labourers in a country, I use another index of labour rights called *labuno*. The index is taken from the Mosley Uno data set that they use in their "Globalization and Collective Labour Rights Racing to the Bottom or Climbing to the Top? Economic Globalization and Collective Labour rights", *Comparative Political Studies* (2007). They created the data set "which consists of annual observations from 1985 to 2002, focusing on the legal rights of workers to freedom of association and collective bargaining, key elements of core labour standards, and respect for these rights (when present) in practice".

Following Kucera's (2002) template, they record 37 types of violations of labour rights in six categories. If there is at least one violation of any particular type out of the 37, the country is given a score of 1 for that year, otherwise 0. Then that score is multiplied by a weighting factor, before adding all 37 together. They also then reversed the index so that lower values of the index mean higher labour standards. This makes interpretation of results easy. Theoretically, their index can range from 0 to 76.5. They collect the data on labour rights violation from the following sources "U.S. State Department Annual Reports on Human Rights Practices; International Labour Organization Committee of Experts on the Applications of Conventions and Recommendations, and Committee on Freedom of Association reports; and the International Confederation of Free Trade Unions (ICFTU) Annual Survey of Violations of Trade Union Rights (ICFTU reports, Weisband & Colvin, 2000)". I have used this index calling it *labuno* as an alternative measure of the condition of labour rights. The *labuno* variable is available for the period from 1985 to 2002. Table 2 is the summary statistic for the variables I have used in my empirical analysis.

4   Results

For the econometric analysis, I have done a cross-country regression with country-fixed effects using a panel data set over the year 1980–2014, adjusted for cluster robust standard errors. Since I have used different specifications, the number of countries and the number of years were different in different equations based on data availability. The maximum number of countries considered is 163. Another point to

Table 2 Summary statistic

Variable	N	Mean	P50	Sd	Min	Max
Lexm	4424	−1.387063	−0.9064129	1.473896	−15.95403	−0.0085644
Lpop	4270	3.650069	3.781378	1.522887	−0.1453724	9.656001
Lenroll	3289	4.035252	4.304307	0.713328	−0.9469046	5.079032
free_asso	4178	1.56989	2	0.72377	0	2
forced_lab	4178	1.707516	2	0.6084915	0	2
Disc	4178	1.637626	2	0.7042001	0	2
child_lab	4178	0.9497367	1	0.8857995	0	2
Fundamental	4178	5.864768	6	2.21561	0	8
Linj	533	−2.557212	−2.488915	1.291608	−9.21034	0.3074847
Lstrike	724	3.146752	2.995732	1.929084	0	7.578146
Lunion	590	3.409722	3.355152	0.8228831	0.2623642	5.630495
Lhou	441	3.731084	3.74242	0.138508	3.104587	4.05889
Labuno	1416	3.032452	3.157	0.4600937	−0.2876821	3.540959

Source Author

remember is that the panel is unbalanced. The time period under consideration also varies under different specifications.

Our general specification is

$$Y_{it} = f(X_{it}, L_{it})$$

where Y_{it} is manufactured exports (*lexm*) of country i at time t as a fraction of country i's merchandise exports at time t, X_{it} refers to a vector of control variables that proxy for the natural determinants of comparative advantage and L_{it} refers to any of the proxies for labour standards outlined in the previous section.

The functional form of the above specification is a log-linear form. In this form, all variables are measured in natural logarithms:

$$\ln Y_{it} = \beta_0 + \beta_1 \ln X_{it} + \beta_2 \ln L_{it} + \mu_i + \varepsilon_{it}$$

μ_i is the country-fixed effect and ε_{it} is the normal disturbance term. I use the fixed effect model because it takes into account time-invariant unobservable country heterogeneity, which could be correlated with the dependent variable, *lexm*. Furthermore, fixed effect model is usually recommended when the number of groups (countries) is less than the number of time periods (years).

Also, to capture if the effect of labour rights on export is different at different level of economic growth, I divide the countries into four categories based on their human development index (HDI) in the year 1990. Then, I look at the effect of labour rights on export for each category of country and see if the effect is different at different levels of income for the country. The results are listed in Table 3.

Table 3 Regression results

Variables	(1) Lexm	(2) Lexm	(3) Lexm	(4) Lexm	(5) Lexm	(6) Lexm
Lpop	0.493 (0.2416104)	0.904 (0.1290931)	−0.0408 (0.972708)	2.048** (0.0010723)	0.685* (0.0477405)	0.930 (0.0761128)
Lenroll	0.307 (0.1424265)	0.114 (0.6362259)	0.143 (0.6672277)	0.539 (0.4459242)	−0.00738 (0.9747039)	0.555 (0.2003024)
Linc	0.137 (0.3455045)	−0.225 (0.4206177)	0.0993 (0.5059766)	−0.266* (0.0252164)	−0.412*** (0.0004154)	0.464 (0.4886492)
Fundamental	0.301* (0.0331073)					
fundamental_inc	−0.0364* (0.0275752)					
Labuno		−0.518 (0.3556718)				
labuno_inc		0.0736 (0.3455462)				
Linj			−0.218 (0.265599)			
linj_inc			0.0270 (0.2422162)			
Lstrike				−0.193 (0.3325992)		
lstrike_inc				0.0210 (0.3475672)		
Lunion					−0.804** (0.0015474)	

(continued)

Table 3 (continued)

Variables	(1) Lexm	(2) Lexm	(3) Lexm	(4) Lexm	(5) Lexm	(6) Lexm
lunion_inc					0.107** (0.0027951)	
Lhou						1.127 (0.462707)
lhou_inc						
_const	-5.453*** (2.32e-06)	-3.632 (0.0998928)	-2.127 (0.4952651)	-9.055*** (7.23e-03)	-0.00991 (0.9909202)	-10.43 (0.1562472)
N	3141	998	413	584	481	364

Source Author
p values in parentheses
*p < 0.05, **p < 0.01, ***p < 0.001

The interaction term between fundamental and income is negative and significant. This means that if a richer country ratifies more labour conventions, its effects on exports will be less positive than what will occur if a comparatively poorer country ratifies the conventions. This is different from our conventional wisdom. Next, I look at the labour rights index by Uno. The coefficients are insignificant. Next, the four equations run regression of different metrices of actual condition of labour rights and their interaction with income. Out of all the metrices, only the interaction term between *lunion* and income is significant. For all other metrices, the coefficients are insignificant. In *lunion*, the interaction term is positive. This result says that as for lower income countries, the negative effect of greater unionization on export is greater than for richer countries. However, if we look at other metrices, we can find no such relation being significant. Although no definite relation comes out between labour rights and export, we can see that the result could depend on whether it is a poor or rich country.

Next tables are regressions done by categorizing countries in three groups based on their 1990 HDI index—high, medium and low. The last equation in each table includes all countries together.

In Table 4, I use free_asso, disc, forced_lab and child_lab as control variables to count how many of the eight core ILO conventions have been ratified by a country.

Table 4 ILO ratification

Variables	(1) (HDI high) Lexm	(2) (HDI medium) Lexm	(3) (HDI low) Lexm	(4) (All countries) Lexm
Lpop	−0.541 (0.4264395)	1.035** (0.0076558)	1.400* (0.0113318)	0.565 (0.1417195)
Lenroll	0.948* (0.0463016)	0.0952 (0.7217355)	0.129 (0.644562)	0.343 (0.1013199)
free_asso	0.147 (0.2096109)	0.274 (0.1698795)	0.120 (0.3417939)	0.343 (0.0604514)
forced_lab	−0.251 (01700512)	−0.171 (0.0570621)	−0.228 (01842495)	−0.198 (0.12476)
Disc	−0.0347 (0.7353269)	−0.0445 (0.7886814)	−0.150 (0.2763615)	0.0350 (0.6731997)
child_lab	−0.0713 (0.2148912)	−0.127* (0.0185727)	−0.0173 (0.8720494)	−0.0734 (0.1593923)
_const	−2.539 (0.420775)	−5.040*** (7.35e−09)	−6.680*** (1.72e−06)	−4.938*** (6.27e−06)
N	1230	919	701	3191

Note Some countries in our sample did not fit into the classification of high, medium and low HDI countries. Therefore, their aggregate number (Column 1 + Column 2 + Column 3) do not equal all countries (Column 4)

Source Author

p values in parentheses

*$p < 0.05$, **$p < 0.01$, ***$p < 0.001$

The only significant result that I find is for middle HDI countries. It shows that if more child labour conventions are ratified, there is a negative effect on exports. Another interesting thing is that free_association has a positive coefficient with exports (although not significant) across all categories of countries, while the rest of the variables capturing ILO core convention ratification like forced labour, discrimination and child_lab has mostly negative coefficient (again not significant).

In Table 5, I use the Labour Rights Index by Uno and check its effect on exports across different categories of countries; no significant effect in any category of country could be found.

In Table 6, using number of fatal injuries per 100,000 employees as the control, I find a significant and negative relation on exports in high HDI countries, i.e. in high

Table 5 Labour rights index-uno

Variables	(1) Lexm	(2) Lexm	(3) Lexm	(4) Lexm
Lpop	−0.228 (0.9090648)	0.579 (0.3887561)	1.666** (0.0022265)	0.895 (0.0906229)
Lenroll	1.216 (0.140168)	0.544 (0.244441)	−0.354 (0.1229523)	0.107 (0.7022585)
Labuno	0.378 (0.1074672)	−0.0720 (0.2523863)	0.0849 (0.3181808)	0.00535 (0.9297625)
Const	−7.077 (0.4572772)	−5.199*** (5.38e−06)	−6.677*** (0.0009374)	−5.226*** (0.0002958)
N	121	413	334	1010

Source Author
p values in parentheses
*p < 0.05, **p < 0.01, ***p < 0.001

Table 6 Injury

Variables	(1) Lexm	(2) Lexm	(3) Lexm	(4) Lexm
Lpop	−2.016*** (0.0000175)	−0.369 (0.6863297)	1.940*** (0.0002723)	−0.0525 (0.9623101)
Lenroll	0.653** (0.0011231)	1.326 (0.1203402)	−0.283 (0.0639346)	0.176 (0.607672)
Linj	−0.0362* (0.024114)	0.0106 (0.8798574)	−0.0532 (0.3860048)	−0.000900 (0.9732771)
Const	5.490*** (0.0001001)	−5.357*** (4.48e−06)	−8.061*** (0.0001462)	−1.434 (0.6677647)
N	225	81	118	434

Source Author
p values in parentheses
*p < 0.05, **p < 0.01, ***p < 0.001

HDI countries, better labour conditions when measured in terms of actual injuries have a significant positive effect on exports. There is no such significant relation between *linj* and *lexp* for middle and low HDI countries.

Table 7 uses extent of strikes in a country as a control, and I could not find any significant effect on exports in any category of countries.

Tables 8 and 9 use trade union density and average hours worked as controls but in neither case could I find any significant effects on export in any category of countries.

From Tables 4, 5, 6, 7, 8 and 9, one common thing that can be observed is that given small sample size, we do not often get significant results but still it suggests that the effects of labour rights on exports is different in countries at different stages of development.

Table 7 Strikes

Variables	(1) Lexm	(2) Lexm	(3) Lexm	(4) Lexm
Lpop	0.0941 (0.7796465)	0.982** (0.0030866)	1.508 (0.115254)	10697l** (0.0098739)
Lenroll	0.0615 (0.6150207)	−0.965 (0.248108)	0.256 (0.7843356)	0.537 (0.4589703)
Lstrike	−0.0207 (0.1962182)	−0.0221 (0.5195374)	−0.0325 (0.7565194)	−0.00961 (0.710336)
Const	−1.012 (0.3401405)	−13.41*** (0.0000147)	−8.237*** (0.0004447)	−9.850*** (7.32e−08)
N	303	144	121	586

Source Author
p values in parentheses
p < 0.05, **p* < 0.01, ***p* < 0.001

Table 8 Trade union density

Variables	(1) Lexm	(2) Lexm	(3) Lexm	(4) Lexm
Lpop	−0.282 (0.3305051)	0.419 (0.4678411)	2.172 (0.1035732)	0.361 (0.3448108)
Lenroll	0.124 (0.2668958)	0.0478 (0.8597926)	−0.740 (0.077984)	0.0617 (0.7343584)
Lunion	0.0296 (0.7253037)	−0.0585 (0.3110582)	0.162 (0.25111)	0.0351 (0.6735284)
Const	−0.186 (0.8701854)	−2.343 (0.2105973)	−8.562 (0.0895013)	−2.410* (0.0249517)
N	328	101	52	481

Source Author
p values in parentheses
p < 0.05, **p* < 0.01, ***p* < 0.001

Table 9 Average hours worked

Variables	(1) Lexm	(2) Lexm	(3) Lexm	(4) Lexm
Lpop	0.478 (0.2449212)	2.472 (0.1569097)	0.400 (0.5545235)	0.730 (0.0584)
Lenroll	0.455 (0.1829141)	0.218 (0.8919357)	0.124 (0.7684215)	0.494 (0.3268562)
Lhou	0.566 (0.1471442)	−1.175 (0.3084337)	0.0426 (0.9370185)	0.0723 (0.8672028)
Const	−5.781* (0.0328725)	−5.421 (0.3456334)	−3.350 (0.3484128)	−5.148* (0.0297518)
N	221	84	54	364

Source Author
p values in parentheses
*$p < 0.05$, **$p < 0.01$, ***$p < 0.001$

5   Conclusion

This paper has examined the effects of labour standards on export performance of countries. I have tried to test the conventional wisdom and belief that low labour standards give a country some advantages in the form of export competitiveness. I also tested if the effect of labour rights on export is different at different levels of economic growth. I found that although no definite relation emerges between labour rights and export performance, the result could depend on whether it is a poor or rich country. Specifically, if a richer country ratifies more labour conventions, its effects on exports will be less positive than what will occur if a comparatively poorer country ratifies the conventions.

But as mentioned at the end of the previous section, although insignificant, we do see in some cases, some of the proxies of labour standards having a positive impact on export performance. This signifies that countries do have an incentive to strengthen their labour conditions to improve export performance, especially if it is a poorer country. Therefore, we may say that the conventional belief that these countries deliberately engage in a race to the bottom may not be true since that may actually harm their interest.

References

Alden, D., Steenkamp, J. E., & Batra, R. (1999). Brand positioning through advertising in Asia, North America, and Europe: The role of global consumer culture. *Journal of Marketing, 63,* 75–87.

Anderson, K. (1996). *Environmental standards and international trade.* University of Adelaide, Centre for International Economic Studies.

Bartley, T. (2007). Institutional emergence in an era of globalization: The rise of transnational private regulation of labor and environmental conditions. *American Journal of Sociology, 113*(2), 297–351.

Brautigam, D. (2009). *The dragon's gift: The real story of China in Africa.* Oxford: Oxford University Press.

Brown, D. K. (2000). *International trade and core labour standards.*

Dehejia, V. H., & Samy, Y. (2008). Labor standards and economic integration in the European Union: An empirical analysis. *Journal of Economic Integration,* 817–847.

Dion, C., Lanoie, P., & Laplante, B. (1997). *Monitoring environmental standards: Do local conditions matter?* Policy Research Working Paper 1701. World Bank: Policy Research Department.

Elliott, K., & Freeman, R. B. (2001). *White hats or don quixotes? Human rights vigilantes in the global economy.* Cambridge: National Bureau of Economic Research.

Guarín, A., & Knorringa, P. (2014). New middle-class consumers in rising powers: Responsible consumption and private standards. *Oxford Development Studies.*

Henderson, J. (2008). China and global development: Towards a global-Asian era? *Contemporary Politics, 14*(4), 375–392.

Kaplinsky, R., & Farooki, M. (2010). *What are the implications for global value chains when the market shifts from the north to the south?* (Working Paper No. 5205). Washington, DC: World Bank.

Kaplinsky, R., & Messner, D. (2008). Introduction: The impact of Asian drivers on the developing world. *World Development, 36*(2), 197–209.

Kaplinsky, R., Terheggen, A., & Tijaja, J. (2011). China as a final market: The Gabon timber and Thai cassava value chains. *World Development, 39*(7), 1177–1190.

Krueger, A. B. (1996). *Observations on international labor standards and trade* (No. w5632). National Bureau of Economic Research.

Kucera, D. (2002). Core labour standards and foreign direct investment. *International Labour Review, 141*(1–2), 31–69.

Lee, J., & Gereffi, G. (2015). Global value chains, rising power firms and economic and social upgrading.

Mah, J. S. (1997). Core labour standards and export performance in developing countries. *The World Economy, 20*(6), 773–785.

Maskus, K. E. (1997). *Should core labor standards be imposed through international trade policy?*

Mosley, L., & Uno, S. (2007). Racing to the bottom or climbing to the top? Economic globalization and collective labour rights. *Comparative Political Studies, 40*(8), 923–948.

Nadvi, K. (2014). "Rising powers" and labour and environmental standards. *Oxford Development Studies, 42*(2), 137–150.

O'Neill, J. (2001). *Building better global economic BRICs* (Goldman Sachs Global Economics Papers No. 66). London: Goldman Sachs.

O'Rourke, D. (2003). Outsourcing regulation: Analyzing nongovernmental systems of labor standards and monitoring. *Policy Studies Journal, 31*(1), 1–29.

Power, M., Giles, M., & Tan-Mullins, M. (2012). *China's resource diplomacy in Africa: Powering development?* London: Palgrave Macmillan.

Sengerberger, W., & Campbell, D. (1994). *Creating economic opportunities: The role of labour standards in economic restructuring.* Geneva: ILO.

Srinivasan, T. N. (1998). Trade and human rights. In *Constituent interests and US trade policies* (Vol. 1, pp. 225–253).

Stephenson, S. M. (1997). *Standards and conformity assessment as nontariff barriers to trade.*

Timmer, M. P., Erumban, A. A., Los, B., Stehrer, R., & de Vries, G. J. (2014). Slicing up global value chains. *Journal of Economic Perspectives, 28*(2), 99–118.

Trumbull, G. (2006). *Consumer capitalism: Politics, product markets, and firm strategy in France and Germany.* Ithaca, NY: Cornell University Press.

OECD, W. UNCTAD. (2013). *Implications of global value chains for trade, investment, development and jobs.* Prepared for the G-20 Leaders Summit, Saint Petersburg, Russian Federation.

Weisband, E., & Colvin, C. J. (2000). An empirical analysis of International Confederation of Free Trade Unions (ICFTU) annual surveys. *Human Rights Quarterly, 22*(1), 167–186.

Weiss, T. G., & Thakur, R. (2006). *The UN and global governance: An idea and its prospects.*

White, B. (1996). *Globalization and the child labour problem.* The Hague: Institute of Social Studies.

WTO. (2011). *International trade statistics 2011.* Geneva: World Trade Organization.

Yeung, H. W.-C. (2009). Regional development and the competitive dynamics of global production networks: An East Asian perspective. *Regional Studies, 43*(3), 325–351.

Part II
Sustainability Standards in Sectoral and Country Contexts

Chapter 8
The Changing Landscape of Sustainability Standards in Indonesia: Potentials and Pitfalls of Making Global Value Chains More Sustainable

Clara Brandi

1 Introduction

Development pathways have to be altered to make them both more environmentally sustainable and socially inclusive.[1] To be environmentally sustainable, development must be reconciled with planetary boundaries. To reduce poverty, development must be inclusive, such that it benefits all members of society. These two approaches can entail both synergies and conflicts. For instance, solar panels can give poor people access to low-carbon energy. Meanwhile, ecologically sustainable energy or food production may increase costs and consumer prices, or production of biofuels may crowd out food production, thereby compromising food security. Synergies have been investigated in focusing on concepts such as the "Green Economy" (UNEP, 2011), "Green Growth" (OECD, 2011) and "Inclusive Green Growth" (World Bank, 2012). UNEP's Green Economy Initiative sets the stage for the transition to a green economy that is low carbon, resource efficient and socially inclusive. OECD's Towards Green Growth Initiative provides a framework for achieving economic growth and development while preventing environmental degradation. World Bank's Inclusive Green Growth sets out a pathway to sustainable development. These concepts explicitly focus on the positive and reinforcing interlinkages between environmental sustainability and development. The related trade-offs, however, have not been in the limelight yet (Brandi, 2016). Against this background, this chapter assesses the potential trade-offs between socio-economic and green dimensions of development in the

---

[1]Substantial parts of this chapter have previously been published in Brandi (2016), "Sustainability Standards and Sustainable Development: Synergies and Trade-offs of Transnational Business Governance", *Sustainable Development*, 25(1), 25–34.

C. Brandi (✉)
German Development Institute/Deutsches Institut Für Entwicklungspolitik (DIE), Bonn, Germany
e-mail: clara.brandi@die-gdi.de

context of sustainability standards for palm oil and proposes practical ways to address these trade-offs.

Palm oil gives rise to both substantial positive socio-economic as well as negative environmental and social impacts, generating important questions at the nexus of environmental sustainability and socio-economic development issues (Brandi, 2015). On the one hand, the palm oil sector poses a lucrative source of income by offering a high return on land and labour and can function as an important engine for rural socio-economic development. At the same time, the palm oil sector has serious negative impacts regarding environmental sustainability, including reduced biodiversity and massive greenhouse gas emissions when forest and peatland are replaced (Danielsen et al., 2009; Sheil et al., 2009). Hosting tropical forests and peatlands that count among the world's largest, Indonesia serves as a good example to illustrate the increasing relevance of sustainability standards in the sector.

Over the last years, rising sustainability concerns regarding palm oil have triggered various standard-setting and certification initiatives. The most important initiative is the Roundtable on Sustainable Palm Oil (RSPO), a private-driven multi-stakeholder standard and certification scheme that entails third-party verification that the product under consideration is in compliance with the given principles and criteria of the RSPO standard. In recent years, there has been a significant increase in regulatory initiatives to develop private voluntary sustainability standards. The literature refers to this boom as the rise of "civil regulation" (Vogel, 2008) or the "certification revolution" (Conroy, 2007).

At the same time, lately, the landscape has started to change. For example, in Indonesia, the government recently introduced the "Indonesian Sustainable Palm Oil" (ISPO) initiative, a mandatory government-led certification scheme. The rise of ISPO illustrates the recent trend in terms of public actors reclaiming certification authority through state-led, mandatory schemes, undermining the private transnational certification institutions in support of government-driven certification regimes (Hospes, 2014; Giessen et al., 2016; Wijaya & Glasbergen, 2016). The interaction between private and public authorities in the governance of environmental and social challenges is still an understudied field of global governance. This paper will shed light on it with a particular emphasis on the effects for smallholders and potential trade-offs between socio-economic and green dimensions of sustainable development.

It is essential to include smallholders into certification schemes—both from an environmental sustainability and from a socio-economic development perspective. Any sustainability standard is more effective from an economic, environmental and social perspective if it includes this important group. At the same time, certification of smallholders is challenging, as it demands a set of financial, managerial and agronomic capacities that smallholders in most cases lack. While smallholder certification can be a promising instrument in order to contribute to inclusive green growth, there are important potential trade-offs between environmental sustainability and inclusive development: First, there is a worry that the diffusion of private standards that aim at enhancing environmental sustainability may undermine the socio-economic situation of smallholders—in so far as standards generate market exclusion. Second, while smallholder certification can generate socio-economic benefits for farmers who are a part of certification schemes, these benefits may have perverse implications for environmental sustainability—in so far as they increase incentives to expand palm oil plantations, including into forested areas. This chapter analyses these trade-offs and discusses practical implications with a view to fostering the synergies between economic and environmental sustainability in the context of sustainability standards and smallholder certification. The chapter focuses on the private-driven RSPO but also discusses the public-driven ISPO and examines what their interaction might imply for the above-mentioned trade-offs.

The findings in this chapter are based on secondary sources as well as primary data collected through a smallholder survey as well as interviews with various stakeholders. To collect the data, field research was conducted within the context of four RSPO smallholder certification projects in four different provinces in Sumatra, comprising both independent and scheme smallholders. The survey was conducted with 196 independent smallholders. In addition, 71 semi-structured interviews with smallholders, heads of small smallholder groups, mill and plantation company staff, and experts were conducted.

The remainder of the chapter is structured as follows. Section 2 underlines the importance of smallholder certification and Sect. 3 outlines the benefits of RSPO certification for smallholders and assesses trade-offs between socio-economic and green dimensions of development in the context of private-driven sustainability standards for palm oil. Section 4 discusses the implications of the interaction between private- and public-driven certification schemes for the trade-offs under consideration. Section 5 offers concluding comments, focusing on how trade-offs in the context of smallholder certification can be managed and what lessons may emerge for other sectors as well as for other countries.

2 The Importance of Smallholder Certification

Rising concerns about the negative effects of palm oil production have led to the emergence of sustainability standards and certification schemes. For palm oil, RSPO is the most prominent private-driven standard-setting body so far (Brandi, 2016, p. 26). RSPO, a multi-stakeholder voluntary initiative founded in 2004, brings together major actors from the palm oil supply chain with NGOs in order to promote the growth and use of sustainable palm oil through credible global standards. Through multi-stakeholder consultations, the Roundtable has developed a set of principles and criteria (P&C) for sustainable palm oil production and has been implementing independent certification of growers according to these P&C since 2008. RSPO standards cover a broad range of sustainability aspects with regard to the environmental and social effects of palm oil production. The relevant certification criteria require the following aspects: compliance with laws and regulations; transparency; economic long-term planning; good agricultural practices; social responsibility for employees and the rights of communities; environmental responsibility; and the protection of high conservation value areas (RSPO, 2007). For each of the criteria, indicators exist that are verified on the ground by auditors during the certification process.

Including smallholders into certification schemes is essential—in the palm oil sectors and beyond it (Brandi, 2016, p. 26). Overall, smallholders account for around 85% of the 525 million farmers worldwide (Nagayets, 2005, p. 2; FAO, 2012, p. 56). These smallholders and their livelihoods are important both from a development as well as from an environment perspective. They can be both a hurdle for the "main-streaming" of certification (Steering Committee of the State-of-Knowledge Assess-ment of Standards and Certification, 2012) or play the beneficial role of "managed ecosystems" (Swinton, 2008). In Indonesia, more than one million smallholders are an essential element of the palm oil sector. They account for 38% of cultivation area and 35% of production output (Indonesian Palm Oil Commission, 2012) and are of central relevance for processes of sector change. A social and sustainability-oriented transformation of the palm oil sector can only be realized on the basis of their cooperation and inclusion in sustainability standards and certification schemes.

Certification schemes have to include the important group of smallholders for two main reasons: for environmental reasons and in order to help smallholders to improve yields and quality of their production and to avoid potential exclusion from standard-sensitive markets.[2]

Environmental Reasons for Smallholder Inclusion The large-scale environmental impacts from oil palm cultivation stated above—greenhouse gas emissions through land-use conversion, loss of biodiversity and deforestation—occur through the expan-sion of large plantations and through smallholder palm oil expansion and production alike. Smallholder certification can be regarded as a potentially promising comple-mentary instrument to the enforcement of environmental laws and regulations in establishing more sustainable oil palm cultivation (Brandi, 2016, pp. 29–30).

Certification causes smallholders to improve their often poor agronomic prac-tices, thereby reducing small-scale negative environmental impacts. Smallholders often use poor agronomic practices when they lack the relevant knowledge relating to integrated pest management, correct application of agrochemicals, soil manage-ment via intercropping, modalities of land conversion (use of fire to clear forest) and the illegality of hunting protected animal species, of which there have been increasing reports over the past several years. Knowledge and capacity-building as well as rising environmental awareness in the process of preparing for the certifica-tion of sustainability standards can generate spill-over effects and help in other fields of environmental action in rural regions. Smallholders using better agronomic prac-tices offer the potential to realise yield increases on already existing cultivation areas. In this way, overall palm oil production can potentially be increased in a sustainable way without converting primary forests.

RSPO aims at reducing negative environmental impacts, including large-scale concerns such as deforestation and associated negative effects on ecosystems. On the ground, as the empirical findings of this study suggest, a private standard like RSPO

---

[2]The remainder of this section is based on Brandi (2016), pp. 29–31.

struggles to effectively combat large-scale problems within the existing institutional framework. At the same time, voluntary standards can contribute towards reducing negative environmental impacts on a small scale. Potential small-scale environmental benefits include reduced chemical usage via the application of an integrated pest management system, soil quality improvements (e.g. higher soil fertility), erosion control, improved waste management and buffer zones near rivers.

Economic Reasons for Smallholder Inclusion Smallholder certification can generate a number of important economic benefits for smallholders, including increases in yields and better quality of fruit and price premiums (Brandi, 2016, p. 29). The improvement of capacities in the process of gaining certification leads to spill-over effects on other activities. The training smallholders receive for better agronomic management, and organisational and economic planning is expected to strongly improve the efficiency of their agricultural and economic activities. Moreover, the potential premium for certified sustainable palm oil paid in international markets or the direct sale of certificates like Green Palm can potentially generate additional income for smallholders and contribute to improving their livelihoods. The certification of smallholders thus offers economic development opportunities, especially for rural regions. Smallholder development and its social multiplier effects are the main drivers for rural development, thus making it essential that smallholders realise the above-stated market access and benefit via certification. Additionally, the certification process can incorporate stronger supply chain cooperation, thus lowering production costs, raising productivity to a better quality level and stabilizing supply through risk diversification.

There are two types of smallholders in Indonesia. While scheme smallholders are tied to a formal partnership, Nucleus Estate Smallholder (NES) scheme, with a palm oil company and are receiving important technical assistance, knowledge and inputs, independent smallholders, on the other hand, operate independently through all phases of production. This chapter puts the spotlight on the latter since information on the certification of independent smallholders is particularly scarce. There have been few smallholder certifications so far, especially independent ones. In 2010, the first Indonesian scheme smallholders were certified under RSPO. In 2012, the first independent smallholders were certified in Thailand. In Indonesia, the first independent smallholders, a smallholder association in Riau, received certification from the RSPO in 2013, constituting the second such certification of independent smallholders in the world. Subsequently, the association of independent smallholders Tajung Sehati in Jambi was also certified under RSPO.

3 Economic and Environmental Sustainability: The Risk of Trade-Offs

To what extent are there trade-offs between socio-economic and environmental sustainability in the context of private-driven oil palm smallholder certification? This section begins by discussing whether the socio-economic dimension of sustainability is coming under pressure in the context of smallholder certification being used as a tool to foster environmental sustainability before it turns to a discussion on whether environmental sustainability is at risk in the context of supporting smallholders to become certified and comply with sustainability standards in the palm oil sector.[3]

Smallholder Exclusion First, there is a worry that the diffusion of standards that aim at enhancing environmental sustainability may undermine the socio-economic situation of smallholders. Current certification schemes might exclude smallholders because they are dominantly designed for large-scale agro-industry requiring costs and capacities that are often out of reach for most smallholders. The concern is that smallholders may be excluded from international markets that demand certified palm oil.

There is no consensus in the literature regarding the question whether and under which conditions standards cause market exclusion for smallholders. While some studies disagree, the literature frequently suggests that, while their impact is context-specific, private standards may indeed undermine smallholder market participation and that the threat of exclusion in case of non-compliance with certification standards can be significant for smallholders (e.g. Herzfeld et al., 2011; Elbehri et al., 2013; Schuster & Maertens, 2013; Loconto & Dankers, 2014). The underlying fear is that smallholders who are not certified cannot gain access to markets that require compliance with sustainability standards and that non-certified smallholders are excluded from these markets. Moreover, most authors argue that stringent standards imperil smallholder participation in global value chains because sourcing from numerous smallholders is more costly for companies, for example, due to higher transaction costs for monitoring conformity and the need for more intensive farm extension (Reardon et al., 1999; Swinnen, 2007). In other words, certification systems could lead to the exclusion of smallholders from international trade. This is a substantive fear among policy makers and development practitioners.

However, the research conducted on smallholder certification in Indonesia has shown that independent smallholders have so far not been confronted with exclusion from markets in general. Only very few independent smallholders mentioned explicitly that they saw a benefit in being able to contribute to satisfy international demand for sustainable palm oil with their production. For instance, China and India, as well as the domestic Indonesian market, are still largely sourcing non-certified palm oil. Since the demand is strong enough to absorb non-certified palm oil, independent smallholders are still able to sell their production output to non-certified mills. Thus, as long as international demand for non-certified palm oil remains unchanged, or rises, and markets requiring compliance with sustainability standards remain small, non-certified smallholders are not confronted with complete market exclusion.

Perverse Incentives Second, while smallholder certification can generate socio-economic benefits for farmers who are a part of certification schemes, above all by

---

[3]This section is based on Brandi (2016), pp. 30–31.

increasing yields, socio-economic benefits of certification may have perverse implications for environmental sustainability. This in turn can lead to increased economic attractiveness of oil palm cultivation and increased financial capacity of the smallholder to buy land for expanding palm oil plantation areas. If expansion takes place in forested areas, it constitutes a contradiction to a key aim of sustainability standards for palm oil. The survey conducted with palm oil smallholders in Indonesia included a question regarding the expansion of their palm oil plots into forested areas. Almost 40% of smallholders who answered the question stated that they would expand into an area that is covered by forest.

Thus, RSPO certification might lead to a perverse incentive scheme concerning expansion into forest areas. Nevertheless, the decision of the smallholder to expand depends on a variety of factors, such as personal motivation, world market prices of palm oil and other financial needs. Nevertheless, this problem of a possible perverse incentive scheme for independent smallholders has to be taken into account in the context of RSPO certification processes.

4   The Changing Standards Landscape and Its Implications

Recently, with the rise of public-driven standards and certification schemes, the landscape of sustainability standards has begun to change. In 2010, ISPO was established, a mandatory government-led certification scheme. The launch of ISPO is largely driven by a struggle between the national level, especially the government and domestic producer companies, and the international level, above all international NGOs and their influence in the RSPO. For instance, the chair of the Indonesian Palm Oil Committee (IPOC) explicitly characterized the challenge of sustainable palm oil as an Indonesian problem that has to be solved at the national level rather than one that concerns the international community. A second important driver for the launch of ISPO was competition for market shares. For instance, the chair of IPOC made it clear that the aim of ISPO is to enhance the competitiveness of Indonesian palm oil in global markets (Suharto, 2010).

What does the interaction between the private-driven and the public-driven certification schemes imply for the trade-offs mentioned above? Overall, ISPO is (even) less demanding than RSPO. First of all, ISPO imposes less stringent requirements for many environmental issues. ISPO lacks 11% of the indicators found in the RSPO, including an indicator on high conservation value (HCV) (Salim, 2014). Moreover, in the context of ISPO, many key social issues are missing or vaguely worded (Paoli, 2013). For instance, ISPO does not contain the concept of "free, prior, informed consent" (FPIC), wherein consent for plantation development or local community land-use change is to be obtained in a "free, prior and informed" way from affected individuals and communities.

What does the launch of ISPO imply for smallholders? On the one hand, the interplay of public and private standards can give rise to inefficiencies and put a burden on producers, especially small ones, if they have to become certified under different standards. On the other hand, public-driven schemes may take better account of small producers or smallholders than private-driven ones in so far as states "claim back their regulatory power, playing back their role in granting and enforcing citizens' rights" (Bartley, 2014). While the potentially dysfunctional interaction of public and private standards can burden producers, especially small ones, the case at hand suggests that the public-driven scheme may actually take better account of small producers or smallholders than private-driven ones. The high financial and administrative costs make certification almost impossible for small producers and smallholders without additional support, potentially leading to their exclusion from the international market. With state-driven schemes like ISPO, states seem to re-claim their role in taking care of their citizens. Indeed, ISPO has put a spotlight on certifying smallholders, arguably a stronger one than the private-driven RSPO, despite efforts to include smallholder interests in that context as well. It is sometimes even argued that ISPO was introduced to eventually develop a standard that is better applicable to smallholders. In 2015, the Indonesian Ministry of Agriculture and UNDP began the process of pilot testing the guidelines for ISPO smallholder certification (UNDP, 2015), addressing the need to focus on smallholders (Salim, 2014). At the same time, smallholders would still be likely to face severe challenges when adopting ISPO (Jong, 2018). Moreover, since there is no comprehensive roadmap for integrating smallholders, the implementation of ISPO in that context might end up being ineffective (Yuliawati, 2016).

Overall, the above-mentioned trend towards more public-driven initiatives might affect potential trade-offs between social and environmental dimensions of sustainability. The case of palm oil suggests that while the public-driven scheme may take better account of small producers or smallholders than the private-driven one, ISPO is less demanding than RSPO in terms of a number of relevant environmental challenges.

5 Conclusion

While sustainability standards and smallholder certification have the potential to create substantial socio-economic benefits for smallholders, large-scale environmental benefits focussing on deforestation and greenhouse gas emissions are found to be difficult to achieve.[4] Only small-scale environmental benefits such as reduced usage of agrochemicals seem realistic. One major reason for limited effectiveness in environmental terms is that sustainability standards like RSPO are not without loopholes and face implementation and control challenges. Overall, private sustainability standards alone can hardly solve all relevant environmental problems of palm oil production, for example, indirect land-use change. In order to be effective, standards

---

[4]*See also* Brandi (2016), pp. 31–32.

need a favourable economic and institutional environment. The formulation of a standard's P&C implies difficult trade-offs thus private sustainability standards cannot provide all-encompassing solutions for all problems. As discussed above, sustainability standards are meant to contribute to solving dilemmas such as that between a lucrative sector of the economy producing income and jobs, on the one hand, and its negative environmental impacts, on the other hand. Yet, the development and implementation of such standards creates new dilemmas.

This chapter has shown that aiming for "sustainable development" or "inclusive green growth" on the basis of smallholder certification is challenging and can entail major trade-offs. First, there is a worry that the diffusion of standards that aim at enhancing environmental sustainability may undermine the socio-economic situation of smallholders. Since smallholders can access certified markets only through group certification, they need to organize cooperatives or other types of smallholder groups. Even more importantly, smallholder certification usually requires external support as it demands capacities that smallholders often lack. The concern is that, without external support, smallholders may, in the future, be excluded from international markets that demand certified palm oil.

Second, while smallholder certification can generate socio-economic benefits for farmers who are a part of certification schemes, these benefits may have perverse implications for environmental sustainability. Training associated with certification can increase the smallholders' productivity and thus their income from palm oil. This in turn can lead to increased economic attractiveness of oil palm cultivation and increased financial capacity of the smallholder to buy land for expanding palm oil plantation areas. If expansion takes place in forested areas, it constitutes a contradiction to a key aim of sustainability standards for palm oil. The current specification of the RSPO P&C thus entails a potential contradiction between RSPO goals to foster socio-economic and environmental sustainability at the same time. Productivity gains related to RSPO certification can potentially lead to increased expansion into forest or protected areas. This perverse incentive scheme might contradict the aim of RSPO to combat deforestation. In order to avoid such contradictory outcomes, control and safeguard mechanisms should be implemented—especially in smallholder certification projects.

More recently, the landscape of sustainability standards has begun to change. In the light of the rise of private-driven certification initiatives, there is a need for more research on the interaction between private- and public- driven certification schemes and its implications for smallholders and for the trade-offs examined in this chapter. In the shorter run, the introduction of state-driven schemes like the one assessed in this chapter arguably creates more fragmentation by being added to the existing ones—especially since they seem to be triggering the introduction of even more national standards in other sectors and in other countries that are following the example set by ISPO. For example, the Indonesian Ministry of Forestry created a mandatory certification system for the forest sector (Giessen et al., 2016) and after the establishment of ISPO, the Ministry of Agriculture initiated a similar approach for the rubber sector asking a third party for the creation of a draft for a national rubber certification scheme. Moreover, the launch of ISPO has triggered the introduction of additional, potentially competing and national standards for palm oil. In 2015, the Government of Malaysia, ranked second in terms of volume after Indonesia, introduced the MSPO standard, explicitly "following in the footsteps of Indonesia" (Adnan, 2013). Moreover, Brazil has also introduced national schemes for palm oil and soy (Hospes, 2014).

More research is also needed on how the shift towards national public-driven certification schemes and their interaction with private-driven governance initiatives affects the environmental, social and economic sustainability of the sectors under consideration in the longer run. In the shorter run, the introduction of national public-driven schemes, at least in the case at hand, seems to be beneficial for smallholders but appears to lead to the introduction of a lower standard, especially from the point of view of environmental sustainability.

How can the trade-offs between economic and environmental sustainability in the context of smallholder certification be managed? One possible approach could be that when joining a smallholder group, smallholders should sign a contract forbidding the establishment of new plots in forested areas—be it nearby or in other provinces. The breach of such a contract should attract the withdrawal of the certificate of the whole group or exclude the particular member of the group in order to generate social pressure. In addition, special training should be provided that focuses on the benefits of environmentally sustainable production for the smallholders. Overall, the environmental aims of smallholder certification should be given the same attention, from the beginning, as the socio-economic aims. Possible contradictions between these two sets of goals should be managed, or at least be made transparent—both in the Indonesian palm oil sector but also in other sectors and in other countries as well.

References

Adnan, H. (2013). National palm oil standard soon. *The Star*. 21 March. Available at URL: http://www.thestar.com.my/Business/Business-News/2013/03/21/National-palm-oil-standard-soon.aspx.

Bartley, T. (2014). Transnational governance and the re-centered state: Sustainability or legality? *Regulation & Governance, 8*, 93–109.

Brandi, C. (2015). Sustainability standards for palm oil—Challenges for smallholder certification under the RSPO. *The Journal of Environment & Development, 24*(3), 1–23.

Brandi, C. (2016). Sustainability standards and sustainable development: Synergies and trade-offs of transnational governance. *Sustainable Development, 25*(1), 25–34.

Conroy, M. E. (2007). *Branded! how the certification revolution is transforming global corporations.* Minneapolis: Consortium Book.

Danielsen, F., et al. (2009). Biofuel plantations on forested lands: Double Jeopardy for biodiversity and climate. *Conservation Biology, 23*, 348–358.

Elbehri, A., Segerstedt, A., & Liu, P. (2013). *Biofuels and the sustainability challenge: A global assessment of sustainability issues, trends and policies for biofuels and related feedstocks.* Rome: FAO.

FAO (Food and Agriculture Organization of the United Nations) (2012). *The state of food and agriculture.* Rome: Author. Retrieved from http://www.fao.org/docrep/017/i3028e/i3028e.pdf.

Giessen, L., Burns, S., Sahide, A., & Wibowo, A. (2016). Governance to government: The strengthened role of state bureaucracies in forest and agricultural certification. *Policy and Society, 35*(1), 71–89.

Herzfeld, T., Drescher, L., & Grebitus, C. (2011). Cross-national adoption of private food quality standards. *Food Policy, 36,* 401–411.

Hospes, O. (2014). Marking the success or end of global multi-stakeholder governance? The rise of national sustainability standards in Indonesia and Brazil for palm oil and soy. *Agriculture and Human Values, 31*(3), 425–437.

Indonesian Palm Oil Commission. (2012). *Indonesian palm oil statistics 2010.* Jakarta: IPOC.

Jong, H. N. (2018). Are small farmers ready as Indonesia looks to impose its palm oil sustainability standard on all? Available at URL: https://www.eco-business.com/news/are-small-farmers-ready-as-indonesia-looks-to-impose-its-palm-oil-sustainability-standard-on-all/.

Loconto, A., & Dankers, C. (2014). *Impact of international voluntary standards on smallholder market participation in developing countries—A review of the literature.* Rome: FAO.

Nagayets, O. (2005). *Small farms: Current status and key trends.* Information brief prepared for The Future of Small Farms Research Workshop at Wye College, UK. Retrieved from http://citeseerx.ist.psu.edu/viewdoc/download?doi=10.1.1.146.4632&rep=rep1&type=pdf.

Organization for Economic Co-operation and Development (OECD). (2011). *Towards green growth.* Paris: Author.

Paoli, G. D., & Yaap, B. (2013). *A comparison of leading palm oil certification standards applied in Indonesia: Towards defining emerging norms of good practices.* Bogor: Daemeter.

Reardon, T., Codron, J. M., Busch, L., Bingen, J., & Harris, C. (1999). Global change in agrifood grades and standards: Agribusiness strategic responses in developing countries. *International Food and Agribusiness Management Review, 2*(3), 421–435.

RSPO. (2007). *RSPO principles & criteria for sustainable palm oil production.* Kuala Lumpur: Roundtable on Sustainable Palm Oil.

Salim, T. (2014). Palm oil certification gets int'l support. *The Jakarta Post.* 4 October. Available at URL: http://www.thejakartapost.com/news/2014/10/04/palm-oil-certification-gets-int-l-support.html.

Schuster, M., & Maertens, M. (2013). Do private standards create exclusive supply chains? New evidence from the Peruvian Asparagus export sector. *Food Policy, 43,* 291–305.

Sheil, D., et al. (2009). The impacts and opportunities of oil palm in Southeast Asia. In *Occasional Paper,* Centre for International Forestry Research (ed.). Bogor: Centre for International Forestry Research.

SCSKASC (Steering Committee of the State-of-Knowledge Assessment of Standards and Certification). (2012). *Toward sustainability: The roles and limitations of certification.* Washington, DC: RESOLVE Inc.

Suharto, R. (2010). Why Indonesia needs ISPO. *The Jakarta Post.* December 2. Available at URL: http://www.thejakartapost.com/news/2010/12/02/why-indonesia-needs-ispo.html.

Swinnen, J. F. M. (2007). *Global supply chains, standards and the poor.* Oxon: CAB International.

Swinton, S. M. (2008). Reimagining Farms as Managed Ecosystems. *Choices, 23*(2), 28–31.

UNDP (United Nations Development Programme) (2015). Indonesia palm oil platform (InPOP). *Newsletter, 15*(1). Jakarta: Author. Available at URL: http://www.undp.org/content/dam/undp/library/Environment%20and%20Energy/Green%20Commodities%20Programme/UNDP%20NewsLetter%20Final%20Final.pdf.

UNEP (United Nations Environment Programme). (2011). *Towards a green economy: Pathways to sustainable development and poverty eradication.* Nairobi: Author.

Vogel, D. (2008). Private global business regulation. *Annual Review of Political Science, 11,* 261–282.

Wijaya, A., & Glasbergen, P. (2016). Toward a new scenario in agricultural sustainability certification? The response of the Indonesian national government to private certification. *The Journal of Environment and Development, 25*(2), 219–246.

World Bank. (2012). *Inclusive green growth: The pathway to sustainable development*. Washington, D.C.: World Bank.

Yuliawati, Devi. (2016). *Power dynamic in smallholders' participation in sustainable certification: A case study of Indonesian sustainable palm oil certification*. Department of Human Geography: University of Lund.

Chapter 9
The Programme for the Endorsement of Forest Certification (PEFC) and Its Contribution to Sustainable Forest Management in Indonesia

Pratiwi Kartika, Hariyadi, and Cerdikwan

1 Introduction

Indonesia has an extensive tropical forest, which accounts for almost half of its land. This signifies not only plentiful resources but also numerous problems such as forest fires, deforestation and illegal logging. Although the government has put in place several regulations to address them, these problems persist. Effort was also taken at the international level, with the international community offering an internationally-recognized, private certification to companies practicing sustainable forest management (SFM). Since the effort is initiated by a private agent, this certification is voluntary. The International Trade Centre (ITC, 2012) reports that there are 17 types of voluntary standards that have been implemented in many countries with many types of products certified. In forest management, so far, there have been two internationally-recognized voluntary sustainability standards (VSS) which can be obtained by any forest concession holder in Indonesia—Forest Stewardship Council (FSC) and Programme for the Endorsement of Forest Certification (PEFC).

VSS, or private voluntary standards (PVS), emerged at a time when inter-state negotiations on collective action for social and environmental concerns had reached a deadlock. Private actors, namely multinational corporations (MNCs) and non-governmental organizations (NGOs) came up with some agreement over good social and environmental practices, known as sustainability standards (Djama, 2011). In many cases, VSS are seen as a more effective way to enforce sustainable practices

P. Kartika
Independent Consultant, Amsterdam, The Netherlands

Hariyadi
Research Centre, Secretariat General of the House of Representatives, Jakarta, Indonesia

Cerdikwan (✉)
Ministry of National Development Planning/National Development Planning Agency (Bappenas), Jakarta, Indonesia
e-mail: cerdikwan@gmail.com

145

amongst the producers than government regulations (Hagen & Alvarez, 2011; Djama, 2011). Thus, VSS are deemed to weaken governments' role. In terms of actual practice, private and public standards are often seen as duplicating, but sometimes, complementing each other (Hagen & Alvarez, 2011). Multiple standards may be harmful for producers due to the larger compliance cost (Hagen & Alvarez, 2011; Ruslandi, Klassen, Romero, & Putz, 2014).

This chapter investigates whether PEFC complements the mandatory standard as well as the FSC, and whether it plays an important role for sustainability practices in the Indonesian forest industry. We focus on PEFC since little attention has so far been given to this standard. FSC, which was introduced in Indonesia in the 1990s, has received much more attention (Ruslandi et al., 2014; Romero et al., 2015). This chapter further aims to analyse whether PEFC is likely to be widely applied in Indonesia and thus help address the forest management problems in the country. This research is based on interviews conducted with a forestry research institution, an Indonesian association of forest concession holders—Indonesian Forestry Certification Cooperation (IFCC) (through which PEFC was introduced in Indonesia) and a certification body. In addition, this research is based on an analysis of documents of PEFC, FSC and of the public mandatory standard, Sustainable Forest Production Management (PHPL).

This chapter proceeds as follows. Section 2 describes forest management problems in Indonesia and a series of government regulations addressing these problems. Section 3 reviews a number of standards existing in the country both in the past and in the present, and discusses whether the PEFC fills in for what was lacking in the PHPL, SVLK (Timber Legality Assurance System), and FSC. Section 4 explores several features indicating PEFC's acceptability in Indonesia and its role in contributing to SFM in the country. Section 5 provides a conclusion on whether PEFC is likely to be widely applied in Indonesia to help remedy the unsustainable practices in Indonesian forestry.

2 Forest Management in Indonesia

Indonesia has an extraordinary biodiversity and huge size of tropical forest. In accordance with Act No. 41/1999 on Forestry, forest area includes conservation forest, protection forest and production forest. Referring to the Forestry Statistics of Indonesia 2013, the total forest including inland water, and coastal and marine ecosystems accounted for 129.43 million hectares (MOEF, 2014) while later statistics (2017) placed the figure at 125.92 million hectares (MOEF 2018). However, Indonesia has been facing daunting challenges to protect and manage its forest resources due to its high rates of deforestation, illegal logging, social frictions over forest rights between the government and local communities, etc. The underlying sources of many, if not most, of these challenges rest on the confusion and disagreement over who should control or own Indonesia's forests (Contreras & Fay, 2005). Research on land-use and remote sensing data reveals that significant forest areas are in fact community-planted agro-forests, agricultural lands and grasslands. The government, however, views them as natural forests or lands to be reforested for timber production, and this often results in conflicts (Contreras & Fay, 2005). Other serious challenges include forest fires and deforestation. The deforestation rate inside and outside forest areas in Indonesia remains high; for the period of 2011–12, it reached a figure of 613,480 ha per year (MOEF, 2014). Through tougher efforts, the government has succeeded in reducing the deforestation rate to 480,010 ha per year for the period of 2016–2017 (MOEF 2018).

To respond to these challenges, the government has in fact launched several tough policies and efforts. Reinforcing the existing legal framework, the government passed the so-called *lex specialis* Act No. 18/2013 on the *Deterring and Combating of Forest Deteriorating Actions*. Partly, these policies aim at reinforcing previous progressive initiatives relating to the reduction of carbon emissions from the forest sector that was launched in October 2009 wherein Indonesia committed to reducing national emissions by 26%, or by as much as 41% against business-as-usual by 2020 with international support (G-20 Leaders Summit, September 2009). Apart from designing related policies to achieve this target, Indonesia embarked on two consecutive two-year moratoriums on forests and peat lands concessions. In 2011, the government issued a presidential decree on the national action plan to reduce GHG emissions. With the new administration, through midterm national development planning 2015–2019, the government embarked on a more ambitious policy route to upgrade SFM and conservation measures (Appendix I, Presidential Decree No. 2/2015). For the post 2020 period, the government envisions a progression beyond its existing commitment to emission reductions. Based on the country's emissions level assessment, the government has set an unconditional reduction target of 29% and a conditional reduction target of up to 41% of the business-as-usual scenario by 2030 (UNFCCC, 2016).

Forest management and conservation measures and policies have evolved dynamically over time and they have been determined by both societal values as well as socio-economic and political conditions. Making them work effectively is a serious challenge (Maryudi, 2015). In order to promote SFM in the light of the growing scepticism about the effectiveness of governmental policies and initiatives, and the perceived failure of a global intergovernmental mechanism to stop deforestation and forest degradation, voluntary certification schemes were seen as a viable alternative to sustain nationally existing mandatory policies and regulations (Maryudi, 2015; Van Bueren, 2010).

3   Forest-Related Standards in Indonesia

Forest certification is not new to Indonesia. The country has engaged with forest certification since 1990. Indonesia has its own national forest certification system, called Indonesia Ecolabelling Institute (LEI—*Lembaga Ekolabel Indonesia*), which was introduced in 1997. In 2000, this institute signed a Joint Certification Program (JCP) with the FSC (Muhtaman & Prasetyo, 2006). FSC certification, as an international certification system, has also been available in Indonesia for some years. In 2009, the government started the mandatory certification programmes—PHPL (Sustainable Production Forest Management) and SVLK (Timber Legality Assurance Scheme).

PHPL was endorsed through several government regulations, i.e. Govt. Reg. No. 6/2007 *junto* No. 3/2008 on Forest Governance, the Establishment of Forest Management Plans and Forest Utilization, and MOEF Reg. No. 38/Menhut-II/2009 *junto* Permenhut P.68/Menhut-II/2011, *junto* Permenhut P.45/Menhut-II/2012, *junto* Permenhut P.42/Menhut-II/2013 on Standards and Guidelines for the Assessment of the Sustainability Performance of Production Forest Management and for Timber Legality Assurance for Concession Holders or People's Forests (Nurtjahjawilasa, Duryat, Yasman, Septiani, & Lasmini, 2013). This programme aims to enforce the existing laws in order to ensure that forest management is subject to sustainability principles. Since this programme is a mandatory government instrument, it does not relate to the technical issue of trade of forest products and is not targeted at fulfilling market demands. The programme sets five basic criteria relating to the following aspects: (1) legality and security of forest resources; (2) product sustainability; (3) conservation, ecology and environment; (4) economic benefits and (5) institutions (Nurtjahjawilasa et al., 2013). To measure the degree to which PHPL is performed by a forest management unit, there is measurement guidance and standardization. This standardization and guidance are then used as instruments for the certification process by an independent assessor.

SVLK is a mandatory tracking system, effective since 2009, which was developed by involving multistakeholders to ensure the legality of sources from which timber is being traded in Indonesia. The system seeks to improve forest management and to maintain the credibility and legality of Indonesian timber. It was eventually integrated into the PHPL programme. Pursuant to the Ministry of Trade's Regulation No. 64 in 2012, there are 40 timber-based products obliged to obtain the SVLK certificate. The SVLK audit is performed by a certification body which has been certified by the National Accreditation Committee (KAN) to be a Timber Legality Verification Body (LV-LK) in line with MOEF's Decree. This policy reflects the government's commitment to fight illegal logging and illegal timber trading and to fulfil international market demand for certified legal timber—in particular from the European Union (EU), USA, Japan and Australia. This system can be seen as a "national incentive" to respond to the increasing demand for timber legality certification schemes from abroad, such as FSC and PEFC (Ministry of Environment and Forestry/MOEF, 2016). By the end of 2016, about 24 million hectares of forest and 2843 forest-based industries were SVLK certified (The Jakarta Post, 2016).

Obtaining certification is not always easy, and there are several barriers that prevent or discourage voluntary certification in particular. Bartley (2010) and Ruslandi et al. (2014), in their study of FSC certification in Indonesia, point to a lack of market incentive as one of the barriers. The EU, as the most green-conscious market, is apparently not Indonesia's largest export destination for timber and timber products. Another barrier is the high cost of achieving the standards required by

Table 1 Forest management components and their references to FSC and PEFC principles

Forest management components used in this study	FSC principles	PEFC principles
Compliance with laws and satisfaction of financial obligations	1	1
Implementation of reduced-impact logging	5, 6, 7, 8	2, 3, 4, 6
Social impact assessment and community development programs	3, 4	9, 10
Environmental management and monitoring plans	6, 8	2, 6, 3, 4
Biodiversity conservation	9	7
Worker rights, health and safety	4	11
Yield sustainability and silviculture	7, 8, 10	2, 3, 5, 8

Source Columns 1 and 2 from Ruslandi et al. (2014); Column 3 authors' elaboration

FSC. To obtain the certificate, a concession has to pay audit fees, make infrastructure improvements and forgo the profits from unsustainable practices. From the five concession areas that Ruslandi et al. (2014) focus on in their research, the concessions needed time as long as from 3 to 10 years to get the FSC certificate. Another international voluntary certificate introduced in Indonesia is PEFC. The Indonesia Forest Certification Cooperation (IFCC), which introduced PEFC in Indonesia, was established in 2011, and the standards of PEFC Indonesia were endorsed in 2014.

Comparison of PEFC, FSC and Government Regulations

To get an idea of whether PEFC, FSC and government regulations are substitutable or complementary, the three standards are compared across seven forest management components. Each component is matched to its reference in PEFC and FSC principles, respectively (Table 1).

Referring to the seven forest management components above, Table 2 comparatively displays governmental regulations, FSC and PEFC requirements. Features of the requirements of the two voluntary certification schemes will be elaborated subsequently.

With regard to *compliance with regulations and satisfaction of financial obligations*, both PEFC and FSC strengthen government regulations. However, PEFC explicitly mentions that concessions have to comply with the SVLK—the public mandatory standard. This implies that in this regard, PEFC does not want to be contradictory to government regulations. In addition, PEFC has some additional requirements such as to identify an adequate infrastructure for delivery of goods and protection of ecosystem, and to carry out R&D activities. However, in general, PEFC has many similarities with FSC, e.g. concessions have to abide with national legislations, pay all of the financial obligations to the government, and state explicitly their commitment to SFM.

As for the *implementation of reduced-impact logging (RIL)*, the PEFC requirement is similar to that of FSC as it includes criteria, e.g. on tree felling, bucking and log yarding, as well as on soil and water protection functions. Since the implementation

Table 2 Comparing governmental regulations and voluntary certification schemes' requirements

Forest management components	Government regulations	FSC requirements	PEFC requirements
Compliance with regulations and satisfaction of financial obligations	Comply with TPTI rules; Comply with labour and environmental laws; Pay reforestation fees (DR) and forest royalties (PSDH); Compensate local communities (about USD1/m^3 in Kalimantan and USD10/m^3 in Papua); Issuance of annual cutting permits and license renewals conditional on legal compliance, as determined by external auditors (SVLK)	In addition to complying with national and local laws, concession should recognize and respect local community rules; negotiate and make an agreement on the compensation fee for the communities; deal with FSC rules that sometimes contradict national regulations (e.g. SILIN rules require unsustainable logging intensities); provide evidence of balanced attention to social, ecological, and production issues and provide documentation for forest delineation and resolve any related conflicts	Similar to FSC requirements, with additional requirement that concessions explicitly comply with SVLK, to identify an adequate infrastructure for delivery of goods and protection of ecosystem, and to carry out R&D activities
Implement reduced-impact logging (RIL)	RIL is the MOEF's principal proxy for SFM in their mandatory forest certification program (PHPL); Prepare tree position maps and plan logging roads, but these are only administrative requirements	Pre-harvest timber inventories and contour mapping; Harvest plans to reflect established standards for operations, environmental protection and utilization; Felling and bucking methods to prioritise worker safety, ensure efficiency, and minimize logging waste Efficient and low environmental impact skidding with planning and operational controls down to the individual tree level Deactivation activities (e.g.post-logging road and skid trail closure) to reduce soil erosion and restrict illegal access Construct and maintain logging roads so as to minimize soil erosion and facilitate log transport Monitor compliance with RIL guidelines and ensure company-wide utilization RIL training and supervision	Similar to FSC requirements, RIL is a must in PEFC, which includes requirements on tree felling, bucking and log yarding as well as on soil and water protection functions

(continued)

Table 2   (continued)

Forest management components	Government regulations	FSC requirements	PEFC requirements
Environmental management and monitoring plan	Prepare environmental management and monitoring plans (*Analisis Dampak Lingkungan*-AMDAL) for reduction and monitoring of soil erosion, protection of flora and fauna, and community development programs; Prepare annual reports on plan implementation	Integration of monitoring protocols and results into forest management plans as well as making public the results of these monitoring activities; Infrastructure changes generally required for fuel handling, recycling and general waste management	Requiring the documentation of measures regarding land use, forest protection functions, and forest fire prevention, amongst others. In contrast to FSC, PEFC also requires an R&D plan. However, PEFC does not mention detailed requirements
Biodiversity conservation	No explicit regulations require biodiversity conservation at the concession level. Small portions of concessions should be set aside to protect genetic resources	Extensive training and substantial investments in external consultants are required for HCVF surveys and development of biodiversity management plans; Other required HCVF-related activities include stakeholder consultations and incorporation of habitat protection and monitoring of planning and operational procedures	Identify, maintain and repair the habitat of protected flora and fauna, endemic, rare and threatened/endangered species and features of special biological interests in accordance with the regulations/conventions; Identify key protected and endangered fauna species, their habitats and migration patterns, including landscape consideration; and apply appropriate management measures to minimize the pressure of forest operations on those species as well as to minimize potential negative impacts of those species on local communities; Carry out environmental impact assessment of the potential impacts on protected flora and fauna, endemic, rare and threatened/endangered species; and incorporate measures to mitigate those impacts and disruptions;The protected and endangered flora and fauna species shall not be exploited for commercial purposes

(continued)

Table 2 (continued)

Forest management components	Government regulations	FSC requirements	PEFC requirements
Social impact assessment and community development programs	Concessions are required to develop social programs for local people (MOEF Decree691/Kpts-II/1991)	Social baseline surveys and social impact assessments; Help with community development programs using participatory processes; Monitor social impacts and evaluate programme effectiveness; Resolve land tenure and other rights issues on a case-by-case basis using procedures developed by the concession; All activities that affect communities need to be preceded by community consultations with broad stakeholder participation	Identify, honour, recognize and respect customary rights of the indigenous peoples in compliance with the national legislation and taking into account ILO Convention 169 and the UN Declaration on the Rights of Indigenous Peoples of 2007; Ensure that forest management does not threaten or diminish, either directly or indirectly, the resources or tenure rights of indigenous peoples and minimize any negative impact; Establish a participatory and equitable agreement to manage the forest area based on customary and/or legal rights of the communities; Establish a conflict resolution mechanism, which shall be designed in a participatory manner, and mutually accepted and agreed; Carry out a social impact assessment of forest management activities
Worker rights, health and safety	Concessions should follow the labour law (Law 13/2003) and related regulations	Comply with all national regulations and international conventions related to workers; Proper safety equipment provided and utilized; Adequate training and supervision provided and documented	Comply with all national regulations and international conventions related to normative rights of the workers; Give workers access to support for their collective bargaining; Provide workers with adequate facilities and infrastructure; To have systems to detect and avoid/respond to potential threats to the health and safety of workers and their workplace environment

(continued)

Table 2 (continued)

Forest management components	Government regulations	FSC requirements	PEFC requirements
Yield sustainability and silviculture	Comply with TPTI (MoF Decree 485/Kpts/II/ 1989 and MoFDecree P.11/Menhut- II/2009)	Intensive growth and yield monitoring are required; Harvest levels should be revised based on monitoring results; Logging intensities should be reduced, and logging cycles lengthened	PEFC requires merely general things about yield sustainability and silviculture. It only mentions that the management plan has to include silviculture technique and that the harvest rate must not exceed the rate of sustainable production

Source Columns 1, 2, and 3 from Ruslandi et al. (2014); Column 4 authors' elaboration

level of government regulations on RIL is low (Ruslandi et al., 2014), PEFC and FSC requirements on RIL strengthen government regulation.

Regarding their *environmental management and monitoring plan*, PEFC requires concessions to provide documentation of measures relating to land use, forest protection functions and forest fire prevention. It also requires an R&D plan. In this regard, the PEFC requirement is in line with those of the government and FSC. However, the FSC requirement is more detailed than that of PEFC. For instance, FSC lists examples of particular activities that have to be mentioned in the evaluation report if those activities are to be conducted by concessions in future. FSC also requires concessions to include particular measures such as water flow management in their plan.

Biodiversity conservation and protection: Compared to governmental regulations and FSC, the PEFC scheme has set at least two important emphases: (1) the importance of not only maintaining the (key) protected flora and fauna, endemic, rare and threatened/endangered species and their habitats in accordance with the national regulations and international conventions but also repairing their habitat and features of special biological interests and (2) the obligation to carry out the environmental impact assessment (EIA) indicated in point (1) and to incorporate measures to mitigate those impacts and disruptions.

In the framework of forest management components, the PEFC requirements reinforce the existing ones and provide more comprehensive parameters compared to government regulations, i.e. the mandatory PHPL, and also compared to the existing voluntary certification scheme, the FSC. For the government, this is quite important because there are no explicit regulations that require biodiversity protection and conservation at the concession unit level, nor in the framework of the national legislation agenda to amend the specific law concerning biodiversity (Act No. 5/1990) (Prolegnas, 2015; Ruslandi et al., 2014).

Social impacts and community development: Compared to the mandatory PHPL and the FSC, the PEFC provides more detailed parameters on the fulfilment of certification requirements regarding the customary and legal rights of indigenous people.

Several specific aspects of the PEFC scheme can be summarized as follows: (1) the strengthening of the credibility of conflict resolution within the framework of forest management, which is closely related to the customary and legal rights of the indigenous people/community, through a participatory and equitable agreement and institutionalized mechanism; (2) the ambitious obligation to carry out a social impact assessment of forest management activities regarding indigenous people and/or local communities, prior to their implementation; and (3) the obligation for the holder of the forest concession to identify the forest resources that have important value for recreation purposes and to protect them from the negative impacts of recreation activities. This parameter is thus strengthening governmental regulations, which were seen to have failed to enforce community development programmes as an obligation for forest concession holders (Ruslandi et al., 2014).

Workers' normative rights: Both the FSC and the PEFC set more or less comparable requirements regarding the obligation of the forest concession holders to fulfil all related normative rights of workers employed in these sectors in compliance with national regulations and international conventions, both in their operations and workplace infrastructure. However, compared to the FSC scheme, PEFC requirements seem to be slightly more imperative in this case in terms of the workers' rights to collective bargaining with their company. In this regard, the PEFC clearly both complements and strengthens the governmental regulations.

Yield sustainability and silviculture: PEFC requirements are very general, only requiring that silviculture techniques be included in the management plan, and that the harvest rate of forest products not exceed the rate of sustainable production. FSC, in turn, requires regular monitoring of harvest rates and logging cycles as well as their revision if the rates are not appropriate.

In general, PEFC requirements in Indonesia are not as detailed as those of FSC. For example, the FSC document exemplifies significant activities that have to be included in the EIA that a company has to undertake. Meanwhile, PEFC details only the list of prohibited ingredients for pesticides. Another notable difference is that PEFC mentions several times that it requires concessions to be in compliance with national legislation including SVLK. This means that PEFC does not want to be contradictory to government regulations, and perhaps wants to gain the government's endorsement. This also indicates that PEFC does not substitute government regulations.

Having analysed the FSC and PEFC columns in the table above, it seems that PEFC does not add important requirements for SFM. Both FSC and PEFC show many similarities for each forest management component. Therefore, even though FSC and PEFC may not complement each other, both of them complement government regulations.

4 Discussion

4.1 PEFC Acceptability

This section makes an attempt to predict whether PEFC will be widely acceptable in the forest industry in Indonesia. The acceptability depends on PEFC's current status in the country, the nature of its criteria, its differences compared to the existing scheme, i.e. FSC, and the socio-political conditions in the country.

To begin with, it is worth noting that both FSC and PEFC are similar certification systems which focus on source-oriented standards in an effort to achieve SFM and sustainably produced wood. They have the same primary goal, which is to maintain and sustain the ecosystem integrity and its social functions (Van Bueren, 2010) (Table 3). Their mission is, quite simply, sustainable tropical forest management. Therefore, as forest policy analysts say, their proposed solution is developing a set of global sustainable forestry principles and criteria, engaging national and sub-national multi-stakeholder committees to develop regionally appropriate standards, inviting third parties to audit forestry operations for compliance, and finally, certifying those who pass the test (Cashore, Gale, Errol, & Newsom, 2006). However, they are in fact competing agents, and even prominent competitors of one another (Bernstein & Cashore, 2003; Cashore, Gale, Errol, & Newsom, 2006). The FSC, in its operations worldwide, still has to find some accommodation with its competitors (Bernstein & Cashore, 2003).

Normatively, the standards of the PEFC system are adaptable to the national characteristics, involving multiple stakeholders for consensus-based certifications. This system is also developed in a framework of cooperative action and without any negative campaign against any forest management unit. In this regard, the market sees it as a system which is easily accessible. The government itself sees that both the voluntary and mandatory certification systems have different histories, mechanisms and goals, but these schemes continue to have similar frameworks for developing

Table 3 Certification systems relevant to forest management

Source-oriented standards		Goal
SFM/sustainably produced wood	FSC	Maintain and sustain the ecosystem integrity and its social functions
	PEFC international and national systems endorsed by PEFC	
	ISO environment management system	
	RIL standard, Tropical Forest Foundation (USA)	

Source Van Bueren (2010)

Table 4 Comparing voluntary certification schemes and their operations

Dimension	PEFC	FSC
Year of launching	1999	1994
Year of introduction in Indonesia	2014	2000
Area coverage worldwide	304 million hectares	199 million hectares
Area coverage in Indonesia	3.8 million hectares	3.1 million hectares
Number of certificates	60	39
Perception	Forest production industry	Environmental activists
Criteria	Countries create their own standards based on seven meta-standards	Ten rigid principles and criteria, to be applied universally

Sources Buckingham and Jepson (2013); Authors' respondent; FSC (2018); PEFC (2017); IFCC (2018)

criteria and indicators aimed to infuse sustainability principles into forest production and management. Thus, their development and implementation are likely to be mutually reinforcing and synergetic (MOEF, s.a.).

As a market-driven certification scheme, the PEFC system has received relatively positive responses from concession holders. Forest coverage by this certification system has now grown to 304 million hectares worldwide (PEFC, 2017). Meanwhile, the FSC scheme, which was introduced much earlier in 1994, covers only 199 million hectares (FSC, 2018) (Table 4). This suggests that the certification system developed by the PEFC may have wider market acceptability.

In Indonesia, the PEFC certification system was introduced by the Indonesian Forestry Certification Cooperation (IFCC) as its National Governing Body at the end of 2014. Although it is still new and in the development phase, the PEFC scheme has had relatively high acceptability in Indonesia too. Within less than a year following its introduction, for instance, more than 600,000 ha (PEFC, 2015) of the industrial forest plantation (HTI—*Hutan Tanaman Industri*) were certified, a number that reached 3.7 million hectares in early 2018 (IFCC, 2018). At the same point in time, the FSC scheme, which had been introduced in 2000 already, covered Indonesian forest area of 3.1 million hectares (FSC, 2018) (Table 4). This assessment confirms earlier studies suggesting that the attraction to FSC certification remains comparatively weak in developing countries (Bernstein & Cashore, 2003; Cashore, Gale, Errol, & Newsom, 2006). Current data shows that only 23% of FSC-certified forest area is located in developing countries. Under the PEFC scheme, in fact, the share of developing countries in global certified area is even less—at around 9%. Nonetheless, the significance of these numbers should not be exaggerated. Principles introduced within the FSC scheme are universally applied to all countries, while principles under the PEFC scheme are prepared by the respective country and then agreed upon. In this regard, both schemes are rolled out according to their respective characteristics. The FSC scheme is perceived to be designed by environmentalists, whereas the

PEFC is seen to be closer to the interests of forest production industries by analysts such as Buckingham and Jepson (2013). We can easily understand why some studies conclude that getting FSC certification will be time consuming and costly (Bartley 2010; Ruslandi et al., 2014). Requirements and standards imposed by the PEFC are not as tight as those imposed by the FSC. For instance, FSC certification cannot be granted to HTI which was converted from natural forest after November 1994, whereas PEFC certification only \excludes plantation forest which was converted from natural forest after 2010. It is, therefore, the big groups of forest concession holders in Indonesia like the Asia Pulp and Paper (APP) and Asia Pacific Resources International Limited (APRIL Group) that have obtained PEFC certification.

Since the PEFC scheme seems relatively acceptable to the market in terms of its principles and standards, which are nationally adaptable and involve multiple stakeholders, more HTI areas may become PEFC-certified in future. An Indonesian forest business association, for instance, argued that the PEFC system, which is voluntary and market-driven, can be an important instrument to realize SFM as the system is also primarily targeted to achieve economic, social and ecological sustainability. The importance of this ISO-based scheme can also be seen as having strategic value for the market survival of forest concession holders. Indeed, rising concerns of forest companies to join PEFC may hint to its positive economic impact. The voluntary scheme can also strengthen the SFM processes which are normatively imposed by the state institution in charge, namely the MOEF in the context of enforcing the regulation, facilitation and oversight of forest companies' compliance to SFM principles (interview with a business association).

However, forest concession holders in Indonesia continue to face constraints in getting voluntary forest certification—not only because of their different financial capacities to bear the certification costs but also because of different preparation levels (Brockhaus, Obidzinski, Dermawan, Laumonier, & Luttrell, 2012). Companies who got certified have usually applied SFM practices right from the beginning so that they do not have to bear huge certification costs (interview with a forestry researcher).

4.2   The PEFC Scheme's Implications for SFM in Indonesia

As indicated above, PEFC may strengthen the SFM policies that Indonesia has so far undertaken for social and environmental protection including the reduction of carbon emissions from the forest sector. Even though it is comparatively well-accepted by the private sector, this does not mean that PEFC will automatically become the main source of certification. As mentioned before, the government itself has developed and imposed a mandatory certification scheme, PHPL, for forest concession holders. This programme was actually an improved version of a set of voluntary government programmes commissioned by LEI. It resulted from the concerns of environmental activists as well as USA and European tropical timber consumers demanding a certification programme (as a market instrument) for forest products to reduce the pace of tropical forest degradation in the world (MOEF, 2015). However, the programme does not address the technical problem of trade of forest timber and is not targeted to fulfil market demands in the same way as the voluntary certification programmes.

In addition, the Indonesian forest business association has planned to develop a so-called SelfDeclare certification programme. This programme is mandatory for all association members with the purpose of measuring their actual performance in achieving sustainable production forest management. It aims to promote its members' readiness to fulfil the governmental mandatory certification programme and the voluntary market-driven programmes. Since the certification programme is mainly about facilitation, the criteria and indicators used as a basis for evaluation focus on input and processes rather than on output.

Despite the existence of other initiatives, there are prospects for continued and growing acceptance of the PEFC certification scheme in Indonesia. Since the PHPL programme does not necessarily suit market demands, the PEFC scheme, based on nationally adapted principles and standards, may become a viable voluntary alternative.

Indeed, PHPL faces a number of constraints relating to implementing agencies' capacities and poor performance of forestry governance and certain law enforcement activities. The introduction of the FSC and PEFC certification programmes was in part driven by a lack of "market trust". This lack of trust, which had also resulted in the imposition of a due diligence policy for Indonesian forest products earlier on, relates to high corruption levels in Indonesia as well as poor forest management indices (interview with a certification body), amongst other issues. PHPL's performance also depends on the degree to which government-to-government (G-to-G) SFM cooperation mechanisms between Indonesia and the countries of timber product consumers are strengthened. If this is not the case, the credibility of the PHPL scheme as an instrument to achieve SFM may suffer. There is also a growing concern amongst producers that consumers from other major markets outside the USA and Europe are likely to demand tighter certification of forest products as well. In this regard, forest producers have begun to realize that a market-driven voluntary certification scheme such as PEFC is a choice they have to make (interview with a business association).

Overall, the future application and success of the PEFC scheme in Indonesia will be dependent on two significant aspects. First, a high level of support from the main stakeholders, namely civil society, industry and, most importantly, the government, will be required. As in the regional context, voluntary certification programmes in Indonesia have in fact not been getting full support from these main stakeholders. Data shows that the Indonesian government was not supportive enough of some voluntary forest certification schemes, in this case the FSC, while voluntary standards developed by LEI were seen as an important way to preserve national autonomy and sovereignty as well as compatibility with domestic circumstances. In the context of Indonesian industry, the development of LEI standards was at least in part supported by the industry associations. With regard to civil society support, the Rainforest Alliance has played an active role, with its SmartWood programme certifying the first-ever developing country forest operation, *Perum Perhutani*, in

Indonesia in 1990. But, there are also NGOs that have not been supportive of voluntary certification. The World Rainforest Movement, allied with local forestry NGOs such as the Indonesian Forum for the Environment (WALHI—*Wahana Lingkungan Hidup Indonesia*), for instance, called for a moratorium on FSC and LEI certification. This socio-economic and political constellation underlines a viable argument that the Asia-Pacific region basically lacks the general structural conditions for effective forest certification (Cashore, Gale, Errol, & Newsom, 2006).

Second, the legitimacy of PEFC will flow from both domestic and global actors. The importance of the legitimacy issue here can be seen in the context of PEFC's status as a non-state (governance) scheme, which means that it lacks the traditional enforcement capacities associated with the sovereign state in the realm of global governance (Howlett & Ramesh, 1995; Bernstein & Cashore, 2003). Even though voluntary forest certification plays an important role in the absence of binding international law on tropical forest use, its global legitimacy is still contested and this has local repercussions. In terms of domestic legitimacy, stakeholders' hesitant acceptance of FSC is an experience that PEFC should keep in mind. The degree to which the scheme becomes an effective anchor for national SFM in Indonesia and also for the governance of global emissions from the forestry sector remains to be seen.

5   Conclusion

This study investigated whether PEFC as a relatively new forest certification system in Indonesia substitutes or complements the existing forest certification systems, which mainly are FSC and government regulations. In addition, this study also aimed to predict whether concession holders are likely to be further attracted to obtain PEFC certification. In other words, the study sought to understand the role PEFC is likely to play for the purpose of SFM in Indonesia.

This study found that PEFC seems to substitute FSC as both schemes are very similar but FSC requirements are more detailed and stricter than PEFC's and thus attract fewer concession holders. Both PEFC and FSC complement government regulations as both voluntary schemes require higher standards than the government regulations. This indicates that voluntary forest certification schemes can play a role to fill the global forest governance gap in the absence of a binding hard law.

However, to measure PEFC acceptability in Indonesia, two aspects still play an importance role—the degree to which domestic stakeholder support is given, and PEFC's global legitimacy as a non-state scheme. Some of the domestic stakeholders including the government and parts of civil society do not show sufficient support. Thus, its potential contribution to national SFM in Indonesia and, eventually, to the governance of global emissions from the forestry sector remains to be seen.

Future research could delve into the technical requirements of each certification scheme and its applicability in the Indonesian forestry sector. Analysing perceptions of a broad range of stakeholders regarding each scheme is also important in order to determine best practices for forest management.

References

Bartley, T. (2010). Transnational private regulation in practice: The limits of forest and labor standards certification in Indonesia. *Business and Politics., 12*(3), 1–36.

Bernstein, S., & Cashore, B. (2003). Nonstate global governance : Is forest certification a legitimate alternative to a global forest convention? In J. Kirton & M. Trebilcock (Eds.), *Hard choices, soft law: Voluntary standards in global trade, environment and social cohesion in global governance* (pp. 33–64). Ashgate Press.

Brockhaus, M., Obidzinski, K., Dermawan, A., Laumonier, Y., & Luttrell, C. (2012). An overview of forest and land allocation policies in Indonesia: Is the current framework sufficient to meet the needs of REDD+? *Forest Policy and Economics, 18,* 30–37. https://doi.org/10.1016/j.forpol.2011.09.004.

Buckingham, K., & Jepson, P. (2013). Forest certification with Chinese characteristics: State engagement with non-state market-driven governance. *Eurasian Geography and Economics, 54*(3), 280–299.

Cashore, B., Gale, F., Errol, M., & Newsom, D. (2006). Forest certification in developing and transitioning countries. *Environment, 48*(9).

Contreras, A., & Fay, C. (2005). *Strengthening forest management in Indonesia through land tenure reform: Issues and framework for action,* Forest Trends.

Djama, M. (2011). *Articulating private voluntary standards and public regulations.* Paris: CIRAD.

FSC. (2018). *FSC facts & figures.* Retrieved from https://ic.fsc.org/file-download.facts-figures-january-2018.a-3327.pdf.

Hagen, O. v., & Alvarez, G. (2011). *The interplay of public and private standards.* Geneva: International Trade Centre.

Howlett, M., & Ramesh, M. (1995). *Studying public policy: Policy cycles and policy subsystems.* Oxford: Oxford University Press.

IFCC. (2018). *IFCC sustainable forest management certificate holder.* Retrieved from http://www.ifcc-ksk.org/index.php/2015-02-17-06-11-24/2015-02-17-06-12-36.

International Trade Center. (2012). *Market access, transparency and fairness in global trade.* Switzerland: ITC Press.

Maryudi, A. (2015). The political economy of forest land-use, the timber sector, and forest certification. In C. Romero, F. E. Putz, M. R. Guariguata, E.O. Sills, A. Maryudi & Ruslandi (Eds.), *The context of natural forest management and FSC Certification in Indonesia* (Occasional Paper 126). Bogor, Indonesia: Cifor.

Ministry of Forestry. (2014). *Statistik Kementerian Kehutanan 2013.* Jakarta: Ministry of Forestry.

Ministry of Forestry. (2015). *Ministry of forestry, Republic of Indonesia.* Retrieved November 19, 2015, from Kementerian Kehutanan: http://www.dephut.go.id/Halaman/standardisasi_&_lingkungan_kehutanan/info_V02/I_V02.htm.

MOEF. (2016). *What and how SVLK.* Retrieved from http://silk.dephut.go.id/index.php/info/vsvlk/3.

MOEF. (2018). *Statistik Lingkungan Hidup dan Kehutanan Tahun 2017.* Jakarta: Ministry of Environment and Forestry.

Muhtaman, D. R., & Prasetyo, F. A. (2006). Forest certification in Indonesia. In B. Cashore, F. Gale, E. Meidinger, & D. Newsom, (Eds.), *Confronting sustainability: Forest certification in transitioning and developing countries.* Yale School of Forestry and Environmental Study Report no 8.

Nurtjahjawilasa, D. K., Yasman, I., Septiani, Y., & Lasmini. (2013). *Konsep dan kebijakan pengelolaan hutan produksi lestari dan implementasinya (Sustainable forest management/SFM).* Jakarta: Program Terestrial the Nature Conservancy Indonesia.

PEFC. (2015). *Indonesia celebrates its first PEFC-certified forests.* Retrieved from https://www.pefc.org/news-a-media/general-sfm-news/1873-indonesia-celebrates-its-first-pefc-certified-forests.

PEFC. (2017). *PEFC global statistics—SFM & CoC certification.* Retrieved from https://www.pefc.org/images/documents/PEFC_Global_Certificates_-_Sep_2017.pdf.

Prolegnas. (2015 November, 27). *Dewan Perwakilan Rakyat (House of representatives).* Retrieved from Indonesia: http://www.dpr.go.id/uu/prolegnas-long-list.

Romero, C., Putz, F., Guariguata, Sills, E. O., Maryudi, A., & Ruslandi. (2015). *The context of natural forest management and FSC certification in Indonesia.* Bogor: CIFOR.

Ruslandi., Klassen, A., Romero, C., & Putz, F. (2014 June, 1). *Forests under pressure—Local responses to global issues, 32,* 255–272.

UNFCCC. (2016). *First nationally determined contribution, Republic of Indonesia.* Retrieved fromhttps://www.google.com/search?client=firefox-b-d&q=Indonesian+NDC+UNFCCC.

Van Bueren, E. L. (2010). Forest-related standards and certification schemes. *ETFRN News 51,* 11–19. Retrieved from www.etfrn.org/file.php/128/1.2lammerts-van-bueren.pdf.

Chapter 10
Global and National Food Safety and Quality Standards: Implications and Impacts for Farmers in Thailand and India

Sarah Holzapfel and Aimée Hampel-Milagrosa

1 Introduction

In the last three decades, a transformation of the agricultural sector in the developing countries has taken place. The relative importance of staple crops and traditional export commodities (coffee, cacao, tea, sugar, spices and nuts) in agricultural trade and production has declined, and a shift towards high-value products can be observed (Humphrey & Memedovic, 2006; Reardon & Timmer, 2007; World Bank, 2008). In the developing countries, rapid economic growth, urbanization and globalization have induced changes in consumer diets away from staple foods towards an increased consumption of high-value products (Gulati, Minot & Bora, 2007; Pingali, 2007; World Bank, 2008). As a result, the domestic market for high-value products is one of the fastest growing agricultural markets in many developing economies, expanding by 6–7% a year (World Bank, 2008). At the same time, the demand for speciality products and for a year-round supply of highly perishable fruits and vegetables has increased in industrialized countries, creating new exporting opportunities for many developing economies (World Bank, 2008).

However, in recent years, meeting the market requirements in high-value supply chains has become more challenging (Gulati et al., 2007). In particular, high-value export and domestic supply chains in developing countries are increasingly governed by a plethora of public and private food safety and quality standards (Balsevich et al., 2003; Henson & Reardon, 2005). Developed countries' public standards have long been criticized for acting as non-tariff barriers to trade for exports from developing countries (Henson & Caswell, 1999; Henson & Loader, 2001; Otsuki, Wilson

S. Holzapfel (✉)
Office of International Relations and Sustainable Development, Department for Mayoral and City Council's Affairs, Dortmund, Germany
e-mail: Sarah.Holzapfel@gmx.net

A. Hampel-Milagrosa
Asian Development Bank, Mandaluyong, Philippines

© The Editor(s) (if applicable) and The Author(s) 2020
A. Negi et al. (eds.), *Sustainability Standards and Global Governance*,
https://doi.org/10.1007/978-981-15-3473-7_10

163

& Sewadeh, 2001). Private standards, introduced and required by supermarkets, however, often exceed the requirements of public standards and, although voluntary, become mandatory to access high-value markets worldwide (Berdegué, Balsevich, Flores & Reardon, 2005; Dolan & Humphrey, 2000; Elizabeth & Reardon, 2000; Jaffee et al., 2005). The pre-farmgate standard GlobalGAP[1] is the most widely known private standard for good agricultural practices (GAPs). It was developed by a group of European retailers in 1997 with the aim of harmonizing retailers' existing standards and evolved to be a requirement of major retailers worldwide. The main focus of the standard is on food safety, but it also covers aspects of environmental protection, workers' health, safety and welfare, and traceability (GLOBAL GAP, 2012).

There is widespread concern among development practitioners and academics that small-scale farmers will lose access to high-value markets because of their inability to meet stringent private standards, such as GlobalGAP (Graffham, Cooper, Wainwright & MacGregor, 2007; Humphrey & Memedovic, 2006; Jaffee, Henson & Rios, 2011). First, adopting private standards usually entails high compliance and certification costs that disadvantage smallholders. Second, small-scale farmers often lack the technical ability to adapt their farming practices to the requirements of standards (Jaffee et al., 2011; Narrod et al., 2009). Yet, others argue that the challenge can also be turned into an opportunity. Standards are said to encourage new forms of cooperation between producers and agribusinesses, to lead to the upgrading of supply chains and to facilitate access to new remunerative markets (Jaffee, 2003). Moreover, standards are also said to lead to better employment opportunities for rural households, to contribute to better working conditions on farms and to higher welfare for farm workers (Colen, Maertens & Swinnen, 2012; Ehlert, Mithöfer & Waibel, 2014). Seen from this viewpoint, the adoption of standards can lead to higher and more stable incomes and thereby to a reduction of poverty and vulnerability among rural households.

Public and private actors in the developing countries, often supported by development cooperation actors, have reacted to the increased demand for standards in several ways. Public actors have developed national or regional public standards that improve food safety and quality and are more inclusive than international private standards. Private actors, often in cooperation with the public sector, have developed their own national GAP standards that are benchmarked with the international standard GlobalGAP (e.g. ThaiGAP, ChinaGAP, KenyaGAP), but are more adapted to national conditions. More recently, supermarkets in developing countries have started to introduce private GAP standards to substitute for inadequate or missing public standards, to differentiate from produce sold by traditional retailers and to coordinate supply chains (Reardon, Henson & Gulati, 2010).

---

[1] The standard is based on third-party certification, and farmers are audited by certification bodies accredited by Foodplus GmbH, the GLOBALGAP secretariat. GLOBALGAP is jointly governed by retailers and producers. In 2012, 49 retailers and food services were members of GLOBALGAP and 197 producers and suppliers. Of the latter, 32 came from developing countries (GLOBALGAP, 2012).

Given the potential opportunities and challenges of food safety and quality standards, the aim of this chapter is to contribute to the understanding of how public and private actors in developing countries react to global and national standards and to analyse the implications of diverse standards on smallholders in the fruit and vegetable (F&V) value chain. To do this, we have carried out an extensive literature review. In addition, we have conducted semi-structured interviews with farmers, farmer organizations, extension workers, exporters and retailers in the Thai and Indian fruit and vegetable sector, as well as with government officials, researchers and food safety experts.

The proliferation of standards is at different stages in different developing countries. We analyse the evolution and proliferation of standards for the cases of Thailand and India. The two countries differ in several regards: the overall importance of private, international standards, the level of supermarket penetration and the level of engagement of the public and private sectors in standard development and dissemination.

The chapter proceeds as follows. First, we describe how Thailand and India address food safety and quality and how they have reacted to international standards, such as GlobalGAP, by introducing their own local public and private standards. We also discuss the importance of retailers in introducing standards in developing countries' domestic supply chains. Next, we review the literature on the impacts of standards on actors in the Thai and Indian F&V value chain and compare findings among the two country cases. Last, we identify lessons learned from the comparison and provide policy recommendations.

2 Public and Private Food Safety and Quality Standards in Thailand and India

In this section, we look closer into how production and exports have evolved in both countries over the last decade, and into the diversity of food safety and quality standards. This focus is important. While Thailand and India are renowned as strong producers of agricultural commodities in Asia and worldwide, both countries are still plagued with severe food safety and quality problems. Issues of food safety and quality remain a real threat, particularly for exporters who try to respond to heightened global demand while simultaneously adapting to strict global quality standards. With the objective of easing the adaptation process, local governments have assisted producer–exporters by creating domestic standards. However, as the following discussion will show, this has not always been a success.

We begin by describing how production and export of fruits and vegetables have developed in both countries and explain how food safety and quality issues affect exports. We then go on to discuss the evolution of two broad categories of GAP standards that differ in terms of their levels of difficulty and coverage. These are:

Table 1 Types and examples of GAP standards in developing countries

Level 1: Private GAP standards for the high-value export market

- Collective: GlobalGAP
- Chain-specific: Tesco Nature's Choice, Carrefour Quality Line
- National standards developed to achieve GlobalGAP benchmarking status (recognized as GlobalGAP equivalent): ThaiGAP, IndiaGAP and IndGAP

Level 2: Local GAP standards for the high-value domestic market and the export supply chain

- Standards owned by public actors (Q-GAP, revised IndiaGAP)
- Standards owned by private actors (ThaiGAP Level 2, basic IndGAP)

Source Hampel-Milagrosa and Holzapfel (2016)

Level 1 GAP standards for the high-value export market and Level 2 local GAP standards for the high-value domestic market and export supply chain (Table 1).

Level 1 GAP standards are private, third-party standards applied by lead firms in the food chain to meet consumers' concerns over food safety, to differentiate products based on quality attributes, to mitigate commercial risks and to ensure compliance with public regulations. Although voluntary, they are becoming increasingly manda-tory to supply high-value markets worldwide. The most well-known Level 1 standard is the GlobalGAP standard, but there are also several chain-specific GAP standards with similar requirements (e.g. Tesco Nature's Choice). Moreover, both Thailand and India have developed national Level 1 standards (ThaiGAP and IndGAP) with the aim of being recognized as GlobalGAP equivalents. These are more adapted to local circumstances than the GlobalGAP standards, and therefore expected to be easier and less costly to comply with.

Level 2 standards are basic voluntary GAP standards that are introduced either by governments or by private actors or by both collectively as a public–private partner-ship. They are easier to comply with for smallholders than international standards (Level 1) and aim to fulfil two objectives: to ensure food safety in the domestic market and to gradually upgrade food safety systems to facilitate exports and to allow adoption of Level 1 standards (Amekawa, 2013; eFresh Portal, 2016; Korpra-ditskul, Suwannamook, Adulyarattanapan & Damsiri, 2010). Basic GAP standards under Level 2 are diverse: some are not as stringent, whereas others are more chal-lenging to comply with. In our case studies, both the public and private sectors in Thailand and India have introduced their own local Level 2 GAP standards for the high-value domestic markets and the export supply chain, resulting in two coexisting standards and confusion among producers and exporters.

2.1 Production, Exports and Food Safety

Thailand and India are among the largest producers and exporters of horticultural products in the world and among the developing countries most affected by increasing standards (Jaffee et al., 2005; Jairath & Purohit, 2013; Manarungsan et al., 2005). In

2014, India was the second largest producer of fruits (excluding melons) as well as of vegetables (including melons) (FAO, 2010). Thailand was the 14th largest producer of fruits (excluding melons) and the 41st largest producer of vegetables (including melons) (FAO, 2010). Despite high production volumes, Indian fruit and vegetable exports are relatively low. India is the 13th biggest exporter of vegetables (HS 07) and the 21st biggest exporter of fruits (HS 08) (ITC, 2017). One reason for low exports is that production is mainly targeted for domestic consumption. Another reason is producers' failure to adhere to international food safety and quality standards. Thailand, being the 11th biggest exporter of vegetables (HS 07) and the 20th biggest exporter of fruits (HS 08) (ITC, 2017), performs comparably better.

Both Thailand and India suffer from food safety issues which have negatively impacted exports to high-value markets, such as the European Union (EU). Unsafe farming practices are prevalent, resulting in high risks for the consumer and negative health impacts for farmers. Microbial contamination of fruits and vegetables is a problem as a result of poor hygiene practices, the use of untreated manure and polluted irrigation water (Shepard, 2006; UNIDO, NORAD & IDS, 2015). Furthermore, pesticide overuse is common, especially among small-scale farmers, for whom pesticides provide an effective way to manage risks and are frequently applied as a preventive measure. Often, farmers follow a monthly or weekly spraying calendar and apply doses that are higher than what is recommended on the label (Plianbangchang, Jetiyanon & Wittaya-Areekul, 2009; Shepard, 2006). This practice is encouraged by the fact that the physical appearance is the major factor for the determination of the market price in traditional supply chains (Shepard, 2006). For the case of Thailand, a recent study by Wanwimolruk, Phopin, Boonpangrak and Prachayasittikul (2016) showed that EU maximum residue limits (MRLs) were exceeded in 35–71% of the cases, depending on the type of vegetable and the marketing outlet (local market or supermarket).

Thailand's fruit and vegetable exports to the EU fell steadily from 37,414 tons in 2007 to 23,187 tons in 2014 (ITC, 2017) (Table 2),[2] which can partly be attributed to difficulties in meeting the increasingly strict standards in the EU. Within the group of middle-income countries, Thailand has the highest unit and percent rejection rates for exports of agrifood products into the EU and Japan (UNIDO et al., 2015). Thai imports account for 21% of all EU rejections due to pesticide residues (2002–2010), 21% of Japanese rejections due to bacterial contamination (2006–2010) and 22% of Australian rejections on the basis of non-compliance with hygienic conditions/controls (UNIDO et al., 2015).

Similarly, India has also experienced high rejection rates for most of the agricultural commodities it exports. Based on aggregated 2002–2010 data from UNIDO et al. (2015), India ranked fourth among countries with the largest number of agrifood rejections from the EU, with a total of 1145 rejections or equivalent to 127 EU rejections per year. Indian fruits and vegetables rank second to Mexico in terms of

---

[2]HS 0714 (manioc, arrowroot salem, etc.) is excluded from the analysis because almost the entire production of cassava in Thailand is processed into dry chips and pellets and then exported as animal feed (Ratanawaraha, Senanarong & Suriyapan, 2001).

Table 2 Production and export of fruits and vegetables in Thailand and India

Year	Thailand					
	Vegetables (tons)			Fruits (tons)		
	Production[a]	Exports to world[b]	Exports to EU[b]	Production[c]	Exports to world[d]	Exports to EU[d]
2007	2,74,7023	239,281	23,591	12,622,969	752,995	13,823
2008	2,759,375	250,795	22,437	10,993,626	765,847	12,282
2009	3,430,686	251,327	19,036	10,798,782	1,036,019	13,505
2010	3,623,646	220,733	16,333	10,436,562	913,390	11,800
2011	3,833,422	260,643	15,252	10,942,378	1,222,597	11,517
2012	3,817,113	238,359	13,001	11,081,410	1,428,942	15,056
2013	3,903,385	208,473	11,509	10,693,755	1,431,090	10,686
2014	4,112,977	201,548	12,593	11,341,667	1,457,446	10,594
Year	India					
	Vegetables (tons)			Fruits (tons)		
	Production[a]	Exports to world[e]	Exports to EU[e]	Production[c]	Exports to world[d]	Exports to EU[d]
2007	88,532,008	1,524,120	106,756	63,888,880	634,147	119,005
2008	92,214,635	2,262,600	102,825	69,797,425	827,372	153,539
2009	91,441,005	2,483,145	91,034	70,242,281	813,685	130,506
2010	100,652,944	1,716,045	72,823	76,411,205	386,012	121,800
2011	107,050,691	2,177,850	152,743	75,241,396	791,170	114,827
2012	114,332,800	2,347,190	108,255	76,877,434	837,762	121,132
2013	120,992,200	2,621,246	120,320	84,004,249	940,576	182,329
2014	126,578,659	2,533,913	132,597	89,920,608	805,033	144,994

[a] Vegetables Primary (FAOSTAT)
[b] HS 07 edible vegetables and certain roots and tubers, excluding HS 0714 roots and tubers (ICT)
[c] Fruit including melons (FAOSTAT)
[d] HS08 edible fruit and nuts; peel of citrus fruits or melons (ICT)
[b] HS 07 edible vegetables and certain roots and tubers
Sources FAO (2017), ITC (2017)

largest rejection rates for the US market, with a total of 8770 rejections or equivalent to 974 rejections per year (ibid). India joins Turkey, China and Vietnam in having the highest rate of rejections per US$1 million of imports. UNIDO et al. (2015), and Roy and Thorat (2008) report that the most common grounds for rejection of Indian exports to EU are mycotoxins, food/feed additives and bacterial contamination. For produce directed to the American market, the most common reasons for rejection are wrong or inappropriate labelling, unhygienic conditions and bacterial contamination. Such high rates of rejection point to inadequate compliance, or lack thereof, to international standards (ibid). Indian fruit and vegetable exports to the EU, in contrast to Thailand, did not experience a decrease over the period from 2007 to 2014 but increased by 23%. However, the increase in exports is much lower than the increase in exports to world and production increases. Production increased by 42% and exports to the world by 55% over the same period (ITC, 2017).

2.2   Level 1 Standards: Private GAP Standards for the High-Value Export Market

There is considerable evidence that adopting Level 1 private food safety and quality standards such as GlobalGAP is especially challenging for small-scale farmers (Ashraf, Giné & Karlan, 2009; Graffham et al., 2007; Roy & Thorat, 2008). Compliance with standards entails high upfront investments in farm facilities and equipment, which smallholders are often not able to incur, especially if they lack access to credit (Jaffee et al., 2005). In addition, the costs of compliance with standards are, to a large extent, fixed costs, which disadvantage small-scale producers (Chemnitz, 2007; Jaffee et al., 2005). Besides, the technical and information requirements of standards are high. Farmers have to adopt more sophisticated farming practices, and they require producers to be informed about changing requirements of standards. However, acquiring information is also subject to economies of scale (Narrod et al., 2009; Roy & Thorat, 2008). Poor education levels and a lack of access to extension services and training programmes further hinder the implementation of food safety and quality standards by small-scale farmers (Markelova, Meinzen-Dick, Hellin & Dohrn, 2009).

In the light of the above-mentioned challenges, several donors, governments and NGOs in Thailand and India—as in other developing and emerging countries—have initiated development programmes to facilitate the adoption of private standards by small-scale farmers (McCullough, Pingali & Stamoulis, 2008). Most initiatives focused on the GlobalGAP standard, which became increasingly mandatory to supply the European market in the mid-2000s and therewith threatened to exclude small-scale farmers from high-value markets (Humphrey, 2008; Will, 2010). These programmes supported the creation of farmer groups and offered financial assistance, training and information to the groups to achieve certification (Humphrey, 2008; Kersting & Wollni, 2012; Roy & Thorat, 2008). Moreover, public–private partnerships were formed between donors and exporters to enable small-scale farmers to adopt the standard as part of exporter–outgrower schemes (Holzapfel & Wollni, 2014a; Humphrey, 2008; Narrod et al., 2009; Roy & Thorat, 2008).

Notwithstanding these developments, the number of GlobalGAP-certified producers remains low. In 2016, 188 F&V producers in Thailand and 8006 F&V producers in India were GlobalGAP-certified according to the GlobalGAP database. These are low numbers given that there are almost six million farms in Thailand and more than 263 million farms in India. In Thailand, the number of certified producers has even declined. While in 2009, 809 producers in Thailand were certified with GlobalGAP, this number declined continuously until 2015 where only 55 producers were certified (Table 3). In 2016, the number of certified producers again slightly increased to 164 producers (GlobalGAP, 2016). According to Thai experts, the decline in the number of GlobalGAP-certified producers can be explained by a high number of Rapid Alert System for Food and Feed (RASFF) notifications. To avoid a ban by the EU on Thai exports of F&V, the Thai government started in September 2010 to inspect 50% of produce intended for the European market. Earlier, only 10% of produce was randomly sampled. In addition, the government introduced an establishment list for exporters to the EU to increase the level of control. These measures have led to Thai F&V exporters supplying the EU market to limit their production and activities.

A shift from group certification towards individual certification can be observed in the case of Thailand. Compared to individual certification, group certification can make compliance with GlobalGAP feasible for small-scale farmers by reducing the costs of compliance for the individual producers and by making it easier for external service providers to provide farmers with advice and training (Will, 2010). Two main group types exist under GlobalGAP option 2. The first is farmers' association or cooperative where the group is managed by farmers, and the second is an outgrower scheme of a company, where the company organizes smallholders and manages the group (GTZ, 2010). In Thailand, in 2009, only 29 producers were certified under option 1 while 780 farmers were certified in eleven farmer groups. In 2015, only two small producer groups with a total of 12 farmers were certified while the number of producers certified under option 1 increased to 43. This indicates that GlobalGAP adoption by smallholders is extremely challenging and often not sustainable as has also been shown by Holzapfel and Wollni (2014b). The case of India, however, shows that group certification can work. The number of farmers and groups certified in India has steadily increased from 2125 farmers (42 groups) in 2008 to 8006 farmers (87 groups) in 2016.

In addition to programmes supporting smallholders in adopting the GlobalGAP standard, both Thailand and India started developing their own national private standards, ThaiGAP, IndGAP and IndiaGAP, with the aim of achieving GlobalGAP benchmarking status, i.e. recognition as GlobalGAP equivalent. The standards are adapted to local circumstances and are thus expected to be easier and less costly to comply with than the GlobalGAP standard (Indian Agricultural and Processed Food Products Development Authority, 2011; Keeratipipatpong, 2010).

The ThaiGAP standard is a product of cooperation between the Thai Chamber of Commerce, Kasetsart University, the National Food Institute, the National Metrology Institute of Germany and the German Technical Cooperation Agency (Keeratipipatpong, 2010). The standard achieved benchmarking status in 2010, but benchmarking was not renewed for GlobalGAP version 5 due to a low demand for the standard, which is reflected in the decreasing number of GlobalGAP-certified producers. It is not clear to what extent the ThaiGAP standard was successful in lowering costs of compliance and in making compliance less challenging.

The Indian case is rather complicated as there are two national standards with two different owners, namely: IndiaGAP owned by the Bureau of Indian Standards (BIS) and IndGAP owned by Quality Council of India (QCI). Both IndiaGAP and

Table 3 Number of GlobalGAP-certified producers in Thailand and India, 2008–2016

| | Option | Certified individuals (no. of groups) | | | | | | | | |
		December 08	December 09	December 10	December 11	December 12	December 13	December 14	December 15	February 16
Thailand	Individual	15	29	28	33	28	27	41	43	39
	Group	354 (4)	780 (11)	687 (11)	219 (9)	246 (8)	107 (5)	65 (5)	12 (2)	125 (4)
	Total	369	809	715	252	274	134	106	55	164
India	Individual	405	311	158	133	127	140	122	93	101
	Group	2125 (42)	1528 (34)	2103 (34)	2961 (43)	3191 (38)	4007 (51)	6666 (55)	7701 (69)	8006 (87)
	Total	2530	1839	2261	3094	3318	4147	6788	7794	8107

Source GlobalGAP (2016)

IndGAP still seek benchmarking against GlobalGAP (Punjabi & Mukherjee, 2015; see www.qcin.org). The IndiaGAP, owned by BIS, was drafted by the Agriculture and Processed Food Export Development Authority (APEDA) in 2007 but was first officially released in 2010. Though a public standard, APEDA designed the IndiaGAP closely around the GlobalGAP but fitted to Indian conditions. IndiaGAP aims to help in the adoption of good agricultural practices all over the country and is oriented for Indian producers (both big and small farmers) that are in the high-value export market for agricultural products. Similar to the GlobalGAP, under the IndiaGAP certification scheme, farmers have two options for certification: individual and group certifications. It is expected that if IndiaGAP is properly implemented through certification of model farms, exports will increase by 25–30% (Food Industry India, 2007; see also www.bis.org.in).

The IndGAP was drafted and released by QCI in 2014. According to a 2016 interview with a QCI representative, APEDA, after creating the draft IndiaGAP, turned over the draft documents to QCI to use as the basis for developing IndGAP. So, while APEDA was occupied promoting IndiaGAP, QCI developed IndGAP (national standard for high-value exports) and basic IndGAP (local standard for domestic market). Meanwhile, IndGAP originates from an institution created through private–public partnership (PPP), with up to 50% funding from the government and the rest coming from industry bodies. QCI was set up as an accreditation body in India, and although its chairman is appointed by the Prime Minister, operationally, QCI is liberated from government control. QCI has a third-party verification system for the IndGAP in place.

IndiaGAP from APEDA and BIS is government-owned and government-led. Since its inception in 1980, BIS has been mandated by Parliament to prepare various Indian national standards and therefore had the legal authority to own and publish IndiaGAP. However, its implementation posed some problems. The structure of Indian government ministries is such that the Ministry of Agriculture is responsible for anything related to domestic agriculture whereas the Ministry of Commerce has the mandate for activities related to exports. Thus, since the original IndiaGAP refers to agricultural products that are destined to go outside of India, APEDA and BIS had to deal with two different Indian ministries whose jurisdictions overlap in the implementation of this certification scheme. A second issue is that unlike IndGAP, IndiaGAP does not allow for third-party verification. There is no third-party certification system that was built around IndiaGAP when the standard was drafted, creating problems of legitimacy and robustness of the standard. Thus, although efforts to have IndiaGAP benchmarked against GlobalGAP have been made, its lack of third-party verification needs to be resolved.

2.3 Level 2 Standards: Local GAP Standards for Broad-Scale Adoption

Both the public and private sectors in Thailand and India have introduced local GAP standards for the high-value domestic markets and the export supply chain, resulting in two coexisting standards and confusion among producers and exporters.

2.3.1 Thailand

In Thailand, the government passed the 'Road Map of Food Safety' and introduced the Q-GAP standard, a national voluntary standard for good agricultural practices, in 2004. The aim was to implement effective food safety controls at all levels of the value chain (Ministry of Public Health, 2004; Sardsud, 2007a). The road map defines three goals: to maintain exports of agricultural commodities and food at the current level, to reduce quarantine problems and to reduce the number of illnesses from contaminated food in Thailand (FAO & WHO, 2004).

Q-GAP initially consisted of 31 crop-specific protocols and was later extended to cover 169 commodities (Pongvinyoo, 2015; Sardsud, 2007a, p. 59). The Q-GAP scheme is implemented by the government at all stages. The government sets the standards, the National Bureau of Agricultural Commodity and Food Standards (ACFS) under the Ministry of Agriculture and Cooperatives (MOAC) serves as the accreditation body, and the Department of Agriculture (DOA) acts as a certification body. Since 2010, the certification and advisory function are partly outsourced to the private sector and to farmer organizations (Pongvinyoo, 2015). The Q-GAP is a requirement of several domestic retailers, and a requirement to export (Sardsud, 2007a; Wannamolee, 2008). In 2013, the Q-GAP standard was newly issued as Thai Agricultural Standard (TAS) of food crops and was harmonized with ASEAN GAP (Korpraditskul & Ratanakreetakul, 2015), a standard developed by members of the Association of Southeast Asian Nations (ASEAN) to facilitate harmonization of GAP programmes among ASEAN member countries (ASEAN Secretariat, 2006). The private sector, however, assesses the Q-GAP standard as insufficient.[3] To export to high-value markets, in particular Europe, the GlobalGAP standard is needed, which is challenging to adopt and entails high compliance costs for producers and exporters. Supermarkets operating in Thailand also assess the Q-GAP standard as insufficient.

Recognizing this, the Thai Chamber of Commerce, owner of the ThaiGAP standard, kicked off the development of ThaiGAP Level 2 for the domestic market. The ThaiGAP standard for the domestic market ensures a higher level of food safety than the Q-GAP standard, but is less challenging to comply with than the GlobalGAP/ThaiGAP standard (Wattanavaekin, 2010). It is seen as a tool for local

---

[3]The standard is criticized for lacking credibility because both certification and accreditation are in the hands of the government and the agencies responsible for certifying farmers lack adequate financing (Sardsud, 2007).

producers to gain and maintain access to retailers and supermarkets in Thailand (Korpraditskul & Ratanakreetakul, 2015). It is also used to promote the fruit and vegetable sector after the export crisis. The development of the ThaiGAP standard for the domestic market was supported by the Thai Retailers Association and several Thai supermarkets, among them Siam Makro, Tops Supermarket, Tesco Lotus and CP All Plc. Participating retailers aim to use ThaiGAP to ensure consumer safety and to differentiate their products. Thai consumers have been found to be sensitive to food safety and to shift from wet markets to supermarkets because they expect a higher level of food safety (Reardon et al., 2010; Reardon, Timmer & Minten, 2012). The first producers became certified against the ThaiGAP standard for the domestic market in 2015.

2.3.2   India

Similarly, in India there are two parallel standards: the government-owned IndiaGAP—initiated by the BIS in cooperation with APEDA in 2010—and the IndGAP standard, introduced in 2014 by a (semi-)private actor, QCI. Like ThaiGAP, both IndiaGAP and IndGAP have two levels: Level 1 for the high-value export market and Level 2 for the domestic market and to allow gradual upgrading to international standards. At Level 2, the revised IndiaGAP that was introduced in 2013 originated from BIS/APEDA while the basic IndGAP that was introduced in 2014 was developed by QCI (Punjabi & Mukherjee, 2015; Jairath & Purohit, 2013). The revised IndiaGAP was a simpler and less stringent certification scheme that would allow farmers to get used to domestic standards so that transition of crop production practices towards IndiaGAP and GlobalGAP accreditation would be easier. Both Level 2 local GAP standards were set up to address the fact that the GlobalGAP and IndiaGAP/IndGAP schemes that are currently in operation in India are meant only for the export market and are being operated by large farmers and farmer groups, overlooking the domestic market. Moreover, both schemes recognize the difficulties smallholders face in getting their produce accredited in order to enter high-value domestic markets. A Level 2 national accreditation is a small step that might eventually make Level 1 accreditation much easier for smaller farmers.

There has already been a certified model farm for IndGAP according to QCI. As of now, both the revised IndiaGAP and basic IndGAP are rather new and therefore no empirical evidence on their impact is available. However, our earlier research in India has shown that the majority of retailers, including international retailers, do not apply food safety and quality standards in India although they might apply them elsewhere (interview with IFPRI, 2014; Hampel-Milagrosa et al., 2017). Primary data from producers and retailers that were interviewed in the state of Andhra Pradesh show that modern retailers tend to implement basic product standards for fruits and vegetables but do not apply farm-level GAP standards. Supermarkets, for their fruits and vegetables portfolio, do not abide by public and private food safety standards (Cohen, 2013). Thus, modern Indian retailers' main criteria for selection of produce tend to neglect critical issues of food safety, including pre- and post-harvest practices, and workers' health and safety.

In addition, traditional markets still encompass a majority of the market share for fruits and vegetables in India, a contributing reason why standards are difficult to implement in the country (Babu, 2012; Gulati, 2007). Foreign direct investment (FDI) in retail is currently the key that allows modern retail chains to operate in the country, but actual investment is still very low (Baskaran, 2012). Many experts believe that once retail FDI enters on a bigger scale, stricter standards that conform to international criteria may be implemented and lead to improvements in the whole sector (interview with Global Agrisystems, 2014; Chari & Madhav Raghavan, 2012).

3 Implications and Impacts of Standards on Farmers

This section summarizes the existing literature on the implications and impacts of standards on smallholders in Thailand and India. The analysis is carried out separately for Level 1 and Level 2 standards. In addition, we distinguish between Level 2 standards promoted by public actors and those demanded by domestic retailers since these were found to differ in their level of difficulty.

3.1 Level 1 GAP Standards for High-Value Export Market

Research on Level 1 standards focuses on the GlobalGAP standard. Findings from both countries on the factors influencing adoption, the impacts of adoption and the sustainability of certification show a similar pattern. Studies from India (Roy & Thorat, 2008) and Thailand (Kersting & Wollni, 2012) on the factors influencing GlobalGAP adoption find that if farmers are supported by external actors in the adoption process, such as a donor, an exporter or a marketing partner to a producer cooperative, it is not land size, but farmers' human and organizational capacities that are the main determinants of adoption. Small-scale farmers are unlikely to adopt the standard without support and need external assistance at all stages of the adoption process: to obtain the relevant information, to decide on whether or not to adopt the standard and to implement the requirements at farm level (Roy & Thorat, 2008).

Studies show that once farmers have adopted the GlobalGAP standard, on an average, they gain from certification (Bourquin & Thiagarajan, n.d.; Holzapfel & Wollni, 2014a, 2014b; Punjabi & Mukherjee, 2015; Roy & Thorat, 2008). Using panel data of 218 farm households in Thailand, Holzapfel and Wollni (2014a, 2014b) find that GlobalGAP adoption, on an average, has a significant positive impact on F&V prices as well as on farmers' household incomes. The impact on prices and household incomes depends highly on the type of institutional arrangement small-holders are certified in. Farmers certified in producer-managed groups had very high benefits and on average received 62% higher prices and 14,678 USD higher net household incomes. In contrast, farmers certified in exporter-managed groups did not benefit from higher prices or incomes. Exporters covered expenses for certification and provided trainings, but farmers were not paid higher prices. Holzapfel and Wollni (2014b) also find that larger farmers in producer-managed certification groups realize high net income gains while smaller farmers only benefit as long as they do not have to incur the costs of compliance, i.e. as long as certification costs and costs for technical assistance, equipment and laboratory analyses are paid for by a donor.

For the case of India, Bourquin and Thiagarajan (n.d.) analysed the impact of a USAID-funded project supporting mango producers in India and found that GlobalGAP-certified farmers selling to the domestic high-value market receive 20–30% more and farmers selling to the export market 50% higher returns than farmers selling through traditional channels. However, they also found that the additional revenue is not sufficient to pay for the costs of certification during the first year. Similarly, Punjabi and Mukherjee (2015) found that grape growers contracted by an exporter and producing under GlobalGAP have a 60% higher gross margin than farmers supplying to the traditional market. In addition, contracted farmers benefit from a lower price risk because of a minimum guaranteed price and from lower production risks. The export company's extension agents regularly inform farmers on weather and infestation risks and provide advice on the issues.

Small-scale farmers, however, need continuous support to make GlobalGAP certification sustainable. Holzapfel and Wollni (2014b), for the case of Thai F&V producers, find that certification in donor-supported producer-managed groups is not sustainable. There are two main reasons for this. First, when donor support ends, small-scale farmers are often not able to cover the recurrent costs of compliance. Second, donor support focused on initial adoption and one-time certification and not on improving the long-term capacities of farmers and farmer groups to manage certification on their own. The results also showed that farmers certified in exporter-managed groups had a 85% higher probability of becoming re-certified (Holzapfel & Wollni, 2014b). Exporters continued to support their contract farmers after donor support ended through extension services, input provision and management of the quality management system and by covering the certification costs.

A lack of sustainability of donor-supported GlobalGAP certification was also found in a USAID project supporting GlobalGAP certification of mango farmers in India. Only 26 out of 62 farmers who became certified in 2006 and 2007 sought recertification in 2008 (Bourquin & Thiagarajan, n.d.). One of the lessons learned from the projects is that farmer groups that were not artificially formed for GlobalGAP certification but that had existed before (self-help groups, cooperatives, clusters) are more successful (Bourquin & Thiagarajan, n.d.). Punjabi and Mukherjee (2015) also stress the importance of longer-term support to GlobalGAP-certified small-scale farmers. Record keeping about farm practices (e.g. pesticide and fertilizer use, and hygiene) is a particular problem for small-scale farmers. Extension agents of the contracting exporting company help farmers to maintain records for the first 2–3 years of certification until farmers acquire the capacity to fulfil the task themselves.

The case of Mahagrapes (Roy & Thorat, 2008), a marketing partner to producer cooperatives in India, shows a very successful example of collective action and farmer-led GlobalGAP certification. Mahagrapes provides a range of services to its member cooperatives and to farmers, such as procurement of information on standards and export markets, negotiation of contracts, provision of inputs, and training about grape growing and handling methods. It succeeded in providing GlobalGAP certification to all its member cooperatives. Member farmers only have to pay $28 annually for certification due to economies of scale, which is much lower than has been found in other studies. The grape sector in India is a success story, and 6409 of the 8107 farmers in India currently certified against GlobalGAP are certified for grapes.

3.2   Level 2 GAP Standards

As shown above, Level 2 GAP standards for fresh fruits and vegetables exist in both Thailand (Q-GAP/TAS/ThaiGAP) and India (basic IndGAP/revised IndiaGAP). However, since basic IndGAP and the revised IndiaGAP have recently been introduced in India and only one farmer had been certified till 2015, the impacts on farmers are yet to be assessed. For this reason, this section focuses on the GAP standards in Thailand. The case of Thailand provides important lessons learned for India and other countries that have initiated basic voluntary GAP standards.

3.2.1   Level 2 GAP Standards Promoted by Public Actors

The TAS (previously Q-GAP) is widely known in Thailand. In 2016, 112 thousand farms in Thailand were certified against the standard (Department of Agriculture, 2016). This is almost as many producers as are certified with GlobalGAP worldwide (GLobalGAP, 2014),[4] but a huge decline from more than 220,000 producers that were Q-GAP-certified in 2012 (Amekawa et al., 2017). The decline started with the introduction of the TAS in 2013 (TAS 9001-2013), which replaced Q-GAP and made it more challenging for Thai farmers to obtain a certificate.[5,6] The revision of the Q-GAP standard is an attempt of the Thai government to improve the effectiveness of the standard and to increase its acceptance in international markets. Several studies

---

[4] According to GlobalGAP (2014), more than 139,000 certified producers in over 110 countries were certified in 2014.

[5] The TAS standard has 116 control pointsand farmers have to comply with 100% of 23 control points and with 60% of 41 control points. A total of 54 control points are recommendations (Amekawa et al., 2017). In comparison, the Q-GAP standard has only 84 control points and farmers were required to comply with only 51% of the control points (Amekawa, 2013).

[6] The GlobalGAP Integrated Farm Assurance standard Version 5 includes 218 control points, thereof 87 major must (100% compliance), 113 minor must (95% compliance) and 18 recommendations (GlobalGAP, 2015).

have dealt with the impacts of the Q-GAP standard on food safety and farm practices and have analysed the benefits and problems associated with the standard.

Amekawa (2013), based on 64 structured interviews with Q-GAP-certified pomelo producers in Northern Thailand, analysed farmers' understanding of the Q-GAP standard and the effect of Q-GAP on farming practices and pesticide use. They find that only half the producers surveyed were able to relate the Q-GAP standard to the official food safety goal, the proper use and control of agrochemicals and other production practices. They also find that the level of implementation of Q-GAP requirements is low (especially record keeping) and that changes in pesticide management undertaken by farmers were unrelated to Q-GAP. Similarly, Schreinemachers et al. (2012), who compared pesticide use and handling practices among Q-GAP adopters and non-adopters, showed that a Q-GAP certificate does not have a significant effect on the amount of pesticides used nor on pesticide handling practices. It did, however, have a small impact on the use of hazardous and banned pesticide and has increased farmers' awareness of the dangers of hazardous substances.

The impact of Q-GAP on prices and income has been analysed by Krause, Lippe and Grote (2014) for cut orchids and by Pongvinyoo, Yamao and Hosono (2014) for coffee. Both find that Q-GAP does not influence prices and that certified and non-certified producers sell to the same buyers and markets. The lack of economic incentive for farmers to comply with Q-GAP requirements can be named as one of the reasons for farmers' non-compliance with Q-GAP requirements (Krause et al., 2014). More importantly, however, there are several problems associated with the design and implementation of the Q-GAP standard which lead to a low level of adoption of the standard requirements and ultimately to a lack of credibility.

First, accreditation and certification are both in the hands of the Ministry of Agriculture and Cooperatives, which creates doubts about the credibility of the certification system (Sardsud, 2007a). Second, overambitious targets to certify at least 145,000 farmers from 2004 to 2008 have put too much pressure on the responsible government agencies who lack capacities to carry out appropriate training, or inspection and certification services (Sardsud, 2007a). This has resulted in farmers applying for Q-GAP receiving insufficient training and in lax audit and control. For example, Schreinemachers et al. (2012) state that according to the DOA there are only 120 DOA auditors in Northern Thailand but more than 140,000 registered farms. The government has decided to outsource auditing to private contractors, but these are often only insufficiently trained. Third, auditing has focused mostly on final stages of production (pesticide residue testing and record keeping of pesticide applications) although the Q-GAP standard covers a much broader range of issues. Moreover, farmers are not sufficiently provided with alternatives to the use of synthetic pesticides, such as integrated pest management (IPM) methods (Schreinemachers et al., 2012).

Experiences from Thailand with the implementation of the Q-GAP standard provide important lessons for India. It is important that the APEDA and the QCI, which have launched IndiaGAP and IndGAP, ensure that farmers have access to sufficient information and training, that the quality of infrastructure is upgraded and that certification bodies have adequate capacities to carry out inspections. The development of a joint standard shared between APEDA and QCI is an option that we recommend. Not only will this joint standard unify the two seemingly competing public (IndiaGAP) and semi-private (IndGAP) standards but also reduce confusion among producers and among international buyers with regard to which standard has authority. Joining forces to create a joint standard will also increase capacities in terms of certification. There is always a trade-off between certifying as many farmers as possible and investing in training and auditing to ensure that farmers know and apply GAP principles and that certified farmers comply with the requirements of the standard.

3.2.2 Private Level 2 GAP Standards Imposed by Domestic Retailers

The impact of private standards applied by retailers in the domestic market is still very low in India but much stronger in Thailand where supermarkets have a much higher market share. With increasing market share of supermarkets and rising consumer concerns for food safety and quality, the impacts of standards are expected to increase significantly over the next decade.

As described in Sect. 2.3, supermarkets in India do not yet apply GAP standards. The situation in Thailand is different. Thai supermarkets use labels for fruits and vegetables, such as the Q-mark, pesticide-free or organic. In addition, supermarkets have introduced supply chain management programmes to ensure a basic level of food safety, developed their own food safety standards (e.g. Makro) or require certification with Q-GAP (e.g. Tops). This has certain implications for producers. For example, a case study of Tops carried out in 2006 showed that Tops, following a supply chain restructuring programme, significantly reduced its involvement with smallholders. Following a screening, Tops only chose those farmers as suppliers who already applied 'intelligent pesticide management' and started to require Q-GAP certification from suppliers (Buurma & Saranak, 2006).

Fruits and vegetables are 2–6 times more expensive in supermarkets compared to local open-air markets (Wanwimolruk et al., 2016). Thai consumers are prepared to pay the price also because they expect produce to be safe. Wanwimolruk et al. (2016) in a recent study, however, found that fruits and vegetables from supermarkets exceed MRLs at a rate of 35% for Chinese kale (local markets 48%), at a rate of 55% for *pak choi* (local markets 71%) and at a rate of 49% for morning glory (local market 42%). A similar study by the Thai Pesticide Alert Network (Thai-PAN) showed that produce labelled as Q-GAP-certified exceeded MRLs in 57% of the cases and produce labelled as organic in 25% of the cases (Thailand PAN, 2016). These findings put high pressure on supermarkets as well as on ACFS which is responsible for the Q-GAP standard. Under these circumstances, the ThaiGAP standard for the domestic market, which is now piloted, may receive a boost.

There are not yet many experiences with the ThaiGAP standard for the domestic market, because the standard has only recently been introduced and uptil 2015, only 18 producers had received a certificate. Like GlobalGAP, the ThaiGAP (domestic

Table 4 Comparison of the ThaiGAP standard for the domestic market with GlobalGAP

ThaiGAP domestic		ThaiGAP/GlobalGAP
General regulation ruled by Thai chamber of commerce		General regulation ruled by food plus
All farm base	27	51
Crop base	83	113
Fruit and vegetable	57	70
Traceability (QR code)		Traceability (QR code)
Certification body of ISO 17065		Certification of ISO 17065 GLOBALGAP

Source Korpraditskul and Ratanakreetakul (2015)

market) standard is a private, voluntary standard, but is adapted to the local circumstances and has a significantly lower number of control points (Table 4). The standard owner, the Thai Chamber of Commerce, has decided to offer only one certification option, individual certification for ThaiGAP (domestic market). The main reason provided by Thai Chamber of Commerce is that the experience of the GlobalGAP option 2 project has shown that the group certification process, especially the quality management system, is too complex.

It is yet to be seen whether ThaiGAP (domestic market) will also be an option for small-scale farmers. The 16 farmers that have already obtained a certificate have been proposed by the supermarkets involved in the ThaiGAP project. All of them are large-scale farmers that own between 8 and 32 hectares, which is much larger than the Thai average of 3.6 hectares (Pongsrihadulchai, 2009). However, some smallholders have been included in the certificates via contract farming arrangements.

Potentially, the ThaiGAP standard can play a big role in future in Thailand. Almost all major supermarkets in Thailand have supported the development of the standard which shows their high demand for safe fruits and vegetables. If applied at a broader scale and eventually made a requirement of Thai supermarkets, the standard is likely to improve the level of food safety for the domestic consumer and to decrease adverse environmental and health effects of pesticides. At the same time, there is the risk that small-scale farmers who are not able to comply will lose access to the lucrative supermarket channel. It is therefore important to identify ways to also enable small-scale farmers to adopt the standard.

4   Conclusion and Recommendations

Donor programmes on food safety and quality over the past decade have mainly focused on the GlobalGAP standard (Level 1 standard). The results of studies in Thailand and India show that even if access to donor support is available, it is the wealthier and more educated small-scale farmers who adopt and benefit from the GlobalGAP standard, indicating that the poorest segment of smallholders has not benefited from donor interventions. In addition, the vast majority of smallholders serve domestic markets or lower value export markets, where GlobalGAP is not a requirement.

Local Level 2 GAP standards applied in developing countries' domestic supply chains can potentially reach a much larger number of producers and as a result may have a much higher impact. On the one hand, if imposed by supermarkets, local standards may lead to changes in the supply chain. Although the standards applied to the domestic market are usually less stringent than GlobalGAP, they pose a similar threat and may lead to the loss of market access for resource-poor small-scale producers with limited human and social capital. On the other hand, they play an important role in introducing more sustainable agricultural practices and in improving the level of food safety for domestic consumers.

We found coexisting and overlapping local GAP standards (Level 2) initiated by public and private actors in both Thailand and India. In Thailand, the public sector has introduced the Q-GAP (now TAS) in 2004. The standard is a requirement for export, and the Q-GAP label is used by domestic supermarket chains. However, studies found that the level of implementation of standard requirements among certified farmers is low. The government lacks the resources and capacity to monitor compliance, and credibility is low because both certification and accreditation are in the hands of the government. As a result, the standard is assessed as insufficient by the private sector. Recognizing this, the private sector decided to develop its own local GAP standard, the ThaiGAP standard. ThaiGAP is a third-party standard based on Glob-alGAP standard, but more adapted to local circumstances and with lower number of requirements. The four largest major supermarket chains in Thailand participated in the development of ThaiGAP, and if made a requirement, ThaiGAP may have major impact on the F&V value chain.

In India, we found IndiaGAP (introduced by APEDA—a public institution) and IndGAP (introduced by QCI—a public/private institution) as two competing GAP standards geared for the same producers that are in the same high-value export market. Similar to Thailand, levels of implementation of standard requirements among farmers are low for both standards. However, whereas IndiaGAP was intro-duced much earlier with dismal certification rates among farmers, the IndGAP was only recently introduced and uptake could still increase. Also, similar to the case of Thailand, lack of resources hounds both institutions and the capacity to monitor compliance among farmers is low. The decision to introduce revised IndiaGAP (APEDA) and basic IndGAP (QCI) came in order to allow farmers to gradually ease into GlobalGAP standards. This was equally an opportunity to certify smaller farmers in India and provide assurance of food safety and quality to local consumers. Owing to the large numbers of smallholders in India, proper and widespread imple-mentation of revised IndiaGAP and basic IndGAP is expected to have a profound impact on domestic markets.

Parallel standards—as found in both Thailand and India—lead to high transac-tion costs and uncertainty among producers, exporters and consumers. We therefore encourage public and private actors to harmonize existing GAP standards. Instead of aiming to certify as many smallholders as possible, governments are recommended to invest in upgrading the quality of the infrastructure needed for standard adoption (in particular, metrology and accreditation) and in extension programmes and media campaigns that disseminate GAP on a larger scale. The widespread awareness and application of GAP principles are particularly important to improve the level of food safety for domestic consumers.

Moreover, institutional arrangements that allow large numbers of small-scale farmers to adopt local GAP standards should be supported. Here, lessons can be learnt from the example of GlobalGAP, in which large-scale producers and enterprises support small-scale farmers in adopting standards. In addition, the support of service providers and producer cooperatives that offer access to financing and training to enable standard adoption by small-scale farmers is crucial. The grape sector in India is a particularly successful case, showing how large numbers of smallholders can be sustainably integrated into GlobalGAP group certification schemes and benefit from certification.

References

Amekawa, Y. (2013). Can a public GAP approach ensure safety and fairness? A comparative study of Q-GAP in Thailand. *The Journal of Peasant Studies, 40*(1), 189–217. https://doi.org/10.1080/03066150.2012.746958.

Amekawa, Y., Ng, C. C., Lumayag, L., Tan, G. H., Wong, C.S. et al. (2017). Producers' perceptions of public good agricultural practices and their pesticide use: The case of MyGAP for durian farming in Pahang, Malaysia. *Asian Journal of Agriculture and Rural Development, 7*(1), 1-16.

ASEAN Secretariat. (2006). *Interpretive Guide for ASEAN GAP. Good agricultural practices for production of fresh fruit and vegetables in ASEAN countries. Food safety module.* Retrieved from http://www.asean.org/storage/images/2012/publications/ASEAN%20GAP_Food%20Safety%20Module.pdf.

Ashraf, N., Giné, X., & Karlan, D. (2009). Finding missing markets (and a disturbing epilogue): Evidence from an export crop adoption and marketing intervention in Kenya. *American Journal of Agricultural Economics, 91*(4), 973–990.

Babu, H. S. (2012). SWOT Analysis for opening of FDI in Indian Retailing. *European Journal of Business and Management, 4*(3).

Balsevich, F., Berdegué, J. A., Flores, L., Mainville, D., & Reardon, T. (2003). Supermarkets and produce quality and safety standards in Latin America. *American Journal of Agricultural Economics, 85*(5), 1147–1154.

Baskaran, K. (2012). The FDI for multi brand retail trading in India—Green signal or red signal. *Business Intelligence Journal, 15,* 175–186.

Berdegué, J. A., Balsevich, F., Flores, L., & Reardon, T. (2005). Central American supermarkets' private standards of quality and safety in procurement of fresh fruits and vegetables. *Food Policy, 30*(3), 254–269. https://doi.org/10.1016/j.foodpol.2005.05.003.

Bourquin, L. D., & Thiagarajan, D. (n.d.). *PFID: F&V India Mango Market Development Project.* Retrieved from: https://www.researchgate.net/publication/267834146_PFIDFV_India_Mango_PFIDFV_India_Mango_Market_Development_Project_Market_Development_Project.

Buurma, J., & Saranak, J. (2006). Supply-chain development for fresh fruits and vegetables in Thailand. In R. Ruben, M. Slingerland, & H. Nijhoff (Eds.), *Agro-food chains and networks for development.* Den Haag: Springer.

Chari, A., & Madhav Raghavan, T. C. A. (2012). Foreign direct investment in India's Retail Bazaar: Opportunities and challenges. *The World Economy, 35*(1), 75–90.

Chemnitz, C. (2007). *The Compliance Decision with Food Quality Standards on Primary Producer Level; A Case Study of the EUREPGAP Standard in the Moroccan Tomato Sector. 103rd EAAE Seminar 'Adding Value to the Agro-Food Supply Chain in the Future Euromediterranean Space', Barcelona, Spain*. Retrieved from http://purl.umn.edu/9440.

Cohen, A. J. (2013). Supermarkets in India: Struggles over the Organization of Agricultural Markets and Food Supply Chains. *University of Miami Law Review, 68*(19–86).

Colen, L., Maertens, M., & Swinnen, J. (2012). Private standards, trade and poverty: GlobalGAP and horticultural employment in senegal. *The World Economy, 35*(8), 1073–1088. https://doi.org/10.1111/j.1467-9701.2012.01463.x.

Department of Agriculture. (2016). Retrieved from http://gap.doa.go.th/.

Dolan, C. and Humphrey, J. (2000). Governance and Trade in Fresh Vegetables: The Impact of UK Supermarkets on the African Horticulture Industry. *The Journal of Development Studies, 37*(2), 147–176. https://doi.org/10.1080/713600072.

eFresh Portal. (2016). Good Agricultural Practices—Basic GAP for Small & Marginal Farmers Retrieved from http://efreshglobal.com/eFresh/indgap_home.aspx.

Ehlert, C. R., Mithöfer, D., & Waibel, H. (2014). Worker welfare on Kenyan export vegetable farms. *Food Policy, 46*, 66–73. https://doi.org/10.1016/j.foodpol.2014.01.004.

Elizabeth, M. M. Q. F., & Reardon, T. (2000). Agrifood grades and standards in the extended Mercosur: Their role in the changing agrifood system. *American Journal of Agricultural Economics, 82*(5), 1170–1176.

FAO. (2010). FAOSTAT. Retrieved from http://faostat.fao.org/.

FAO. (2017). *FAOSTAT*. Retrieved from: http://www.fao.org/faostat/en/#data/QC.

FAO, & WHO. (2004). *Strengthening official food safety control services. Paper prepared by Thailand.* Paper presented at the Second FAO/WHO global forum of food safety regulators, Bangkok, Thailand, 12–14 October 2004. http://www.fao.org/tempref/docrep/fao/Meeting/008/y5871e/y5871e02.pdf.

Food Industry India. (2007). India to notify standards for Agro products. Retrieved from: http://www.foodindustryindia.com/newfood/detailnews.jsp?n=India%20to%20notify%20standards%20for%20agro%20products&id=214 website.

GLOBALGAP (2015). *Control points and compliance criteria in IFA version 5 fruit and vegetables. Summary of Changes*. Retrieved from Cologne: http://www.globalgap.org/export/sites/default/.content/.galleries/documents/150630_Summary_Changes_V5-0_CPCC_AF_CB_FV_en.pdf.

GLOBALGAP (2012). GLOBALG.A.P. website. Retrieved from: http://www.globalgap.org/uk_en/for-producers/crops/FV/.

GLOBALGAP (2014). *Building a global solution through partnership and collaboration. GLOBALG.A.P. annual report 2013–2014*. Retrieved from Cologne.

Graffham, A., Cooper, J., Wainwright, H., & MacGregor, J. (2007). *Fresh Insights Number 15. Small-scale farmers who withdraw from GLOBALGAP: Results of a survey in Kenya*. Retrieved from: http://r4d.dfid.gov.uk/PDF/Outputs/EcoDev/60506-Fresh-insights-15.pdf.

Gulati, A. (2007). Re-energizing Agricultural Sector of Andhra Pradesh: From Food Security to Income Opportunities *IFPRI Discussion Paper Series*. New Delhi: International Food Policy Research Institute (IFPRI).

Gulati, A., Minot, N., Delgado, C. L., & Bora, S. (2007). Growth in high-value agriculture in Asia and the emergence of vertical links with farmers. In J. F. M. Swinnen (Ed.), *Global supply chains, standards and the poor: How the globalization of food systems and standards affects rural development and poverty* (pp. 91–108): CAB International.

Hampel-Milagrosa, A., Brannkamp, H., Cremer, T., Haddad, A., Pannwitz, K., Wehinger, F., et al. (2017). *Retail FDI Liberalisation and the transformation of agrifood value chains in India*. Bonn: German Development Institute/Deutsches Institut für Entwicklungspolitik.

Hampel-Milagrosa, A., & Holzapfel, S. (2016). *Diversity and implications of food safety and quality standards in Thailand and India*. Bonn: German Development Institute/Deutsches Institut für Entwicklungspolitik.

Henson, S., & Caswell, J. (1999). Food safety regulation: an overview of contemporary issues. *Food Policy, 24*(6), 589–603. https://doi.org/10.1016/S0306-9192(99)00072-X.

Henson, S., & Loader, R. (2001). Barriers to agricultural exports from developing countries: The role of sanitary and phytosanitary requirements. *World Development, 29*(1), 85–102. https://doi.org/10.1016/S0305-750X(00)00085-1.

Henson, S., & Reardon, T. (2005). Private agri-food standards: Implications for food policy and the agri-food system. *Food Policy, 30*(3), 241–253. https://doi.org/10.1016/j.foodpol.2005.05.002.

Holzapfel, S., & Wollni, M. (2014a). Innovative business models in the Thai horticultural sector: a panel data analysis of the impacts of global GAP certification. In R. D. Christy, C. A. D. Silva, N. Mhlanga, E. Mabaya, & K. Tihanyi (Eds.), *Innovative institutions, public policies and private strategies for agro-enterprise development* Rome and Singapore: Food and Agriculture Organization of the United Nations; World Scientific Publishing Co. Pte. Ltd.

Holzapfel, S., & Wollni, M. (2014b). Is GlobalGAP certification of small-scale farmers sustainable? Evidence from Thailand. *Journal of Development Studies, 50*(5), 731–747. https://doi.org/10.1080/00220388.2013.874558.

Humphrey, J. (2008). *Private standards, small farmers and donor policy: EUREPGAP in Kenya. Working paper series, 308.* Retrieved from Brighton. https://opendocs.ids.ac.uk/opendocs/bitstream/handle/123456789/4167/Wp308.pdf?sequence=1&isAllowed=y.

Humphrey, J., & Memedovic, O. (2006). Global value chains in the agrifood sector.

Indian Agricultural and Processed Food Products Development Authority. (2011). Requirements for GAP—IndiaGAP (Draft Indian Standard), 18. Retrieved from: www.bis.org.in/sf/fad/FAD 22(2200)C.pdf website.

ITC. (2017). *Trade map—international trade statistics.* Retrieved from: http://www.trademap.org/tradestat/Index.aspx.

Jaffee, S. (2003). *From challenge to opportunity: Transforming Kenya's fresh vegetable trade in the context of emerging food safety and other standards in Europe. Agriculture and Rural Development discussion paper no.2* Retrieved from Washington, DC. http://documents.worldbank.org/curated/en/2003/12/5558962/challenge-opportunity-transforming-kenyas-fresh-vegetable-trade-context-emerging-food-safety-other-standards-europe.

Jaffee, S., Henson, S., & Rios, L. D. (2011). Making the grade: Smallholder farmers, emerging standards, and development assistance programs in Africa. *A Research Program Synthesis. Washington DC: World Bank. Report*(62324-AFR).

Jaffee, S., Meer, K. v. d., Henson, S., Haan, C. d., Sewadeh, M., Ignacio, L., … Lisazo, M. B. (2005). *Food Safety and Agricultural Health Standards: Challenges and Opportunities for Developing Country Exports.* Retrieved from Washington, D.C.: http://siteresources.worldbank.org/INTRANETTRADE/Resources/Topics/Standards/standards_challenges_synthesisreport.pdf.

Jairath, M. S., & Purohit, P. (2013). Food Safety and Regulatory Compliance in India: A Challenge to Enhance Agribusinesses. *Indian Journal of Agricultural Economics, 68*(July-September 2013), 430–448.

Keeratipipatpong, W. (2010). *Thai farm product standard certified.* Bangkok Post: ThaiGAP will help reduce trade barriers.

Kersting, S., & Wollni, M. (2012). New institutional arrangements and standard adoption: evidence from small-scale fruit and vegetable farmers in Thailand. *Food Policy, 37*(4), 452–462.

Korpraditskul, R., & Ratanakreetakul, C. (2015). *THAI Good Agricultural Practice. Submitted for the FFTC-KU International Workshop on Risk Management on Agrochemicals through Novel Technologies for Food Safety in Asia, November 10–14, Sampran Riverside, Nakorn Pathom, Thailand.* Retrieved from: http://ap.fftc.agnet.org/ap_db.php?id=558.

Korpraditskul, R., Suwannamook, S., Adulyarattanapan, S., & Damsiri, W. (2010). *Comparison study of GlobalGAP, IGAP and ASEANGAP.* Retrieved from.

Krause, H., Lippe, R. S., & Grote, U. (2014). *Do Thai Cut Orchid Producers Benefit from Q-GAP Certification?* Paper presented at the Tropentag 2014, Conference on International Research on Food Security, Natural Resource Management and Rural Development organised by the Czech

University of Life Sciences Prague., September 17–19, 2014, Prague, Czech Republic. http://www.tropentag.de/2014/abstracts/full/648.pdf.

Manarungsan, S., Naewbanij, J. O. & Rerngjakrabhe. (2005). *Costs of compliance with SPS standards: Thailand case studies of shrimp, fresh asparagus, and frozen green soybeans.* Retrieved from Washington, DC.

Markelova, H., Meinzen-Dick, R., Hellin, J., & Dohrn, S. (2009). Collective action for smallholder market access. *Food Policy, 34*(1), 1–7. https://doi.org/10.1016/j.foodpol.2008.10.001.

McCullough, E., Pingali, P. L., & Stamoulis, K. G. (Eds.). (2008). *The transformation of agri-food systems, globalization, supply chains and smallholder farmers.* UK and USA: MPG Books Ltd, Bodmin.

Ministry of Public Health. (2004). *Road map of food safety.* Retrieved from Bangkok: http://www.fao.org/docrep/meeting/008/ae183e/ae183eApp.pdf.

Narrod, C., Roy, D., Okello, J., Avendaño, B., Rich, K., & Thorat, A. (2009). Public–private partnerships and collective action in high value fruit and vegetable supply chains. *Food Policy, 34*(1), 8–15. https://doi.org/10.1016/j.foodpol.2008.10.005.

Otsuki, T., Wilson, J. S., & Sewadeh, M. (2001). Saving two in a billion: quantifying the trade effect of European food safety standards on African exports. *Food Policy, 26*(5), 495–514. https://doi.org/10.1016/S0306-9192(01)00018-5.

Pingali, P. (2007). Westernization of Asian diets and the transformation of food systems: Implications for research and policy. *Food Policy, 32*(3), 281–298. https://doi.org/10.1016/j.foodpol.2006.08.001.

Plianbangchang, P., Jetiyanon, K., & Wittaya-Areekul, S. (2009). Pesticide use patterns among small-scale farmers: a case study from Phitsanulok, Thailand. *Southeast Asian Journal of Tropical Medicine and Public Health, 40*(2), 401.

Pongsrihadulchai, A. (2009). *Use of farmers' registration for agricultural policy implementation in Thailand.* Retrieved from Bangkok.

Pongvinyoo, P. (2015). *Development of Good Agricultural Practices (GAP) in Thailand: A case study of Thai National GAP selected products.* Retrieved from https://ir.lib.hiroshima-u.ac.jp/files/public/38533/20151210144618141003/k6765_3.pdf.

Pongvinyoo, P., Yamao, M., & Hosono, K. (2014). Factors affecting the implementation of good agricultural practices (GAP) among coffee farmers in Chumphon Province, Thailand. *American Journal of Rural Development, 2*(2), 34–39. https://doi.org/10.12691/ajrd-2-2-3.

Punjabi, M., & Mukherjee, A. (2015). *Grape exports under GLOBALGAP certification: the Mahindra and Mahindra initiative in India.* Retrieved from http://www.fao.org/fileadmin/user_upload/ivc/PDF/Asia/22_Punjabi_and_Mukherjee_Mahindra_GlobalGAP_grape_India.pdf.

Ratanawaraha, C., Senanarong, N., & Suriyapan, P. (2001). *Status of cassava in Thailand: Implications for future research and development. A review of cassava in Asia with country case studies on Thailand and Viet Nam.* Rome: Food and Agriculture Organization of the United Nations.

Reardon, T., Henson, S., & Gulati, A. (2010). Links between supermarkets and food prices, diet diversity and food safety in developing countries. In B. C. Hawkes C, Henson S, Drager N, Dubé L (Ed.), *Trade, food, diet and health: perspectives and policy options* (pp. 111–130). Hoboken, NJ: Wiley-Blackwell.

Reardon, T., & Timmer, C. P. (2007). Chapter 55 Transformation of markets for agricultural output in developing countries since 1950: How has thinking changed? In R. Evenson & P. Pingali (Eds.), *Handbook of agricultural economics* (Vol. 3, pp. 2807–2855): Elsevier.

Reardon, T., Timmer, C. P., & Minten, B. (2012). Supermarket revolution in Asia and emerging development strategies to include small farmers. *Proceedings of the National Academy of Sciences of the United States of America, 109*(31), 12332–12337. https://doi.org/10.1073/pnas.1003160108.

Roy, D., & Thorat, A. (2008). Success in high value horticultural export markets for the small farmers: The case of Mahagrapes in India. *World Development, 36*(10), 1874–1890. https://doi.org/10.1016/j.worlddev.2007.09.009.

Sardsud, V. (2007). *National experiences: Thailand challenges and opportunities arising from private standards on food safety and environment for exporters of fresh fruit and vegetables in Asia: experiences of Malaysia, Thailand and Viet Nam* (pp. 53–68). New York and Geneva: United Nations.

Schreinemachers, P., Schad, I., Tipraqsa, P., Williams, P. M., Neef, A., Riwthong, S., et al. (2012). Can public GAP standards reduce agricultural pesticide use? The case of fruit and vegetable farming in northern Thailand. *Agriculture and Human Values, 29*(4), 519–529. https://doi.org/10.1007/s10460-012-9378-6.

Shepard, A. W. (2006). *Quality and safety in the traditional horticultural marketing chains of Asia.* Retrieved from Rome.

Thailand Pesticide Alert Network. (2016). ผลการเฝ้าระวังสารเคมีกำจัดศัตรูพืชตกค้างในผักและผลไม้ประจำปี *2559.* Retrieved from http://www.thaipan.org/sites/default/files/file/pesticide_doc25_press_4_5_2559.pdf.

UNIDO, NORAD, & IDS. (2015). *Meeting standards, winning markets. Trade standards compliance.* Retrieved from Vienna.

Wannamolee, W. (2008). *Development of Good Agricultural Practices (GAP) for Fruit and Vegetables in Thailand.* Retrieved from Bangkok: http://www.dld.go.th/organic/news52/audotor_3-5Mar09/Aj.Wiboonwan/ThailandsGAP_report.doc.

Wanwimolruk, S., Phopin, K., Boonpangrak, S., & Prachayasittikul, V. (2016). Food safety in Thailand 4: Comparison of pesticide residues found in three commonly consumed vegetables purchased from local markets and supermarkets in Thailand. *PeerJ Preprints 4*:e1928v1.

Wattanavaekin, W. (2010). *Certification for international export markets Bangkok.* Retrieved from Bankgkok.

Will, M. (2010). *Integrating smallholders into global supply chains. GLOBALGAP option 2 smallholder group certification generic manual: lessons learnt in pilot projects in Kenya, Ghana, Thailand and Macedonia.* Retrieved from Eschborn.

World Bank. (2008). *Agriculture for development. World Development Report.* Washington, D.C.: Author.

Chapter 11
Making the Local Work for the Global Best: A Comparative Study of Vehicle Efficiency Standards Implementation in China and Mexico

Juan Carlos Mendoza and CAO Jiahan

1 Introduction

The invention and dissemination of road vehicles globally constituted a major technological shift in the transportation, economic productivity and competitiveness paradigms. While the social and economic benefits flowing from this innovation are overwhelming, the use of fuels to get this technology "on the move" has had a deep ecological impact, resulting in adverse local as well as climate change effects. The transport sector is a key contributor to worldwide greenhouse gas emissions (GHGs) and other volatile compounds, and over 63.7% of the world's total oil consumption is related to fuel usage (IEA, 2014, p. 33), making the transport sector responsible for approximately 23% of the total energy-related CO_2 emissions (6.7 $GtCO_2$ in 2010) (Sims et al., 2014, p. 602). Road transportation represents 73% of such contributions, making it one of the top priority areas for formulating and achieving mitigation efforts globally. Due to accelerated urbanization processes, economic and population growth, transport demand per capita is expected to grow at a faster rate in the developing and emerging countries in the coming decades (Sims et al., 2014, p. 603).

In order to address the ever-increasing concerns about climate risks, fuel efficiency norms and standards have been key policy tools to lead the transformation towards achieving a drastic reduction in the use of fuel and/or the total amount of aggregated emissions derived from light and heavy-duty vehicles. Through technological and market adjustments and institutional arrangements, it is estimated that potential GHG emissions reduction coming from the adoption of vehicle efficiency standards could go up from 1.6 to 3.5 $GtCO_2$ by 2030 (Stec & Baraj, 2009, p. 304)—a figure higher

J. C. Mendoza (✉)
Deutsche Gesellschaft Für Internationale Zusammenarbeit (GIZ), Mexico City, Mexico
e-mail: juancarlosmenr@gmail.com

C. Jiahan
Shanghai Institutes for International Studies (SIIS), Shanghai, China

© The Editor(s) (if applicable) and The Author(s) 2020
A. Negi et al. (eds.), *Sustainability Standards and Global Governance*,
https://doi.org/10.1007/978-981-15-3473-7_11

than the total amount of $GtCO_2$ emissions in Latin America and Africa together in 2012 (EIA, 2015). The adoption of such standards becomes more relevant in emerging economies where along with population dynamics and economic growth, fuel use, vehicle fleets and automotive industries show major growth trends.

Fuel efficiency norms and standards are not only relevant in terms of climate change mitigation[1] but also because of the co-benefits they provide locally. According to the Global Fuel Economy Initiative (GFEI, 2010), the implementation of such standards could lead to cleaner and healthier cities, foster green mobility, ensure sustainable energy use and improve economic opportunities (GFEI, 2015). Accordingly, the multi-dimensional effects of fuel efficiency relate to the global development agenda framed by the Sustainable Development Goals (SDG),[2] and for specific sectoral supporting agendas such as the Global Energy Efficiency Accelerators Platform promoted by the UN's Sustainable Energy for All Initiative (SE4All), aiming to double the global rate of improvement in energy efficiency in six key sectors (including transport)[3] by 2030.

While the global benefits of fuel efficiency standards are well accepted, their implementation at the national level varies from country to country. Although there is no "one-size-fits-all" global standard on fuel efficiency, there are two general reference standards: those used in the European Union[4] and those used in the USA.[5] Both regulations cover elements and parameters regarding the automotive sector production processes such as technologies to improve litre per kilometre efficiency, CO_2 grams per kilometre measurement, time frames, testing methods, fleet requirements, etc. The selection of those parameters is based on the industry and market production necessities and consumption patterns, satisfying and prioritizing the criteria to be covered on a dominant technological basis.

---

[1] The IPCC AR5 recognized in 2014–2015 that one of the key developments in the transport sector in terms of GHG emissions reduction potential has been the fuel economy standards and GHG vehicle performance standards implemented for light and heavy-duty vehicles (Sims et al., 2014, p.605).

[2] The goals that have a direct link to the fuel efficiency standards in the final adopted document at the UN Sustainable Development Summit in September 2015 are: Goal 3: Ensure healthy lives and promote well-being for all at all ages; Goal 7: Ensure access to affordable, reliable, sustainable and modern energy for all; Goal 9: Build resilient infrastructure, promote inclusive and sustainable industrialization and foster innovation; Goal 11: Make cities and human settlements inclusive, safe, resilient and sustainable; Goal 12: Ensure sustainable consumption and production patterns and; Goal 13: Take urgent actions to combat climate change and its impacts.

[3] According to the SE4All Agenda, these sectors are: lighting, electrical appliances, building, industry, district heating/cooling and fuel efficiency.

[4] Road transport contributes about one-fifth of the EU's total emissions of CO_2. While these emissions fell by 3.3% in 2012, they are still 20.5% higher than in 1990. Transport is the only major sector in the EU where greenhouse gas emissions are still rising.

[5] Japan's experience in fuel efficiency standards shouldn't be, however, diminished. Japan has historically had the lightest, most fuel-efficient vehicle fleet in the world. Historically, Japan's fuel economy standards have been rigorous in comparison to other countries, but in the current conditions it has set lower targets for the coming years. For the purpose of this research project, we aim to focus on the EU and US regulations.

This chapter analyses the implementation of fuel efficiency standards in two developing economies: China and Mexico. The second section introduces the methodology used for the comparative analysis. The third section analyzes the use of fuel efficiency standards in emerging economies, underlining the idea that the local economic, political and institutional context must act as the determinant in implementing external standards in national contexts. In two subsections, both national cases are discussed while a third subsection comparatively analyses determinants and barriers in both cases regarding the fuel efficiency implementation process. Challenges and lessons learned are presented in the final section as conclusions.

2 Methodology

The methodology applied in this study is a comparative analysis based on the typology[6] proposed by the International Council of Clean Transportation (ICCT) on fuel and vehicle groups (Kodjak, 2015). Countries that have implemented policy actions towards fuel efficiency are divided into three main groups based on the implementation stage/policy action status. Under this typology, Mexico and China share certain attributes; both employ processes involving clean, low-sulphur, available or planned standards, but both also partially adopt external (de facto "global") standards (Euro or US EPA). Derived from this categorization of countries, it is possible to draw a two-country case-oriented comparison based on interpretation of literature and review of policies rather than bearing a set of variables. The study is focused on making an appropriate comparison in respect of fuel efficiency implementation processes in emerging economies.

Due to the governance and economic asymmetries between these two countries, the strategy adopted was based on a "Most Different Systems Design" method. According to Lor (2012), this method implies a selection of different countries that share a phenomenon which constitutes a societal challenge based on attributes rather than merely variables. The strategy aims to define a boundary of comparability useful for limiting the scope of the comparison. Nevertheless, the typology is used for reference purposes only because several countries even within the proposed groups may differ in their implementation stages of fuel efficiency standards. The criteria offered by this strategy are logical and consistent for the purposes of the research objectives.

---

[6]Mouton and Marais (1990, p. 137) define a typology as a conceptual framework in which phenomena are classified in terms of characteristics that they have in common with other phenomena.

3   Fuel Efficiency Standards in Emerging Economies

Fuel efficiency standards are understood as having a strong regulatory component; the adoption and scope of implementation of such standards depend on the stage of the value chain where they are intended to be applied. Fuel efficiency standards establish emission limits in the automotive industry; the indirect effect on the private or productive sector entails the adoption or development of new and clean technologies in order to make cars produce fewer emissions by making fuel usage more efficient. The adoption of this technology is voluntary; each company decides where and in which fleet investments would be feasible in order to comply with the standard. Several co-effects result from the adoption of such standards: improved air quality and public health caused by lessening particulate matter, nitrogen oxides and ozone molecule concentrations in the atmosphere, mobility and renewed automotive fleet in urban and peri-urban areas, among others (GFEI, 2010). The interplay between voluntary and/or mandatory standards on fuel efficiency remains in many emerging economies dependent on its implementation stage. For instance, USA and Mexico have both fuel economy and GHG standards, and manufacturers must satisfy both. By contrast, South Korea's light-duty vehicle manufacturers have the option to choose which standard to meet—fuel economy or GHG standard (IEA, 2015a).

In most scenarios, emerging economies usually adopt and implement fuel economy/efficiency standards based on a reference to the EU/US regulations that are modified according to its own national conditions and economic structures. This entails a complex process of norm diffusion from the global to the local level. Such adoption is in some cases mixed—this means incorporating elements from both (and other) regulations into a unique standard; in other cases, it is part of a homologation process on a regional basis. China and Mexico are clear examples of the above. As Mikler (2008, p. 1) suggests, fuel economy/efficiency implies that "sharing sovereignty in the process of making and implementing national regulations produces opportunities for global regulation"; fuel economy/efficiency standards require complex public–private governance where incentives, regulation and communication are vital. Therefore, fuel economy/efficiency standards are key components of a regulation process that could be analysed from the multi-level governance approach (Payne & Phillips, 2015; Evans, 2012), with the benefit of allowing the national implementation to be examined under the light of its own specific conditions without disregarding the global processes. The local–global inter-linkages that a regulation such as the fuel economy/efficiency one creates could be enablers/drivers for societal change (Hughes, 2010), not only in terms of environmental benefits, but under a wider sustainability scope.

The analysis of the China and Mexico cases aims to provide an overview of the implementation process of fuel efficiency standards in particular economies, in order to find their comparability elements. The idea of a differentiated local political and economic arrangement connecting with the global efforts to impulse fuel efficiency underlies this study.

3.1 The Case of China

The Chinese vehicle fuel economy standard is a weight class based, per vehicle and corporate average standard that is mandatory for every domestically made vehicle and is more stringent than its European counterpart (EIA, 2015). Light-duty vehicle manufacturers in China must meet a fuel-consumption standard at each weight class level and must meet an overall corporate average fuel-consumption standard. Vehicle fuel economy standards in China are based on 16 weight classes, ranging from vehicles weighing less than 750 kg (approximately 1500 lb) to vehicles weighing more than 2500 kg, or approximately 5500 lb. Based on the New European Driving Circle (NEDC) testing standard system, China has set a new fuel economy target for 2020, which would require the fleet average fuel economy to reach 5l/100 km. This target could translate into about 53 mpg US equivalent, or about 116 CO_2g/km EU equivalent (Arena & Mezzana, 2014).

China initially based its vehicle emission standard on that of Europe. In 2000, the Chinese government issued the first national emission standard for both heavy and light-duty vehicles that was equivalent to Euro I, followed by several more stringent standards in later years. The China National V emission standard was implemented nationwide by harmonizing the Euro V emission standard. Meanwhile, the China National VI emission standard was announced by the government at the end of 2016 to be implemented nationwide from 2019. Since the EU upgrades emission standards every 4–5 years or so, China sets new targets every 4.5 years on average in order to catch up with EU standards as early as possible, as the implementation of China's national emission standards usually lags behind Europe by 5–9 years (Table 1). With the acceleration of urbanization as well as localization of the auto industry, China has begun to design its own emission standards system. When setting the National VI emission standard for light-duty vehicles, the Chinese government introduced the US (California) standard, but at the same time it also developed a new National VI emission standard for heavy-duty vehicles, with no reference to the EU or the US model.

Table 1 Year of implementation of vehicle emission standards in China and EU

Vehicle emission standards	Year of implementation (all sales and registrations)		Time lag: China versus EU
	China	EU	
China National I (Euro I)	2000	1992	8
China National II (Euro II)	2004	1996	8
China National III (Euro III)	2007	2000	7
China National IV (Euro IV)	2010	2005	5
China National V (Euro V)	2018	2009	9

Source Authors

There were basically two factors that drove China to adopt the EU's emissions standards in the beginning. The first was its social circumstances; China's vast rural areas and population imply widespread need for the use of diesel trucks, rural and non-road vehicles, just as diesel vehicles are prevalent in the European market. The other was the late development of the auto industry, which meant that most of the domestically made vehicles depended on technologies from Europe.

Nowadays, China's urban population has exceeded its rural population and gasoline vehicles, especially passenger cars, have gained a dominating proportion in the cities and even in some rural areas. Meanwhile, although European car companies still retain a certain market share in China, American and Japanese automakers have been enlarging their business, which has diversified China's autoindustry. The changing landscape of China's urbanization and auto industry has led the Chinese government to create its own standards by taking the US (California) standards as reference. China's geographic area covers similar latitudes as those of the USA. What is more, diesel vehicles that enjoy less stringent regulations (when compared to gasoline vehicles) still dominate the European market, while 99% of China's vehicles today are gasoline vehicles, falling into a situation similar to the USA. Adopting fair regulations on gasoline and diesel vehicles, the US standards are a better fit for China's current situation.

In China, it is notable that all the vehicle efficiency standards are set by the central government, with several Ministries and state-owned oil companies involved.[7] These governmental institutions or enterprises with vested interests sometimes have conflicting views with regard to how to formulate vehicle efficiency standards. One typical example is that the Ministry of Ecology and Environment (MEE), which used to lack the authority to set standards, as the lead agency for developing and enforcing vehicle emission standards, can now exert a strong influence on specifying fuel quality parameters. In contrast, the auto industry seems to have a relatively weak voice in the process, while the participation of NGOs is negligible.

Since retail prices of gasoline and diesel have always been set by the National Development and Reform Commission (NDRC) on behalf of the central government in China, it is difficult for the oil industry to recoup capital investments on refinery upgrades without a market pricing mechanism. In addition, small refineries with outdated technologies are not cost effective to upgrade. Concerns about unemployment and other economic impacts from facility closures in some regions where these small refineries are located could cause more delay in tightening fuel standards. This is why China's fuel efficiency standards have consistently lagged behind the fuel requirements corresponding to the emission standards.[8] Since the best vehicle

---

[7]Some of these institutions are the National Development and Reform Commission (NDRC), Ministry of Industry and Information Technology (MIIT), Ministry of Science and Technology (MST), Ministry of Ecology and Environment (MEE), State Administration for Market Regulation (SAMR), China National Petroleum Corporation (CNPC) as well as China Petroleum and Chemical Corporation (SINOPEC).

[8]China's State Council issued the *Air Pollution Prevention and Control Action Plan* in September 2013, vowing to greatly improve air quality by 2017 in most Chinese cities, especially the metropolises. To implement this plan, the central government urged state-owned oil giants to quicken

emission performance can only be achieved if fuel and emission standards are implemented in parallel and a compliance program is established to enforce both fuel and vehicle standards, the staggered implementation of fuel standards has become a major roadblock in bringing down vehicle emissions.

Beijing, being the capital city, was one of the few exceptional places in China that could employ the highest fuel and emission standards simultaneously. For the sake of improving air quality, Beijing has pioneered the setting and implementation of these national standards. Most of the standards, from National I to V, were first piloted in Beijing and then fully applied across the nation after a gap of two or three years. For instance, in 2013, Beijing put the National V emission standard into practice, five years ahead of its proposed implementation nationwide.

3.2   The Case of Mexico

Mexico's fuel economy standard was first set in 2013, after several rounds of negotiations. NOM-163-SEMARNAT-ENER-SCFI-2013 (NOM 163) regulates year-model automobiles starting from 2012 productions. The norm that is referred to is the US Code of Federal Regulations vol. 40 parts 85, 86 and 600 and the Light-Duty Vehicle Greenhouse Gas Emissions Standards and Corporate Average Fuel Economy Standards Final Rule (EPA, 2010). NOM 163 complements the existing regulations on fuel limits and average methods,[9] which, nevertheless, had never included components such as emission goals (g-CO_2/km) and Corporate Average Fuel Economy Standards. When published, this standard became a model in the region, being the first Latin American standard of its type (with other countries such as Peru, Chile and Argentina developing similar schemes), reflecting a complex relation within the North American region.[10]

The major drivers for the implementation of such a standard are linked to air quality (health effects) and climate change. Since the mid-1980s, air pollution became a major problem in urban areas in Mexico, mainly in the Metropolitan area of Mexico City. According to Molina (2005), some policies were implemented aiming to establish major pollutants' permissible limits, gaining some results for certain pollutants

---

their pace on fuel quality upgrading, in order to keep up with the more stringent vehicle emission standards. Chinese Premier Li Keqiang has reiterated the significance of domestic gasoline and diesel standards improvement in coping with environmental pollution. He encouraged further investment and technological innovation by major oil companies, which could lead to an early accomplishment of the set goals.

[9]Mexico uses the US-combined test cycle officially, although several companies—mainly the European ones—may incorporate the New European Driving Cycle (NEDC) into their plants' processes.

[10]In fact, the Mexican standard on fuel efficiency was created with an effort to look for a homologation with the USA standard proposed by then President Barack Obama in 2009, followed by Canada in 2010. The Mexican norm tries to homologate the 2016 USA goals of 35.5 miles per US Gallon (mpg). However, depending on the priorities of the newly elected Mexican Government, the Mexican standard's revision could point to another direction.

(mainly lead, carbon dioxide and sulphur dioxide), but retaining high levels of particulate material (PM_{10} and $PM_{2.5}$), carbon monoxide and ozone. In 2003, norms on vehicles were first issued, trying to reduce smog and limit pollutant emissions, followed by health-related standards on limits to all pollutants. Also, implementation of specific public policies for reducing emissions coming from mobile sources (such as Vehicle Verification Programs or the circulation restriction program (*Hoy no circula*) fostered an awareness of the high impact of transport on air quality.

Mexico has used the US EPA reference and test method as a "global best" reference for its own national standard setting. The Mexican fuel efficiency norm is aligned in design and depth with the US and Canadian standards (ICCT, 2012), trying to equal efficiency levels by 2016. In 2012, then US President Barack Obama announced a new 54.5 mpg (20.9 K/l) goal for USA fuel efficiency by 2025 (The White House, 2012)—considerably higher than the Mexican 2016 goal (whose revision process started in 2018). However, in 2018, the Trump administration announced a new policy shift, abandoning the standards and freezing them to the 2020 values, arguing they were too high and expensive (Walsh, 2018). US EPA announced a new rule named "Safer Affordable Fuel-Efficient" (SAFE) for the years 2021–2025, which was criticized by a group of scientists (Bento, et al., 2018). In order to match this goal, the subsequent Mexican regulation has to be more solid and set higher thresholds. This, however, could be contested by the private sector—as was the case in 2012. This is notwithstanding the recent environmental concerns regarding urban air pollution, alteration and corruption in the vehicle verification testing methods and technologies used by international automotive companies, which undermined fuel efficiency governance, and the regulatory challenges in getting the standard updated on the basis of robust modelling instruments.

The transport sector is therefore a complex issue in terms of standards-related processes in the country, either for climate change reduction schemes or fuel efficiency. During the standards negotiation process, some of the concerns of the automotive sector were the cost effectiveness and terms of its mandate. Mostly dependent on foreign technology, imports would modify the commercial chain of technology associated with autoparts and engines in terms of compliance, posing serious challenges to the industry actors. Another barrier to the implementation of the standard was the absence of an overall standards policy that provides direction to all the standards related to a certain area. Although there is, for instance, a clear relation between the fuel economy standards and both health and climate change policies, the standard was negotiated separately with the automotive industry with a focus on industry implications rather than on health impacts. In-depth analysis is also likely to show that there are significant gaps in the standard setting process (standard cycle), which does not link development planning and normative analysis in a clear fashion. The Mexican experience shows that a wide vision of integral and multi-dimensional policies is needed in order to create a clearly-articulated policy that has governance mandates for all sectors involved.[11]

---

[11] The necessity of updating the NOM 163 in Mexico has been supported, however, by parallel environmental policies. In preparing a new national communication for the United Nations Framework

3.3   China and Mexico: A Comparative Analysis

Both country cases demonstrate that there are several attributes and features related to their fuel efficiency standards implementation processes that are similar. First, the transportation sector in both countries is currently regarded as one of the main contributors to overall GHG emissions, mainly because commercial vehicles have become one of the most important sources of air pollution. In Beijing, Shanghai and other Chinese metropolitan areas, passenger vehicles are major contributors to the overall GHG emissions due to traffic congestion. Similarly, in Mexico the transport sector contributed in 2015 with 25.1% of total GHG emissions in the country, mainly dominated by freight and passenger vehicles (23.4% of total GHG emissions) (INECC, 2018). According to Mexico's Climate Change Special Program, 94% of the current transport GHG-related emissions come from road transportation. Besides, Mexico is the second largest market for new vehicles in Latin America, with a medium annual growth rate of 7.09% from 2013 to 2017 (1.3 million units per year projected average) (PROMEXICO, 2014, p. 16). A future increase in automobile consumption in both countries could exacerbate the global warming effect.[12]

Second, China and Mexico rank among the 15 largest automobile producers (first and thirteenth place respectively in 2018) and are leading automobile exporters in the world (JATO, 2019). According to the International Organization of Motor Vehicle Manufacturers (OICA), Chinese and Mexican car industries represented 30.7% of the global total of cars and commercial vehicle production in 2017 (OICA, 2018). At the same time, light-duty vehicles sales and exports in both countries have been increasing significantly (PROMEXICO, 2014).[13] Through exports, China and Mexico could bring about some indirect impacts for importing countries in terms of their national GHG emissions.

Third, both China and Mexico have to fulfil their individual commitments on combating climate change as a part of the global efforts and seek alignment in climate actions based on their own national interests. By the end of June 2015, both

---

Convention on Climate Change (UNFCCC), Mexico is preparing technological routes in which fuel efficiency standards for light vehicles will play a very relevant mitigation role. Discussions on a new standard for heavy duty-vehicles, and discussions on the energy transition requirements seem to pose new challenges for future debates.

[12] Mexico City entered into an environmental air quality crisis in early 2016 because the Metropolitan Index of Air Quality (IMECA) was surpassed for more than 150 points after 14 years of stability. Allegedly, one of the main causes of this was a court decision in June 2015 that allowed particular vehicle owners to get a protection against the assignation requirements for the vehicle verification programme based on year-model rather than emissions, which changed the criteria allowing for circulating cars. This, along with altered verification schemes, increased the number of cars circulating in the city to more than one million per day.

[13] The new international context for the car industry has affected the traditional car manufacturing geography. While the US, Canada, Japan and France have showed a decline in their production rates, emerging producers such as China, India, Brazil and Korea have showed considerable growth. Although in the last year (April 2018–2019) Mexico showed an important decrease on its car sales (−10.4%), it has shown growth and stability in the period 2012–2016. Investment announcements and growing road infrastructure are complementary elements for these dynamics.

China and Mexico had presented their new climate mitigation and adaptation targets after 2020, under their Nationally Determined Contributions (NDC)[14] to the United Nations Framework Convention on Climate Change (UNFCCC), where the transport sector is a key player.

The standard setting and implementation processes in both China and Mexico have been quite different. Norm diffusion rests on a diversity of factors within each country: socio-economic structure, regulatory framework, private sector engagement, industry and investments and even sub-regional standards application. The key dissimilarity is the adoption of different reference standards: while China has been working under the EU's regulatory framework, Mexico has set a partial homologation with the US EPA regulation. Consequently, the adoption of different targets, indicators, testing methods, fleet targets, penalties, incentives, etc., opens the possibility of analysing how the implementation process of fuel efficiency/economy standards in both economies has aligned with global commitment while at the same time being aligned with their own national development conditions.

4   Conclusion

Fuel efficiency is at the core of a local–global solution for GHG emissions reduction by addressing the negative impacts of vehicle fuel-consumption patterns, and generating significant local impacts that could be translated into global benefits. It is notable that a series of efficiency programs such as Europe's Euro VI and US's EPA 2010 have been undertaken on a global scale, thus becoming the de facto "global" standards, but it is relevant to analyse how this standardization process has been translated and adapted in emerging economies where fuel use, GHG emissions and economic growth will tend to increase.

When applying the European or American models to some emerging economies like China and Mexico, we found a difference in situations. Although EU/US standards are relevant for ensuring comprehensive frameworks for action, standards do not always consider national contexts of the emerging countries, neglecting their specific economic and sectoral conditions. At the same time, although standards are a recognized policy tool and a cost-effective strategy for private investment in many emerging economies (both at the national and local levels), there is a lack of proper standard setting or application processes related to the respective economic and political structure. The result is a domestically challenging multi-stakeholder process that leads to ineffective operations and local–global dialogue, resulting in insufficient mitigation mechanisms that could harm both economic development and environmental balance in emerging markets.

Fuel efficiency standards could be considered as both performance and sustainability standards, for they aim at reducing environmentally and socially harmful

---

[14]Mexico has started the national revision of its NDC mitigation and adaptation goals, under the mandate of Article 4 of the Paris Agreement, for its completion in 2020.

impacts of vehicles. Almost all of these standards are set up by national government agencies to provide legally binding requirements for general market access, thus becoming public mandatory sustainability standards. In terms of the geographic and systemic reach as well as ambition, vehicle fuel efficiency and GHG emissions standards adopted by a single country could also generate sustainability benefits transnationally. Such standards are focused on both product performance and the production process, and will in most cases apply strict criteria for the sake of climate and environment in both the national and international contexts. At the domestic level, frequent interactions between public and private sectors finally shape these standards that become legally mandated. Meanwhile, dialogues between national and international standards or regulations are conducted from time to time. As the International Energy Agency (IEA) suggests (2011, 2015b), fuel efficiency standards are at the core of sound transport and mobility policies that care for environmental and social effects, and promote a technology transition from fossil fuels to clean technologies. Measures such as labelling, eco-driving policies, electric mobility, transport batteries and efficiency together could play a transformational role in re-shaping energy systems nationally and globally.

The application of efficiency standards in emerging economies should guide public policies, investments and other partnerships in a holistic and in-context manner, responding to sustainable development, green economy, climate change and industrial sector priorities. Fuel efficiency standards represent an illustrative example of how this could be translated into practice, with governance playing a key role. "Global" (EU/US) standards should not be considered as a "one-size-fits-all" solution, but rather as a sustainable guideline to reduce emissions worldwide.

References

Arena, F., Mezzana L. (2014), *The automotive CO$_2$ emissions challenge: 2020 Regulatory scenario for passenger cars.* Boston: Arthur D. Little.

Bento, A. M., Gillingham, K., Jacobsen, M. R., Knittel, C. R., Leard, B., Linn, J., … Whitefoot, K. S. (2018). Flawed analyses of U.S. auto fuel economy standards. *Science, 362*(6419), 1119–1121. (Washington).

Environmental Protection Agency. (2010). *Final rulemaking to establish light duty vehicle greenhouse gas emission standards and corporate average fuel standards.* Washington: Regulatory Impact Analysis. EPA.

Evans, J. (2012). *Environmental governance.* London: Routledge.

Global Fuel Economy Initiative (WY), *LDV fuel economy and the G20.* New York: GFEI.

Global Fuel Economy Initiative. (2010). *Improving vehicle fuel economy in the ASEAN region. GFEI, FIA Foundation, International Energy Agency, International Transport Forum, United Nations Environment Program.* London: GFEI.

Global Fuel Economy Initiative (2015), *Fuel economy and the UN´s Post 2015 Sustainable Development Goals.* GFEI- FIA Foundation-Sustainable Energy for All. London. Retrieved from http://www.fiafoundation.org/media/24869/fuel-economy-and-un-post-2015-sdg.pdf.

Hughes, O. (2010). Does governance exist? In S. P. Osborne (Ed.), *The new public governance? Emerging perspectives on the theory and practice of public governance.* London: Routledge.

International Council on Clean Transportation. (2012). *Mexico light-duty vehicle CO_2 and fuel economy standards*. Washington: ICCT.

International Energy Agency. (2011). *25 Energy efficiency recommendations 2011 update*. Paris: IEA.

International Energy Agency. (2014). *Key world energy statistics*. Paris: IEA.

International Energy Agency. (2015a). *Vehicle standards around the world aim to improve fuel economy and reduce emissions*. Paris: IEA.

International Energy Agency. (2015b). *Regional energy efficiency recommendations for Latin America and the Caribbean*. Paris: IEA.

International Organization of Motor Vehicle Manufacturers (OICA). (2018). *Provisional registrations or sales of new vehicles—All types*. Paris: Estimated Figures. OICA.

JATO Dynamics Limited (JATO). (2019). *Global car market remains stable during 2018, as continuous demand for SUVs offsets decline in sales of compact cars and MPVs*. Oxford: JATO.

Kodjak, D. (2015). *Policies to reduce fuel consumption, air pollution, and carbon emissions from vehicles in G20 Nations*. Washington: International Council on Clean Transportation.

Lor, P. (2012). *International and comparative librarianship: A thematic approach*. Munich: De Gruyter Saur.

Mikler, J. (2008). *Sharing sovereignty for global regulation: The cases of fuel economy and online gambling*. Sydney: Blackwell Publishing Asia Pty.

Molina, M. Molina, L. (Coords.). (2005). *La Calidad del Aire en la Megaciudad de México*. México: Fondo de CulturaEconómica.

Mouton, J., & Marais, H. C. (1990). *Basic concepts: The methodology of the social sciences (HSRC studies in research methodology)*. Pretoria: HSRC Press.

National Institute of Ecology and Climate Change (INECC) (2018). *National inventory of greenhouse gas emissions 1990–2015*. Mexico.

PROMEXICO (2014), *IndustriaAutomotriz*. Ministry of Economy. Mexico: ProMéxico.

Payne, A., & Phillips, N. (Eds.). (2015). *Handbook of the international political economy of governance*. London: Edward Elgar Publishing Inc.

Sims, R., Schaeffer, R., Creutzig, F., Cruz-Núñez, X., D'Agosto, M., Dimitriu. D., Figueroa Meza, M.J., Fulton, L., Kobayashi, S., Lah, O., McKinnon, A., Newman, P., Ouyang, M., Schauer, J.J., Sperling, D., Tiwari, G. (2014). *Transport. Climate Change 2014: Mitigation of Climate Change. Contribution of Working Group III to the Fifth Assessment Report of the Intergovernmental Panel on Climate Change*. [Edenhofer, O., Pichs-Madruga, R., Sokona, Y., Farahani, E., Kadner, S., Seyboth, K., Adler, A., Baum, I., Brunner, S., Eickemeier, P., Kriemann, B., Savolainen, J., Schlömer, S., von Stechow, C., Zwickel, T. and Minx, J.C. (eds.)]. Cambridge and New York: Cambridge University Press.

Stec, S., & Baraj, B. (Eds.). (2009). *Energy and environmental challenges to security. Series NATO science for peace and security: Environmental security*. London: Springer.

The White House (2012). *Obama administration finalizes historic 54.5 MPG fuel efficiency standards*. Washington: Press release. Office of the Press Secretary, The White House.

Walsch, D. (2018). *Economists rebuke Trump administration fuel economy standard analysis*. Cambridge: MIT Management Sloan School, MIT.

Chapter 12
Standard-Setting in Water Use and Sustainable Development: A Comparative Critical Analysis of Grey Water Recycling in the Tourism Sector

André Coelho, Alexandre Domingues, Maria Cândida A. de M. Mousinho, and Cassia Saretta

1 Introduction

Tourism is a key sector for studies related to sustainability and the use of natural resources towards truly inclusive development. The sector is responsible for nearly 10% of the world's GDP and for the generation of 280 million jobs. In 2015, approximately 1 billion tourists performed domestic or international trips, circulating trillions of dollars in the world economy (World Travel & Tourism Council, 2016). The number of international tourist arrivals worldwide is expected to increase by an average of 3.3% a year over the period 2010 to 2030 (UNWTO, 2016). Cited by the United Nations (UN) as the strongest sector for job creation (United Nations General Asembly, 2014), it is, however, also responsible for an aggressive use of resources such as water, food, wood and fossil fuels. Despite the fact that it is an industry related to leisure and cultural awareness, the sector has a deep impact on the use of natural resources and natural services.

In contemporary society, water is, in its most simple form of understanding, synonymous with life. It is no wonder that the astronomical sciences search for this natural resource in other spheres of the universe as evidence of the possibility of life. More concretely, the fact is that human beings have always needed this natural

A. Coelho (✉)
Fundação Getulio Vargas (FGV), Rio de Janeiro, Brazil
e-mail: andre.coelho@fgv.br

A. Domingues
Ministry of Planning, Budget and Management, Brasília, Brazil

M. C. A. de M. Mousinho
Federal Institute of Education, Science and Technology (IFBA), Salvador, Brazil

C. Saretta
Ministry of Environment/Brazilian Forest Service (BFS), Brasília, Brazil

© The Editor(s) (if applicable) and The Author(s) 2020   201
A. Negi et al. (eds.), *Sustainability Standards and Global Governance*,
https://doi.org/10.1007/978-981-15-3473-7_12

resource as a source of livelihood and it is an unassailable reality that they will continue to do so. The scientific and technological advances in the areas of food, health, transport, for example, would not have been possible without the systematic use of water, which shows that this source is not only a fundamental need for human existence, but crucial for the realization of all other needs.

The implementation of up-to-date sustainability standards or practices aligned with a multi-stakeholder regulatory framework for water use may complement the international collaboration on new solutions at local, national and regional levels. In order to establish a pilot study, this chapter aims to understand to what extent standards and regulations apply to the sustainable use of water in the hotel industry. The study highlights the multi-stakeholder nature of sustainability standards, using the tourism sector in an exploratory and comparative analysis of the tourist areas of two major cities. Rio de Janeiro, in Brazil, was used as an example of an internationally appealing Latin American city without any formal standards for water use. Berlin, in Germany, was used as a seemingly contrasting example for the implementation of sustainability standards.

2 Tourism and Sustainable Development

Several authors have studied the tourism industry from the perspective of sustainability, focusing on aspects relating to its carbon footprint (Sun, 2014), energy, culture, water and environmental impacts as a whole (Aall, 2011; Collins, Jones, & Munday, 2009; Law & Cheung, 2007; Li, Wichmann, & Otterpohl, 2009; Radwan, Jones, & Minoli, 2012). They have all gained prominent attention in recent years as the notion of the environmental externality of tourism growth has found focus.

The conceptual framework of sustainability seems to be in accordance with the growth of the leisure industry, as the main tourism products (segments) in the world are directly linked to natural resources (Beach & Sun, Ecotourism and Cultural Tourism). Sustainability is a concept that focuses on the fate of the next generations; it is based on the challenge of maintaining the lifestyle of the present in the future (Georgescu-Roegen, 1971). The effects of the increase of tourists circulating in the world are thus not to be measured in terms of their current status but are to be viewed in the context of their long-lasting impact.

The activities of tourists at destinations are additional to those of local residents and regular transit visitors, and their presence adds to the overall environmental impact at the location. Several studies prove that the use of natural resources by someone who is not a local resident is at least two times higher than the optimal use by a local user (Aall, 2011; Gössling et al., 2012; International Network on Regional Economics, Mobility and Tourism & World Tourism Organization, 2012; Law & Cheung, 2007; Martinez-Alier, 2015). According to Li, Yang, Liu, and Zheng (2014), tourist flow has a seasonal diversity, with strong effects in the peak season (usually the summer half of the year in most destinations) and weak effects in the off-season (usually the winter half of the year in most destinations) (Gatt & Schranz, 2015). Local destinations with high tourist flow are certain to experience environmental effects, comparable to cities. Similar to urban island effects in cities, tourist destinations are expected to have destination island effects, in which one or more environmental indexes are significantly higher than those of the surrounding non-tourism areas.

The hospitality business—especially hotels—has been studied as a driver of sustainability standards in tourism as the main employer (workforce) in the sector and as one of the biggest sectors in terms of financial movements for investments (Gatt & Schranz, 2015; Li, Yang, Liu, & Zheng, 2014; Rahman, Dayang-Affizzah, & Edman, 2012). Hotels are involved in several aspects of sustainability, from white papers and corporate commitments to cleaner operation that is recognized by the client, who, sometimes, endorses that by expressing loyalty to the brand. From the used towels that should be hung and reused to solar panels that capture energy to warm up pools and spa areas; from water reuse procedures to roof panels that capture rainwater for gardening use, big chains and small hospitality businesses have been studied in several contexts, but the literature does not show a major concern for expanding the sustainbility impacts of local tourism as a worldwide concern.

Focusing on tourism accommodation as the locus of tourism, water consumption and conventional water indicators are reviewed and discussed, and knowledge gaps identified. From the tourism sector to regular home use, industrial consumption or agricultural irrigation, the use of water is key to pursuing a quality of life. Its use has proved contentious both in economic terms and in socio-cultural and environmental terms. The relationship between humankind and nature sometimes lacks complementarity—as when usage that is necessary for self-sufficiency turns into usage in a hegemonic, exploitative mode.

3 The Use of Water and Sustainability

Not only is water the most important natural resource in all economic cycles, it is central to the very survival of human beings on the planet. How to properly use this source is a crucial challenge in contemporary society—especially considering a scenario in which the demand for water is expected to increase by 55% by 2050. In addition to this, we must consider the lack of accessibility to this source—approximately 800 million people do not have access to quality drinking water in the world. Environmental issues are significant as well—projections indicate change in temporal and spatial distribution of water resources, potentially leading to hydrological disasters (WWAP, 2015).

Water management standards may become the norm in the future (Styles, Schoenberger, & Galvez-Martos, 2015). A general review of the use of water is an urgent issue when it comes to human needs and consumption. Even considering that most of the water available in the world is used in agricultural and industrial operations, regular personal use also needs to be addressed (Charara, Cashman, Bonnell, & Gehr, 2011; Gössling, 2015; Li, Wichmann, & Otterpohl, 2009; Millimet & Roy, 2015; Styles et al., 2015).

Several normative standards apply to a variety of water management and recycling techniques. The International Organization for Standardization (ISO) has more than 200 norms on water recycling systems, from portability criteria to equipment installation processes. Most countries also have local norms that apply and that follow the same path. Table 1 shows examples of ISO standards regarding water reuse.

Thus, the management of water resources does not depend exclusively on public entities, but also on a range of private actors (Jiménez-Cisneros, 2014). The entry of the business sector, taking advantage of an emerging green market (Montibeller-Filho, 2004), was characteristic of environmentalism in the 1990s and a positive factor for sustainable development. It should be noted that, already in the mid-1990s, the concept of sustainable development had been translated into a model to guide business practice that would be economically viable and at the same time socially and environmentally sustainable (Vizeu, Meneghetti, & Seifert, 2012). Similarly, the ever-growing number of voluntary sustainability standards (VSS)—many of them

Table 1 Examples of ISO standards regarding water reuse

Source (Techn. Committee)	Normative standard examples	Further details
ISO/TC 147 Participating countries: 42 Creation date: 1971	Standardisation in the field of water quality, including definition of terms, sampling of water, measurement and reporting of water characteristics	Total number of published ISO standards related to TC 147 and its SCs (number includes updates): 288
ISO/TC 224 Participating countries: 35 Creation date: 2001	Standardisation of a framework for the definition and measurement of service activities relating to drinking water supply systems and wastewater systems	Four published ISO standards under the direct responsibility of ISO/TC 224 (1) ISO 24510:2007—Guidelines for the assessment and for the improvement of the service to users (2) ISO 24511:2007—Guidelines for the management of wastewater utilities and for the assessment of wastewater services (3) ISO 24512:2007—Guidelines for the management of drinking water utilities and for the assessment of drinking water services (4) ISO 24518:2015—Crisis management of water utilities

(continued)

Table 1 (continued)

Source (Techn. Committee)	Normative standard examples	Further details
ISO/TC 282 Water reuse Participating countries: 21 Creation date: 2013	ISO 16075:2015 - Guidelines for treated wastewater use for irrigation projects	Scope: Standardisation of water reuse of any kind and for any purpose. It covers centralized and decentralised or onsite water reuses, direct and indirect ones as well as intentional and unintentional ones. It includes technical, economic, environmental and societal aspects of water reuse. Water reuse comprises a sequence of the stages and operations involved in uptake, conveyance, processing, storage, distribution, consumption, drainage and other handling of wastewater, including the water reuse in repeated, cascaded and recycled ways. The scope of ISO/TC 253 (treated wastewater reuse for irrigation) is merged into the proposed new committee.

Source Authors: compiled from https://www.iso .org

developed by coalitions of non-state actors—have provided market-based mechanisms for sustainability in production and consumption, e.g. for sustainable resource use.

Among the several procedures and practices for the sustainable use of water (which may or may not be required by a specific sustainability standard), the use of grey water is a reference to saving fresh, clean or treated water from regular human use. In the context of this chapter, we will focus on water use by tourists and corresponding opportunities for grey water recycling.

Grey Water as a Driver for the Safer Use of Natural Resources

Grey water is a type of wastewater generated in hotels, households or office buildings from sinks, showers, baths, washing machines or dishwashers. It is considered as containing fewer pathogens than domestic wastewater and is generally safer to handle and easier to treat and reuse onsite for toilet flushing, landscape or crop irrigation and other non-potable uses. The application of grey water reuse in major buildings such as hotels provides substantial benefits for both the water supply subsystem by reducing the demand for fresh clean water as well as the wastewater subsystems by reducing the amount of wastewater required to be conveyed and treated. It is economically viable in most aspects for major operations and simple to implement (Al-Jayyousi, 2003; Gatt & Schranz, 2015; Styles et al., 2015). Grey water, by definition, is different from discharge of toilets and contaminated wastewater, which is designated as black water to indicate that it contains human waste. The implementation of the system is technically feasible; it is basically a matter of civil engineering arrangements to reallocate pipes that will be connected to an alternative discharge system.

4 Methodology

This chapter evaluates two hotel samples in two major tourist cities in the world and checks the use of grey water recycling systems. This is not a statistical study, but an exploratory analysis with both primary and secondary data. Therefore, the process of separation of the sample follows two basic criteria: (1) geographical criteria, which means that the hotel should be in a predominantly tourist area; (2) a qualification criterion, which means that within the selected areas, only the best-evaluated hotels[1] (three to five stars) were selected to respond. After the methodological criteria application, not more than thirty hotels were selected in each city and contacted over telephone in the second half of 2015 to respond to three questions: (1) existence of grey water system; (2) total number of rooms; and (3) number of rooms connected to the system.

The chosen cities were Rio de Janeiro in Brazil and Berlin in Germany. For the Brazilian sample, 27 hotels responded to the research, all located in the Copacabana tourist region. In the German sample, 18 hotels responded to the research, mostly located in Berlin Mitte. All hotels contacted were members of major alliances or had a capacity for meeting international sustainability standards.

The data references were based on the literature for grey water use, which estimates that freshwater consumption for high-end hotels with more than 100 rooms is, for example, 126 litres per day (l/day), considering exclusive individual use (shower/bath/sink) plus the use of 12 l/day for cleaning (Styles et al., 2015). This adds up to 138 l/day, without the consideration of toilet use (aim of this article). Other studies based on Nolde (2000) complement the findings of Gössling (2015) and suggest 95 and 81 l/day as references for individual use (shower/bath/sink). Experiments conducted in a summer hotel on the Spanish island of Mallorca suggest 110 l/day (March, Gual, & Orozco, 2004), a number that was considered for our calculations of annual water use in hotels of the Copacabana region (Sample 1). For hotels in Berlin (Sample 2), a different value (81 l/day) was used to reflect different toilet water discharge equipment, cultural factors and weather conditions influencing water use.

The parameters for toilet discharge of water (not suited for recycling) were also derived from March et al. (2004) for Sample 1 (Copacabana) and amounted to 36 l/day for individual use; Styles et al. (2015) (38 l/day), Nolde (2000) (57 l/day) and Gössling (2015) (21 l/day) do not differ much from this number. For the above-mentioned

---

[1] Evaluations based on Trip Advisor's standards. The hotels were investigated in specific tourist areas.

reasons (technical, cultural and weather-related factors), the lowest number (21 l/day) from this row was again used to calculate annual values for Sample 2 (Berlin).

Given their exploratory and approximate character, the quantitative results in Table 3 (Sect. 5) are not meant to statistically evaluate and rank the two tourist regions under review, but rather to present a broad spectrum of different water use patterns and saving potentials based on two simplified examples.

In addition, eight hotel maintenance managers were willing to complement our quantitative estimates with more detailed interviews. They were interviewed in order to check for two conditions: (1) whether the implementation was driven by an external requirement or by a strategic decision of the hotel managers and (2) whether there were sustainability standards or procedures on grey water to be followed.

5 Results and Analysis

In the hotel business, several procedures are currently applied to mitigate the environmental impacts of major hospitality operations in tourist destinations, but, in most cases, they are driven by internal regulations, market strategies or certification. According to the literature referenced in this chapter, the reuse of grey water is currently one of the easiest procedures used by hotels to reduce the use of freshwater, but its use is restricted to some hotels only and the reasons for this limited application are still not clear.

For the qualitative questions, seven out of eight managers interviewed highlighted that there was no specific sustainability standard mandating them to use grey water systems. In fact, each company implemented the equipment based on its own evaluation. One manager mentioned public incentives for hotels following specific sustainable criteria related to electric energy and water use. Table 2 shows the requirements and standards implemented by hotels.

The qualitative results indicate that hotels using recycling systems were driven by interests related to their own evaluations and expectations—from economic

Table 2 Qualitative interviews with hotel maintenance managers

Sample	Motivation for the implementation of grey water system	Sustainability standards in place
Copacabana group	All managers said that it was an internal strategic decision without any external direction	No sustainability standards, but technical standards for water potability and system installation
Berlin Mitte group	Three managers mentioned that it was an internal decision and one mentioned a possible public fund for sustainability practices, including other activities related to energy	No sustainability standards, but technical standards for water potability and system installation

Source Authors

savings to recognition through clients and contributions to international brands' white papers. This suggests that standards towards sustainable tourism and the common good, unlike standards for technical operations, are not yet common, at least in the sample sector and regions, even though such initiatives in principle exist (e.g. Rainforest Alliance Verification Standard for Tourism Services, Travelife Award, Global Sustainable Tourism Criteria/GSTC and a range of regional/national schemes). Additionally, the companies did not follow any regulatory procedure that could work as an incentive to the implementation of a recycling water system.

The quantitative results are displayed in Table 3. Out of 27 hotels analyzed in Rio de Janeiro, only four had a grey water management system in operation, while out of 18 hotels consulted in Berlin, seven of them had one. Since water use and saving rate per unit were assumed to be higher for the Brazilian sample than for the German one, the total amount of savings was also higher (Table 3) although less hotels had a recycling system in place. In turn, as the proportion of hotels using a recycling system was much lower in the overall Brazilian sample compared to the German one, the amount saved in Rio de Janeiro was proportionally lower than in Berlin. However, even considering that the results for Berlin were better than for the

Table 3 Major quantitative results for water savings

	Total use/savings of the sample (l)	Total use/savings of the samples (M^3)	Olympic pools[g]	% of total use
Total use (Copacabana)[a]	413,043,968.88	413,043.97	165.2	–
Total use (Berlin)[b]	248,847,710.02	248,847.71	99.5	–
Total savings (Copacabana)[c]	28,249,239.24	28,249.24	11.3	6.84
Total savings (Berlin)[d]	20,077,118.46	20,077.12	8.0	8.07
Total possible savings (Copacabana)[e]	101,846,458.08	101,846.46	40.7	24.66
Total possible savings (Berlin)[f]	57,426,394.62	57,426.39	23.0	23.08

Source Authors
[a]Estimated total (fresh) water use per year of the Brazilian sample (27 hotels, all rooms)
[b]Estimated total (fresh) water use per year of the German sample (18 hotels, all rooms)
[c]Estimated water savings in one year of operation of grey water recycling for the Brazilian sample (4 hotels out of 27, only those rooms connected to the system were considered)
[d]Estimated water savings in one year of operation of grey water recycling for the German sample (7 hotels out of 18, only those rooms connected to the system were considered)
[e, f]Total possible savings if 100% of the sample had the system
[g]Average Olympic pool with 2.5 million litres

Brazilian sample, the majority of hotels consulted did not have the system in either country.

Among our findings, there is a clear conclusion that the use of recycling systems for water is relevant in terms of the volume saved in the tourism industry. Just considering water savings in the studied sample, the results show that 6.86% and 8.07%, respectively, of the total water used in one year across the two samples were saved. Translating these results into commonly understood terms, in the Brazilian sample there was a total saving equivalent to 11 Olympic water pools in one year of operation among the rooms with the system installed. In Germany, 8 Olympic water pools could be saved within the sample analyzed. A greater result could be expected if the whole industry in one city would be using this recycling system.

Exploring our data and case studies from literature, on average, hotels using recycling systems may save between 20 and 25% of all the water used in their rooms. Since neither standards nor regulations play a major role across these samples as a driver for sustainability yet, they needed to be rebalanced, especially towards more regulatory procedures. At present, hotels are simply taking their own initiatives.

Towards a Regulatory Framework
The primary research has highlighted a trend. Across the globe, there are significant differences in water consumption with respect to resource endowment, pollution, technical composition, natural cycle, recycling, etc. In addition to estimating and comparing the use of freshwater for human consumption and commercial use we came across a simple conclusion: there is a need to eliminate endogeneity and transform the process of saving this natural resource into a regulatory framework, where private and public sectors could benefit from reduced consumption and from recycling.

The process of "greening" the tourism industry is not an easy task. However, for the cases studied, environmental regulation can exert a significant effect on commercial productivity. It is a matter of implementing voluntary standards and mandatory regulations before relevant economic variables reach the critical point affected by the scarcity of water. Here, we have made an empirical estimation of the threshold characteristics of environmental regulation for tourism, and simple suggestions can already be put in place.

In the voluntary field, the adoption of sustainable practices is already happening in the hotel industry, but, as we could map, even for high-end brands the adoption of technical procedures to save water is not related to political encouragement or pressure but to an economic motivation. This is not a bad thing, but it could be much better executed if there would be an official yet voluntary framework to guide market actions. The Sustainable Development Goals (SDGs) could be a relevant starting point to link voluntary practices of the tourism industry, such as grey water recycling, to broader questions of sustainability and the management of natural resources in the global arena. Voluntary standards for sustainable tourism, as mentioned in Sect. 5, can constitute an important instrument to substantiate and implement the SDGs in this sector.

Within the SDGs framework, there are several topics that relate to the discussion raised in this chapter and the proper adoption of these concepts could lead to better-organized activities for saving freshwater. Table 4 highlights the potential of selected SDGs to guide transformation in three categories related to this chapter: sustainability cooperation, water use and tourism.

In addition to voluntary standards adoption based on SDGs, mandatory regulation may be required. Considering that regulatory actions for protecting the environment vary significantly from industry to industry (including tourism), while different industries may respond differently to the same regulation, it is important to introduce more effective regulatory incentives towards the sustainable use of water. Indeed, environmental regulation has a significant positive correlation with increased environmental productivity

Table 4 Themes of this chapter as reflected in selected SDGs

Sustainability cooperation	Water use	Tourism
17.1 Strengthen domestic resource mobilization, including through international support to developing countries, to improve domestic capacity for tax and other revenue collection 17.14 Enhance policy coherence for sustainable development 17.17 Encourage and promote effective public, public-private and civil society partnerships, building on the experience and resourcing strategies of partnerships	6.4 By 2030, substantially increase water use efficiency across all sectors and ensure sustainable withdrawals and supply of freshwater to address water scarcity and substantially reduce the number of people suffering from water scarcity 6.5 By 2030, implement integrated water resources management at all levels, including through transboundary cooperation as appropriate 6.a By 2030, expand international cooperation and capacity-building support to developing countries in water- and sanitation-related activities and programmes, including water harvesting, desalination, water efficiency, wastewater treatment, recycling and reuse technologies 6.b Support and strengthen the participation of local communities in improving water and sanitation management	8.9 By 2030, devise and implement policies to promote sustainable tourism that creates jobs and promotes local culture and products 12.6 Encourage companies, especially large and transnational companies, to adopt sustainable practices and to integrate sustainability information into their reporting cycle 12.8 By 2030, ensure that people everywhere have the relevant information and awareness for sustainable development and lifestyles in harmony with nature 12.b Develop and implement tools to monitor sustainable development impacts for sustainable tourism that creates jobs and promotes local culture and products

Source Authors' compilation based on the 2030 Agenda for Sustainable Development

A regulatory framework towards the better use of water in tourism and other commercial activities could be the result of an evolution. Continuous changes must be achieved because as the recycling water concept matures, policymakers have to face new challenges. The introduction of mandatory regulation for water use in tourism should be based on at least three considerations:

1. Technological and cost evolution: rigid and at the same time flexible schemes may be required ranging from tax benefits to special financing lines for infrastructure;
2. Socio-economic justice: as water is a natural resource that belongs to everyone, even considering that tourists pay their share for its use, it is still a use that causes social, economic and environmental impacts and this must be registered;
3. New concepts for renewable water sharing: as shares of renewable water use increase, policymakers, managers and the public in general need to address new challenges and priorities, such as sharing the recycled water in neighbourhoods for multipurpose use.

Policymakers play a key role in shaping policy regulatory actions and public support schemes such as financing lines. According to González and Lacal-Arántegui (2016), the proper design of a scheme and of the administrative procedures for accessing it is essential in order to reduce uncertainty. This would not only avoid discouraging investors, but also reduce the overall cost of the support scheme. Higher risk needs to be compensated with higher remuneration levels in order to keep the support scheme attractive for investors. The best sustainability practice is one with clear economic and social benefits and substantial environmental protection, and this seems to be the case for grey water recycling.

6 Policy Recommendations

Regarding the use of water by tourists, it is clear that tourists use more water than regular citizens in similar activities. Recycling systems are the future of water use in major hotels, but the existence of standards does not have any strong relationship to present activities towards sustainability in this matter. In this context, reflection on the sustainable use of water becomes essential. The choice is not between socio-economic development and the environment, but between development models, sensitive or not to the environment. Sustainable development should be underpinned by the ethical idea of avoiding harm to what is necessary to preserve, regardless of the existence of formal restrictions. In the end, it is the behaviour of any social actor that defines outcomes (Sachs, 2015).

To a relevant extent, sustainable development requires good governance: public and corporate. As such, combining public and private initiatives regarding standards and regulations might be a way of moving forward more effectively, given the issue's global scale and the need for transparency as well as participation. Sustainable behaviour begins with voluntary actions as an ethical idea although it is likely that positive and negative incentives are needed.

Free market believers would argue that, in the absence of rules clearly declaring that certain behaviour is not allowed, corporate enterprises would not have a moral obligation to their shareholders to pursue any objective other than maximizing profits, even given that some measures are possible only due to circumstantial legal loopholes (Sachs, 2015). In this light, it is relevant to create social understanding on how society could together reshape thinking that might help tackle ongoing problems and, consequently, develop a more successful path towards sustainability.

Significantly, regulation is a concept that must be addressed in addition to the relevant (voluntary) standardization of sustainable action. The idea that regulation should go hand in hand with standards is much more promising than merely negative incentives, i.e. much more can be done than just restricting behaviour and preventing undesirable activities. It is feasible to develop policies that would enable, or at least facilitate, the flourishing of values through a positive approach. In sum, not only is it important to develop measures to restrict unsustainable behaviour—penalties, sanctions etc.—but it is also necessary to create opportunities for the development of public goods such as funds, technical assistance and capacity building (Baldwing, Cave, & Lodge, 2012). By taking full advantage of positive and negative regulatory approaches, it is possible to handle policy issues with a variety of tools and standards, and consequently achieve better outcomes.

As a contribution to future debates, it is important to highlight some key aspects. First, this chapter aimed to make a pilot study of a sensitive issue that has a massive impact on people's lives: water use. It would be relevant if further research could explore this idea and evaluate what is happening in the other strategic tourist cities of the world. Those studies would allow the creation of more objective evidence-based policies. Moreover, it is clear that the UN World Tourism Organization (UNWTO) should improve its framework in relation to water use standards. The lack of transparency and guidance, on the one hand, makes it difficult for the industry to develop proper voluntary sustainability investment decisions, and, on the other hand, for the consumers to choose wisely between different products. Both sides are acting in the absence of proper information and are not necessarily making the best possible choices. Last and more importantly, it is relevant to take advantage of the SDGs to develop a smart international policy framework on the issue. Taking the SDGs as a reference point seems to be the most effective way of designing balanced (voluntary and mandatory; positive and negative; local and international) governance models to enable not only improvements in touristic practices all over the world but also to tackle instances of improper green washing behaviour.

Finally, as an incentive for further research on the topic, three policy recommendations may be collected from our exploratory research:

1. To expand the case studies on water use, either technical, behavioural, economic or political, in order to achieve substantial knowledge that could underpin evidence-based regulatory policies.
2. To advocate leadership of the UNWTO and other UN agencies in providing guidance towards use of standards and regulations on water use.

3. To use the SDGs framework as a reference for the development of specific voluntary standards and mandatory regulations that could guide stakeholders to achieve the best levels of sustainability, meaning, not only protecting natural resources, but also achieving economic and social development.

References

Aall, C. (2011). Energy use and leisure consumption in Norway: An analysis and reduction strategy. *Journal of Sustainable Tourism, 19*(6), 729–745. https://doi.org/10.1080/09669582.2010.536241.

Al-Jayyousi, O. R. (2003). Greywater reuse: Towards sustainable water management. *Desalination, 156*(1–3), 181–192. https://doi.org/10.1016/S0011-9164(03)00340-0.

Baldwing, R., Cave, M., & Lodge, M. (2012). *Undestanding regulation* (2nd ed.). Oxford: Oxford University Press.

Charara, N., Cashman, A., Bonnell, R., & Gehr, R. (2011). Water use efficiency in the hotel sector of Barbados. *Journal of Sustainable Tourism, 19*(2), 231–245. https://doi.org/10.1080/09669582.2010.502577.

Collins, A., Jones, C., & Munday, M. (2009). Assessing the environmental impacts of mega sporting events: Two options? *Tourism Management, 30*(6), 828–837. https://doi.org/10.1016/j.tourman.2008.12.006.

Gatt, K., & Schranz, C. (2015). Retrofitting a 3 star hotel as a basis for piloting water minimisation interventions in the hospitality sector. *International Journal of Hospitality Management, 50*, 115–121. https://doi.org/10.1016/j.ijhm.2015.06.008.

Georgescu-Roegen, N. (1971). The entropy law and the economic process. *The Economic Journal, 83* (1st ed. Boston: Harvard University Press). http://doi.org/10.2307/2231206.

González, J. S., & Lacal-Arántegui, R. (2016). A review of regulatory framework for wind energy in European Union countries: Current state and expected developments. *Renewable and Sustainable Energy Reviews, 56*, 588–602. https://doi.org/10.1016/j.rser.2015.11.091.

Gössling, S. (2015). New performance indicators for water management in tourism. *Tourism Management, 46*, 233–244. https://doi.org/10.1016/j.tourman.2014.06.018.

Gössling, S., Peeters, P., Hall, C. M., Ceron, J.-P., Dubois, G., Lehmann, L. V., et al. (2012). Tourism and water use: Supply, demand, and security. An international review. *Tourism Management, 33*(1), 1–15. https://doi.org/10.1016/j.tourman.2011.03.015.

International Network on Regional Economics, Mobility and Tourism, & World Tourism Organization (2012). *A closer look at tourism: Sub-national measurement and analysis—Towards a set of UNWTO guidelines*. Madrid: UNWTO Press.

Jiménez-Cisneros, B. (2014). *Comprehensive water quality and purification. Comprehensive water quality and purification*. Amsterdam: Elsevier. https://doi.org/10.1016/B978-0-12-382182-9.00054-2.

Law, R., & Cheung, C. (2007). Air quality in Hong Kong: A study of the perception of international visitors. *Journal of Sustainable Tourism, 15*(4), 390–401. https://doi.org/10.2167/jost637.0.

Li, F., Wichmann, K., & Otterpohl, R. (2009). Review of the technological approaches for grey water treatment and reuses. *Science of the Total Environment, 407*(11), 3439–3449. https://doi.org/10.1016/j.scitotenv.2009.02.004.

Li, G., Yang, X., Liu, Q., & Zheng, F. (2014). Destination island effects: A theoretical framework for the environmental impact assessment of human tourism activities. *Tourism Management Perspectives, 10*, 11–18. https://doi.org/10.1016/j.tmp.2013.12.001.

March, J. G., Gual, M., & Orozco, F. (2004). Experiences on greywater re-use for toilet flushing in a hotel (Mallorca, Island, Spain). *Desalination, 164*(3), 241–247. https://doi.org/10.1016/S0011-9164(04)00192-4.

Martinez-Alier, J. (2015). *International encyclopedia of the social & behavioral sciences*. Amsterdam: Elsevier. http://doi.org/10.1016/B978-0-08-097086-8.91008-0

Millimet, D. L., & Roy, J. (2015). Multilateral environmental agreements and the WTO. *Economics Letters, 134,* 20–23. https://doi.org/10.1016/j.econlet.2015.05.035.

Montibeller-Filho, G. (2004). *O Mito do Desenvolvimento Sustentável: Meio ambiente e custos sociais no moderno sistema produtor de mercadoria*. Florianopolis: UFSC.

Nolde, E. (2000). Greywater reuse systems for toilet flushing in multi-storey buildings ± over ten years experience in Berlin. *Journal of Urban Water, 2*(3), 275–284. https://doi.org/10.1016/S1462-0758(00)00023-6.

Radwan, H. R. I., Jones, E., & Minoli, D. (2012). Solid waste management in small hotels: A comparison of green and non-green small hotels in Wales. *Journal of Sustainable Tourism, 20*(4), 533–550. https://doi.org/10.1080/09669582.2011.621539.

Rahman, D. H. A. A., Dayang-Affizzah, A., & Edman, S. (2012). Tourism and hotels in Sarawak: Economic performance. *Procedia—Social and Behavioral Sciences, 65,* 1020–1026. https://doi.org/10.1016/j.sbspro.2012.11.236.

Sachs, J. (2015). *The age of sustainable development*. New York: Columbia University Press.

Styles, D., Schoenberger, H., & Galvez-Martos, J. L. (2015). Water management in the European hospitality sector: Best practice, performance benchmarks and improvement potential. *Tourism Management, 46,* 187–202. https://doi.org/10.1016/j.tourman.2014.07.005.

Sun, Y. Y. (2014). A framework to account for the tourism carbon footprint at island destinations. *Tourism Management, 45,* 16–27. https://doi.org/10.1016/j.tourman.2014.03.015.

United Nations General Assembly. (2014). *Report of the open working group of the General Assembly on Sustainable Development Goals [A/68/970]*. Madrid: UN.

UNWTO Tourism Highlights. (2016). *In UNWTO Tourism Highlights*, 2016 Edition. https://doi.org/10.18111/9789284418145.

Vizeu, F., Meneghetti, F. K., & Seifert, R. E. (2012). Por uma crítica ao conceito de desenvolvimento sustentável. *Cadernos EBAPE.BR, 10*(3), 569–583. http://doi.org/10.1590/S1679-39512012000300007.

World Travel & Tourism Council. (2016). *Travel and Tourism Economic Impact*. In Tourism. http://www.wttc.org/bin/pdf/original_pdf_file/italy.pdf.

WWAP (World Water Assessment Programme). (2015). *The United Nations world water development report 2015: Water for a sustainable world*. Paris: UN.

Chapter 13
Conclusions

Jorge Antonio Pérez-Pineda, Johannes Blankenbach, and Archna Negi

The complexity of current global challenges necessitates innovative and strategic solutions and, in particular, better models of governance. The twenty-first century began with the launch of the Millennium Development Goals (MDGs), followed by the adoption of the Sustainable Development Goals (SDGs) in 2015. This new set of goals has evolved from a governmental approach to a multi-stakeholder approach, introducing a comprehensive management framework for sustainable development worldwide that goes much beyond the aid-centred focus of the past.

International institutions such as the United Nations (UN) and the Organisation for Economic Co-operation and Development (OECD) have extended support to governments and other actors in achieving development and sustainability goals through various mechanisms and strategies. World summits such as Rio + 20 in 2012, the First High Level Meeting of the Global Partnership for Effective Development Co-operation in 2014 and the Third International Conference on Financing for Development in 2015[1] made it clear that any effort towards economic growth and combating poverty must be achieved with a commitment to environmental sustainability, human rights, inclusion, transparency, accountability and coherence.

Inclusive economic growth, poverty reduction and sustainable development are still considered to depend on "trade as an engine for development" (UNGA, 2015, p. 37) and the World Trade Organisation (WTO), despite the failure of the Doha

---

[1] The Addis Ababa Action Agenda (AAAA) was agreed upon at this conference.

J. A. Pérez-Pineda
Faculty of Economics and Business, Universidad Anáhuac México, Estado de México, Mexico

J. Blankenbach
Business & Human Rights Resource Centre, Berlin, Germany

A. Negi (✉)
Centre for International Politics, Organization and Disarmament (CIPOD), School of International Studies, Jawaharlal Nehru University, New Delhi, India
e-mail: archnanegisingh@gmail.com

215

A. Negi et al. (eds.), *Sustainability Standards and Global Governance*,
https://doi.org/10.1007/978-981-15-3473-7_13

Round and its other troubles, continues to be central to the trade agenda. In addition, we witness increasingly frequent interventions of the private sector in the global development agenda (Severino & Ray, 2010, pp. 8–10). Despite the projected importance of trade for development, when companies from emerging economies and developing countries enter the international markets, their products often face non-tariff barriers (NTBs), which could include a range of sanitary and phytosanitary measures (SPMs) as well as technical barriers to trade (TBTs). Mandatory sustainability regulations as well as voluntary sustainability standards (VSS) may amount to such barriers under certain circumstances. Trade statistics of the United Nations Conference on Trade and Development (UNCTAD, 2015, p. 17) reveal that TBTs impact almost 70% of world trade, whereas SPMs impact around 10% of world trade.

VSS, unless referenced in mandatory regulation, are not formally categorised as NTBs and therefore not covered by official trade rules. A market survey of the International Trade Centre (ITC) for 14 leading VSS found that "all standards in the report continue to show growth of total certified area, albeit not at the same pace as in the past" (Lernoud et al., 2017, p. ii). In the light of such trends, while there needs to be a better understanding of whether and how VSS could be used as a tool to achieve the SDGs, the extent to which they constitue barriers to market entry for emerging economies and developing countries and serve corporate opportunism, also needs to be examined. Within these countries, marginalised regions and small-scale producers seem to be at greatest risk of exclusion (UNFSS, 2016, p. 4). In either case, there exists a clear need to comprehensively review current normative and policy frameworks at the global level relating to sustainability standards and regulations.

The first section of this volume—"Global Governance Frameworks for Sustainability Standards"—introduced the 2030 Agenda for sustainable development as a governance framework, against which to measure the performance of sustainability standards. The 2030 Agenda, by guiding the design of sustainability regulations, standards and corresponding impact assessments, can strengthen the link between sustainable development and the use of sustainability standards and regulations. The mutually reinforcing relationship between the SDGs and human rights is emphasised in this context, as is the importance of implementing the UN Guiding Principles on Business and Human Rights (UNGPs) in order to operationalize corporate respect for human rights across global operations and value chains: "[T]he implementation of the UNGPs can be the single most important contribution by business to the realisation of the SDGs" (Morris et al., 2019, p. 9). Even though the UNGPs recommend a "smart mix" of voluntary and mandatory measures (OHCHR, 2011, p. 5), it remains to be seen whether VSS can play a role in supporting human rights (and environmental) due diligence—the key operational principle put forward by the UNGPs. A matter of concern is that the kind of audits used for certification and verification of VSS have not always proven reliable for detecting human rights and environmental abuses. Also, due diligence is about companies *internalising* processes for human rights and environmental risk assessment, mitigation action and monitoring across their value chains, as well as corresponding reporting and remediation, rather than outsourcing these steps. External VSS initiatives can at best support, but not replace, companies' own due diligence policies and practices—and potentially legal obligation—to respect human rights and the environment across their global operations and value chains.

Regarding other institutionalised frameworks, the WTO is of key importance even though it does not cover private VSS (Henson, 2008, p. 76). It has gathered vast experience in governing the use of SPS as well as technical regulations and standards from public and international sources. Annex 4 of the Second Triennial Review of the WTO's TBT Agreement establishes criteria for international standards: "transparency", "openness", "impartiality and consensus", "effectiveness and relevance", "coherence" and "development dimension" (WTO, 2000, p. 24). These have also been taken up and extended by the International Social and Environmental Accreditation and Labelling Alliance (ISEAL), an umbrella organisation for private standards schemes, notably in its "Credibility Principles" (ISEAL, 2013). Also, in the context of trade, it appears that stagnation at the WTO has led to an increase in bilateral and regional preferential trade agreements (PTAs), which may constitute a new framework of global governance and, as they become "greener", provide a conducive environment for sustainability standards and regulations.

Sustainability reporting, which is discussed as an instrument for sustainability governance in this volume, has also found mention in several other publications that have looked at global reporting as a "multi-stakeholder governance arrangement" (Flohr, Rieth, Schwindenhammer, & Wolf, 2010, p. 219). Legitimacy seems to be the key question here; in their analysis of the Global Reporting Initiative (GRI), Flohr et al. (2010, p. 221) emphasise "the high legitimacy potential of a highly institutionalised and consensus based transnational multi-stakeholder initiative in which corporations act as norm-entrepreneurs". Haufler, as early on as 2001, argued that "all sides view industry self-regulation as a potential new source of global governance", while highlighting that there is disagreement on "whether this is a legitimate and effective means to achieve public policy goals" (Haufler, 2001, p. 1). Several factors that hamper the legitimacy and effectiveness of industry-driven multi-stakeholder initiatives are addressed in this volume, ranging from the lack of means of implementation to the formal or de facto exclusion of crucial local actors and rights-holders from governance arrangements. When it comes to reporting in particular, it should be noted that even where sustainability and/or human rights reporting is required by mandatory national or regional regulation, governments are now being pushed to move towards legally mandating certain types of company *action* rather than mere *reporting,* as the latter has failed to drive real improvements in responsible business conduct across industries. A briefing put forward by the Corporate Responsibility (CORE) Coalition—and endorsed by many others—on the subject of the Modern Slavery Act in the United Kingdom (UK) reads: "[T]he UK Government must now look beyond reporting and introduce an additional legal requirement for companies to carry out human rights due diligence (HRDD) in their global operations, activities, products, services, investments and supply chains." (CORE, 2019, p. 3).

The International Labour Organisation (ILO) Conventions are referred to as concrete requirements in many sustainability standards and regulations, which again underlines their close global governance link. The statistical finding in this volume that strengthening labour standards may in fact improve poorer countries' export performance is an important argument in favour of both public and private initiatives to effectively enforce and respect workers' rights.

While the second part of this volume—titled "Sustainability Standards in Sectoral and Country Contexts"—has a more local focus, implicit global governance linkages remain. The different challenges that are identified in this second part of the volume regarding the national/local implementation of globally operating VSS and their interplay with (local) mandatory regulations underline the need for further research and clarity on the global governance aspects of sustainability standards in the future. Challenges pertaining to sustainability standards take many different forms. In some contexts, there seems to be a contradiction between socioeconomic benefits for smallholders and large-scale environmental benefits such as reduced/halted deforestation. Those farmers that can afford certification may even cause more environmental damage by enlarging their cultivated area, which stands in contradiction to the general purpose of VSS (and at the same time proves that VSS cannot prevent over-production/consumption). The case of PEFC and FSC certification in Indonesia shows that, at a formal level, private standards can complement local regulation well if they comprise more detailed and far-reaching criteria than public stipulations. It seems likely, however, that out of the two VSS under review, more concession holders may opt for PEFC as it is less stringent than FSC.

Comparing various types of global and national food safety and quality standards for farmers, there is a challenge for emerging countries to comply with global standards, particularly in high-value supply chains both for foreign and local markets. Due to the market power of large retailers and supermarket chains, they may, in a purely commercial sense, become de facto mandatory and act as barriers to market entry. There is also a critique that global VSS such as GlobalGAP seem to benefit wealthier and more educated small-scale farmers, whereas local interpretations of the same standard may have broader coverage. However, local interpretations of VSS may also lead to parallel standards (e.g. there are both public and private local GAP versions in Thailand and India) resulting in high transaction costs without necessarily leading to better sustainability outcomes. There is thus a case for standards harmonisation among private and public actors at national levels. Public mandatory sustainability standards (i.e. sustainability regulations) from individual or groups of industrialised countries may have global implications, as the special case of vehicle efficiency standards implementation in China and Mexico shows. However, aligning emerging economies' fuel efficiency norms with EURO VI (European Union) and EPA 2010 (USA) does not always lead to the best results as there may be a mismatch with the specific economic and sectoral conditions on the ground.

The two parts of this volume have sought to shed light on global governance and sustainability standards from within and beyond the analytical mainstream. Not all institutions and processes have got the attention they deserve in this context, such as the UN Treaty process. Negotiations to develop a treaty on business and human rights started in 2015 with the first meeting of the UN Human Rights Council's open-ended intergovernmental working group on transnational corporations and other business enterprises with respect to human rights (OEIWG).[2] It has a mandate to elaborate an international legally binding instrument, requiring companies to respect human rights in their operations including value chains. While negotiations have been difficult so far, this treaty has the potential to become an important global governance framework for responsible business conduct in line with human rights and the SDGs.

Apart from the UNGPs, which have been mentioned above, the ILO Tripartite Declaration of Principles concerning Multinational Enterprises and Social Policy (ILO, 2017a) as well as the OECD Guidelines for Multinational Enterprises (OECD, 2011) also deserve attention. These sets of principles, guidelines and recommendations all strive to promote responsible and sustainable business conduct and must thus even be characterised as global public meta-standards, bridging the gap between public and private actors in global governance. For instance, the ILO Tripartite Declaration is "the only global instrument in this area that was elaborated and adopted by governments, employers and workers from around the world" (ILO, 2017b). The OECD Guidelines, first adopted in 1976, were updated in 2011 to incorporate the UNGPs' notion of human rights due diligence. A more recent OECD document, the Due Diligence Guidance on Responsible Business Conduct (OECD, 2018), spells out the possible steps and design of human rights due diligence in greater detail. It is likely to be "the most authoritative international elaboration of due diligence that is likely to be available for many years" according to civil society network OECD Watch (OECD Watch, 2018, p. 1).

Three of the above-mentioned guidelines are also highlighted in the Group of 20 (G20) Leaders' Declaration adopted at the 2017 Hamburg Summit:

> In order to achieve sustainable and inclusive supply chains, we commit to fostering the implementation of labour, social and environmental standards and human rights in line with internationally recognised frameworks, such as the UN Guiding Principles on Business and Human Rights and the ILO Tripartite Declaration of Principles concerning Multinational Enterprises and Social Policy. Those countries that adhere to the OECD Guidelines for Multinational Enterprises (OECD MNE Guidelines) commit to fostering them and welcome others to follow. (G20, 2017, p. 4)

The Think 20 (T20), one of the G20's outreach groups meant to provide policy advice, suggests a "Global Pact for Sustainable Trade" in its policy brief on "Fostering the Sustainability of Global Value Chains (GVCs)":

> Our proposal is to bring this process of governmental regulations strategies to govern responsibility in complex GVCs in different countries to the global stage, possibly with the participation of the major international institutions, government, business, especially SMEs [small and medium-sized enterprises], and other non-state actors. This would take the form of a Global Pact for Sustainable Trade, which would set minimum standards for environmental protection as well as for labor conditions and human rights protection. (Blumenschein et al., 2017, p. 7)

VSS are covered in the policy brief in the context of both opportunities and challenges. For instance, the authors find that issues of "cost/benefit sharing yet have

---

[2]See the Business & Human Rights Resource Centre's web portal and blog series on a "Binding treaty" at https://www.business-humanrights.org/en/binding-treaty.

to be overcome within and across voluntary standards systems" (Blumenschein et al., 2017, p. 7).

Governments who, for often legitimate reasons, were sceptical of importing countries' sustainability standards and regulations, dismissing them as (Western) protectionism in disguise, seem to have become more open towards them, including private VSS, which bear distinct risks, as some of the chapters discussed. The co-creation of semi-governmental VSS platforms in India (March 2016), Brazil (May/June 2017), China (June 2017) and Mexico (April 2018) for coordination, knowledge-sharing and stakeholder support has been a strong signal that emerging economies, through their national standards bodies, are ready to critically and constructively address the issue of VSS. They are generally moving from being standards-takers to being standards-makers. These platforms as well as other institutions looking into the issue should now ensure proper worker and rights-holder engagement, and also explore legislative options.

The new national VSS platforms were founded jointly with the UNFSS, an initiative of five UN agencies born of the WTO's initial inaction on private standards (UNFSS, 2017; see also Sect. 2). Under UNFSS auspices and with additional support from the Managing Global Governance (MGG) programme of the German Development Institute/*Deutsches Institut für Entwicklungspolitik* (DIE), a global community of experts and stakeholders has started to form, connecting national VSS platforms and actors. Momentum for similar semi-governmental platforms—to address potentials and pitfalls—is also building in South Africa and Indonesia.

There is an indication that sustainability standards, including VSS, are increasingly engaging the attention of policy makers, companies and certification agencies, while awareness of their limitations is also rising. Sustainability standards generally, complemented by multi-stakeholder structures for their national and global governance, can potentially evolve into tools for the realisation of the 2030 Agenda, but reinforced co-operation and, in part, legislation is required on issues of financing, technical co-operation, impact evaluation, multi-stakeholder dialogue, worker voice, as well as accountability and liability. The escalating proliferation of sustainability standards and regulations has the potential to translate into asymmetric compliance burdens for the developing and emerging economies, if simply passed down supply chains, and an effective rationalisation is clearly the need of the hour, along with an assessment of what really works best for workers, communities and the environment. Further, one of the main constraints for smallholders and SMEs in emerging markets, independent of the sector, is the lack of financing for standards implementation, considering that cost-sharing arrangements are still very nascent. Several options may be explored to bridge this gap, such as combining public and private standards to reduce transaction costs or launching funding lines with multilateral development banks and local financial institutions. For instance, "[e]mbedding standards compliance into the terms and conditions of lending contracts would facilitate access to finance on the part of sustainability-oriented SMEs" (Sommer, 2017, p. 61). It will need to be ensured, however, that this does not translate into excessive technical burdens for these SMEs in developing countries and emerging markets but truly supports them in addressing their human rights and environmental risks, while maximizing positive impacts.

The implementation, especially of environmental standards, almost always requires technical skills, appropriate equipment, knowledge of supply chain characteristics and market data, etc. Again, development agencies, local governments and international institutions such as ITC, UNFSS or UNCTAD could provide assistance, complemented by South–South and triangular co-operation. In addition, private enterprises and large-scale producers should offer support to small farmers, through fair purchasing practices and proper supplier engagement, and possibly supported by fundamentally reformed VSS schemes or national multi-stakeholder VSS platforms. While this book has taken shape over the past years, mandatory human rights due diligence and environmental legislation in line with the UNGPs has become a tangible opportunity in European countries, at EU-level and other countries of the world. The objective is to make sure companies' respect for human rights and the environment, including in their global value chains, is no longer an externalized and voluntary option, but an internalized and legal requirement.

There is still a lack of evidence-based assessment of the real impacts of VSS across different sectors and countries. At first sight, it seems obvious that the adoption of standards can potentially have positive impacts on the environment, on society and on the economy. However, as some of the chapters in this volume show, there may be trade-offs and contradictions. It is therefore necessary to collect, compare and analyse more data on the benefits and pitfalls of VSS, shedding light on critical issues such as possible market exclusions at the microlevel and macrolevel, as well as (social) audit failure and lack of accountability. In terms of processes and resources, sustainability standards impact assessment seek synergies with national SDG monitoring and evaluation, for instance, by using joint indicators and data.

There are many concerns at all levels regarding the legitimacy, fairness, quality and effectiveness of multi-stakeholder dialogues, e.g. for the setting or implementation of standards. Power asymmetries are often visible, and some brands and companies may use these initiatives to 'free-ride' on leading practice by others while actually not changing much in the way they do business. Local chambers of commerce, national standards bodies and international organisations should seek to establish mechanisms for better assurance and against unnecessary proliferation, duplication or overlap of standards as this may imply an extra burden of work and extra costs especially for small-scale producers, without necessarily improving developmental, social and environmental outcomes. Coordination tasks may also be undertaken by public–private VSS platforms in more countries under the auspices of the UNFSS. Some of the necessary resources could be channelled through South–South co-operation. UNFSS-facilitated exchange across existing and future platforms may improve the interplay of globally operating private VSS with public VSS and mandatory public regulations in different countries, maximising their contribution to SDG implementation. A network of sustainability standards platforms could also promote public support mechanisms at the national, regional and global scale for smaller producers seeking to implement sustainability standards and practices. And last but not the least, such a network may evolve into a "Southern" building block for global multistakeholder governance of sustainability standards, including VSS, based on common guidelines, rules and "standards for standards".

In the end, it must be remembered that the issue of standards and regulations is not simply a technical issue that can be planned and operationalised in an objective, scientific and neutral way to bring out the optimal results as planned. Standards, in their entire lifecycle—from the moment of conception till the time of operationalisation—are defined by the political and economic environment in which they exist. There are power asymmetries—between the rich and the poor countries, between the large and the small firms, between the large-scale farmers or foresters and the smallholders, between employers and formal or informal workers, and between the cause of growth and that of social and environmental protections—that define the terms of the debate around standards. There are dynamic interfaces—between the public and the private, between states and intergovernmental organisations, between the government and the non-governmental sector and among the host of standardisation agencies—that keep this issue area in a continuous state of flux. Additionally, definitional ambiguity, normative uncertainty and ideational divergences further complicate an already complex canvas. The use of standards as a tool and driver of global governance for sustainable development is commended as well as contested. There is much scope for further research in this issue area and this book, it is hoped, represents an early milestone in a long exploratory journey ahead.

References

Blumenschein, F., Wieland, J., Berger, A., Blankenbach, J., Brandi, C., Dadush, U., Navarro, D., Neligan, A., Jandeisek, I., Johnson, L., Harms, P., & Wickerham, J. (2017). *Fostering the sustainability of global value chains (GVCs)*. Bonn/Kiel: Think 20 Dialogue. Retrieved from http://www.g20-insights.org/wp-content/uploads/2017/03/Trade_Fostering-the-Sustainability.pdf.

CORE (Corporate Responsibility Coalition) (2019). *Briefing for Westminster Hall debate on the independent review of the Modern Slavery Act.* Retrieved from https://corporate-responsibility.org/wp-content/uploads/2019/06/MSA-Review-Joint-Briefing_FINAL_180619.pdf.

Flohr, A., Rieth, L., Schwindenhammer, S., & Wolf, K. (2010). *The role of business in global governance: Corporations as norm-entrepreneurs.* London: Palgrave Macmillan.

G20 (Group of 20) (2017): *Leaders' declaration: Shaping an interconnected world.* Hamburg: Author. Retrieved from https://www.g20.org/Content/EN/_Anlagen/G20/G20-leaders-declaration.pdf?__blob=publicationFile&v=11.

Haufler, V. (2001). *A public role for the private sector: Industry self-regulation in a global economy.* Washington, D.C.: Carnegie Endowment.

Henson, S. (2008). The role of public and private standards in regulating international food markets. *Journal of International Agricultural Trade and Development, 4*(1), 63–81.

ILO (International Labour Organisation) (2017a). *Tripartite declaration of principles concerning multinational enterprises and social policy: 5th edition.* Geneva: Author. Retrieved from http://www.ilo.org/wcmsp5/groups/public/—ed_emp/—emp_ent/—multi/documents/publication/wcms_094386.pdf.

ILO (2017b). *[Information on the] Tripartite declaration of principles concerning multinational enterprises and social policy.* Geneva: Author. Retrieved from http://www.ilo.org/empent/Public ations/WCMS_094386/lang–en/index.htm.

ISEAL (International Social and Environmental Accreditation and Labelling Alliance) (2013). *Principles for credible and effective sustainability standards systems: ISEAL Credibility Principles.* London: Author. Retrieved from https://www.isealalliance.org/sites/default/files/Credib ility%20Principles%20v1.0%20low%20res.pdf.

Lernoud J., Potts, J., Sampson, G., Garibay, S. Lynch, M., Voora, V., Willer, H., & Wozniak, J. (2017). *The state of sustainable markets 2017: Statistics and emerging trends.* Geneva: International Trade Centre (ITC). Retrieved from http://www.intracen.org/uploadedFiles/intracenorg/Content/Public ations/State-of-Sustainable-Market-2017_web.pdf.

Morris, D., Wrzoncki, E., & Lysgaard S. A. (2019). *Responsible business conduct as a cornerstone of the 2030 agenda—A look at the implications.* Copenhagen: The Danish Institute for Human Rights. Retrieved from https://www.humanrights.dk/sites/humanrights.dk/files/media/dokume nter/udgivelser/hrb_2019/responsible_business_conduct_as_a_cornerstone_of_the_2030_a genda_dihr_2019.pdf.

OECD (Organisation for Economic Co-operation and Development) (2011). *OECD guidelines for multinational enterprises: 2011 Edition.* Paris: Author. Retrieved from http://www.oecd.org/daf/ inv/mne/48004323.pdf.

OECD (Organisation for Economic Co-operation and Development) (2018). *OECD due diligence guidance for responsible business conduct.* Paris: Author. Retrieved from http://mneguidelines. oecd.org/OECD-Due-Diligence-Guidance-for-Responsible-Business-Conduct.pdf.

OECD Watch (2018). *Blog: the new OECD due diligence guidance on responsible business conduct.* Retrieved from https://www.oecdwatch.org/2018/06/20/blog-the-new-oecd-due-dilige nce-guidance-on-responsible-business-conduct/.

OHCHR (Office of the High Commissioner for Human Rights) (2011). *Guiding principles on business and human rights.* Geneva: Author. Retrieved from https://www.ohchr.org/documents/ publications/GuidingprinciplesBusinesshr_eN.pdf.

Severino, J.-M. & Ray, O. (2010). *The end of ODA (II): The birth of hypercollective action.* Washington, D.C.: Center for Global Development. Retrieved from https://www.cgdev.org/sites/def ault/files/1424253_file_The_End_of_ODA_II_FINAL.pdf.

Sommer, C. (2017). *Drivers and constraints for adopting sustainability standards in small and medium-sized enterprises (SMEs)* (Discussion Paper 21/2017). Bonn: German Development Institute/Deutsches Institut für Entwicklungspolitik (DIE).

UN GA (United Nations General Assembly) (2015). *Addis Ababa action agenda of the third international conference on financing for development (Addis Ababa Action Agenda).* New York: Author. Retrieved from http://www.un.org/esa/ffd/wp-content/uploads/2015/08/AAAA_Outcome.pdf.

UNCTAD (United Nations Conference on Trade and Development) (2015). *Key statistics and trends in trade policy 2015.* Geneva: Author. Retrieved from http://unctad.org/en/PublicationsLibrary/ ditctab2015d2_en.pdf.

UNFSS (United Nations Forum on Sustainability Standards) (2016). *Meeting sustainability goals: Voluntary sustainability standards and the role of the government: 2nd flagship report.* Geneva: Author. Retrieved from https://unfss.files.wordpress.com/2016/09/final_unfss-report_28092016. pdf.

UNFSS (2017). *About Us: What is the UNFSS?* Geneva: Author. Retrieved fromhttps://unfss.org/ about-us/.

World Trade Organization (WTO) (2000). *Second Triennial review of the operation and implementation of the agreement on technical barriers to trade.* Geneva: Author. Retrieved from http://doc sonline.wto.org/imrd/directdoc.asp?DDFDocuments/t/G/TBT/9.doc.